KAGEKI SHOJO!!

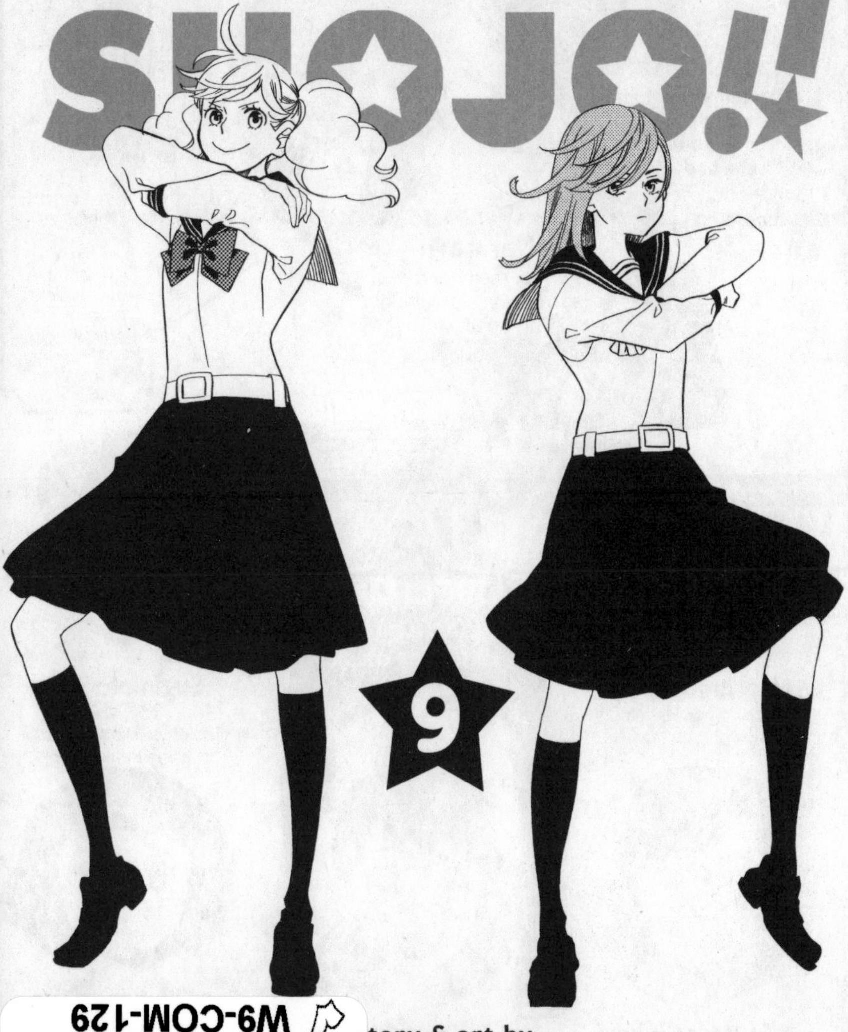

9

story & art by
Kumiko Saiki

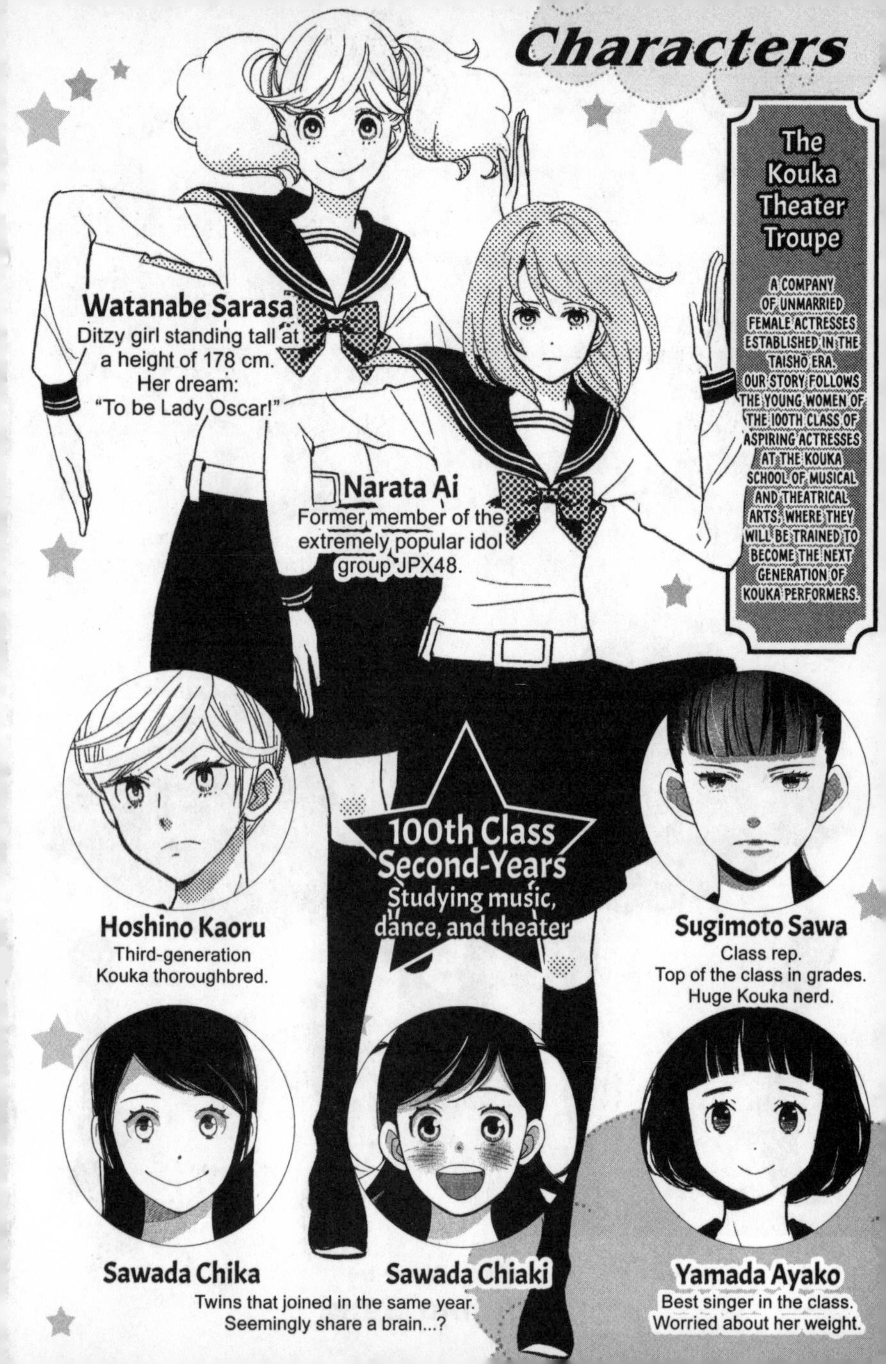

Characters
The Kouka Theater Troupe
A COMPANY OF UNMARRIED FEMALE ACTRESSES ESTABLISHED IN THE TAISHO ERA. OUR STORY FOLLOWS THE YOUNG WOMEN OF THE 100TH CLASS OF ASPIRING ACTRESSES AT THE KOUKA SCHOOL OF MUSICAL AND THEATRICAL ARTS, WHERE THEY WILL BE TRAINED TO BECOME THE NEXT GENERATION OF KOUKA PERFORMERS.
Watanabe Sarasa
Ditzy girl standing tall at a height of 178 cm. Her dream: "To be Lady Oscar!"
Narata Ai
Former member of the extremely popular idol group JPX48.
100th Class Second-Years
Studying music, dance, and theater
Sugimoto Sawa
Class rep. Top of the class in grades. Huge Kouka nerd.
Hoshino Kaoru
Third-generation Kouka thoroughbred.
Yamada Ayako
Best singer in the class. Worried about her weight.
Sawada Chiaki
Sawada Chika
Twins that joined in the same year. Seemingly share a brain...?

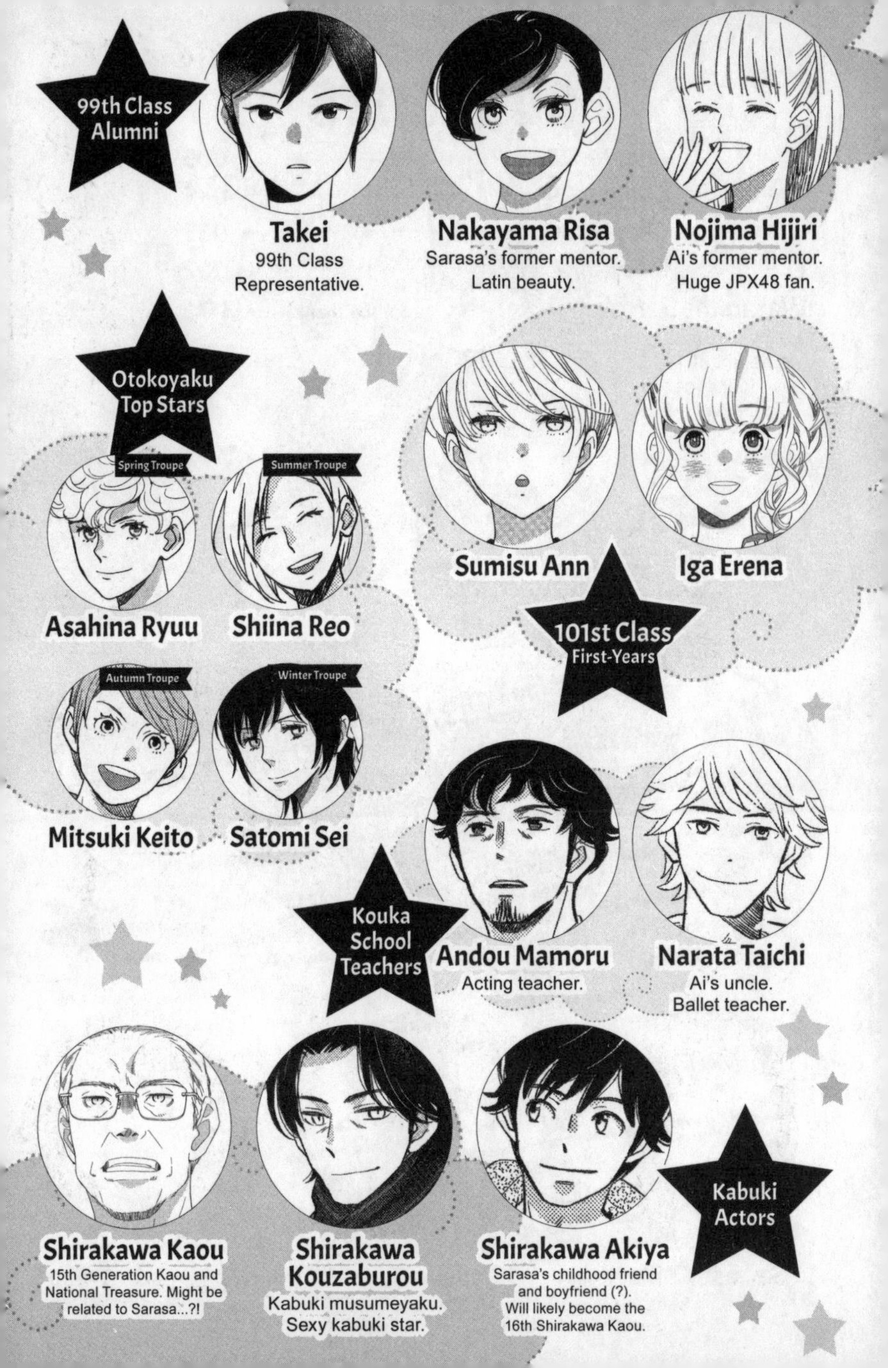
99th Class Alumni
Takei
99th Class Representative.
Nakayama Risa
Sarasa's former mentor. Latin beauty.
Nojima Hijiri
Ai's former mentor. Huge JPX48 fan.
Otokoyaku Top Stars
Spring Troupe
Asahina Ryuu
Summer Troupe
Shiina Reo
Autumn Troupe
Mitsuki Keito
Winter Troupe
Satomi Sei
Sumisu Ann
Iga Erena
101st Class First-Years
Kouka School Teachers
Andou Mamoru
Acting teacher.
Narata Taichi
Ai's uncle. Ballet teacher.
Shirakawa Kaou
15th Generation Kaou and National Treasure. Might be related to Sarasa...?!
Shirakawa Kouzaburou
Kabuki musumeyaku. Sexy kabuki star.
Shirakawa Akiya
Sarasa's childhood friend and boyfriend (?). Will likely become the 16th Shirakawa Kaou.
Kabuki Actors

CONTENTS

No.

Date

Kouka Troupe Terms to Know! ★

Kouka Theater Troupe
Founded a hundred years ago as a theater troupe comprised of young, unmarried women.
Split into four troupes (Spring/Summer/Autumn/Winter). Main theater is in Kobe.

Otokoyaku / Musumeyaku
Designated roles for the gender of characters actresses play. Otokoyaku actresses play male or
masculine characters, while musumeyaku actresses play female or feminine characters.

Top Star
The actress who heads her troupe. Each troupe has an otokoyaku top star and musumeyaku top star.
Top stars appear in every major production.

Kouka School of Musical and Theatrical Arts
Two-year prep school where the next stars of the Kouka Troupe are forged.
Girls can apply anytime between 9th and 12th grade!

First-Year Students vs. Second-Year Students
While first-year students primarily focus on their studies, second-year students are tasked both
with their studies and mentoring the first-year students, as well as managing their cleaning
schedule and helping them with lifestyle adjustments.

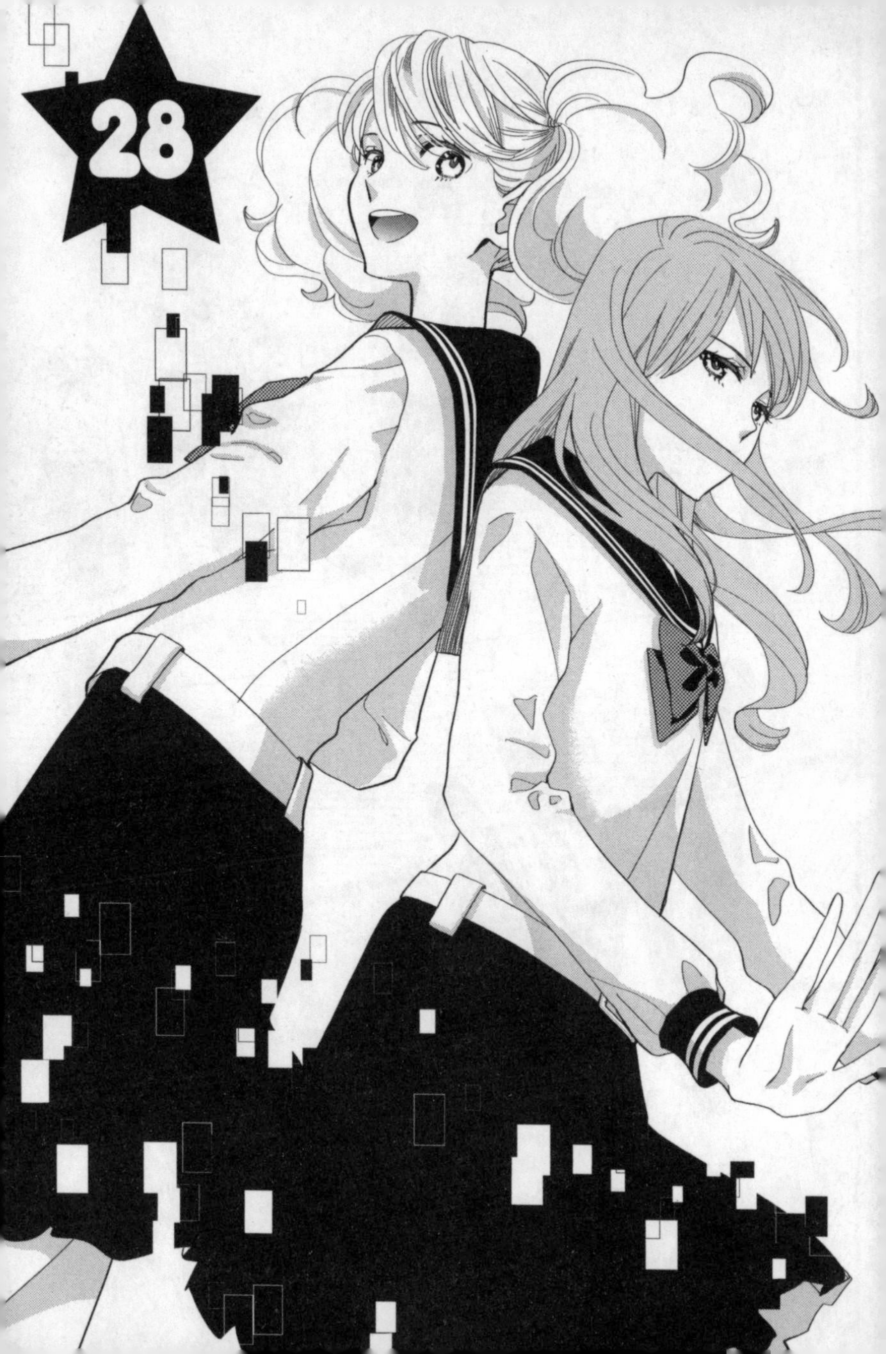
28

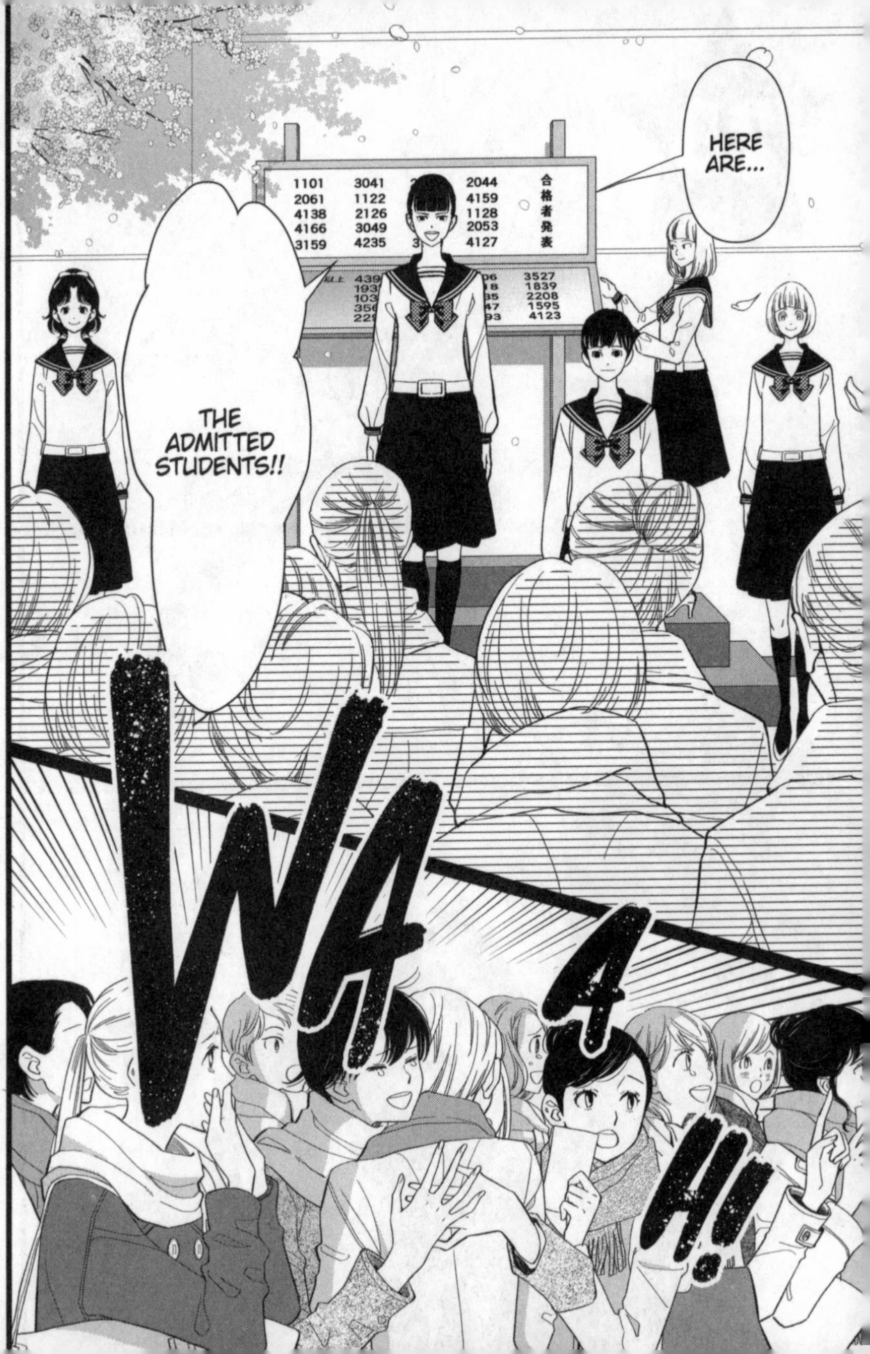
HERE ARE...
THE ADMITTED STUDENTS!!
合格者発表
2044 4159 1128 2053 4127
3041 1122 2126 3049 4235
1101 2061 4138 4166 3159
3527 1839 2208 1595 4123
WAAH!!

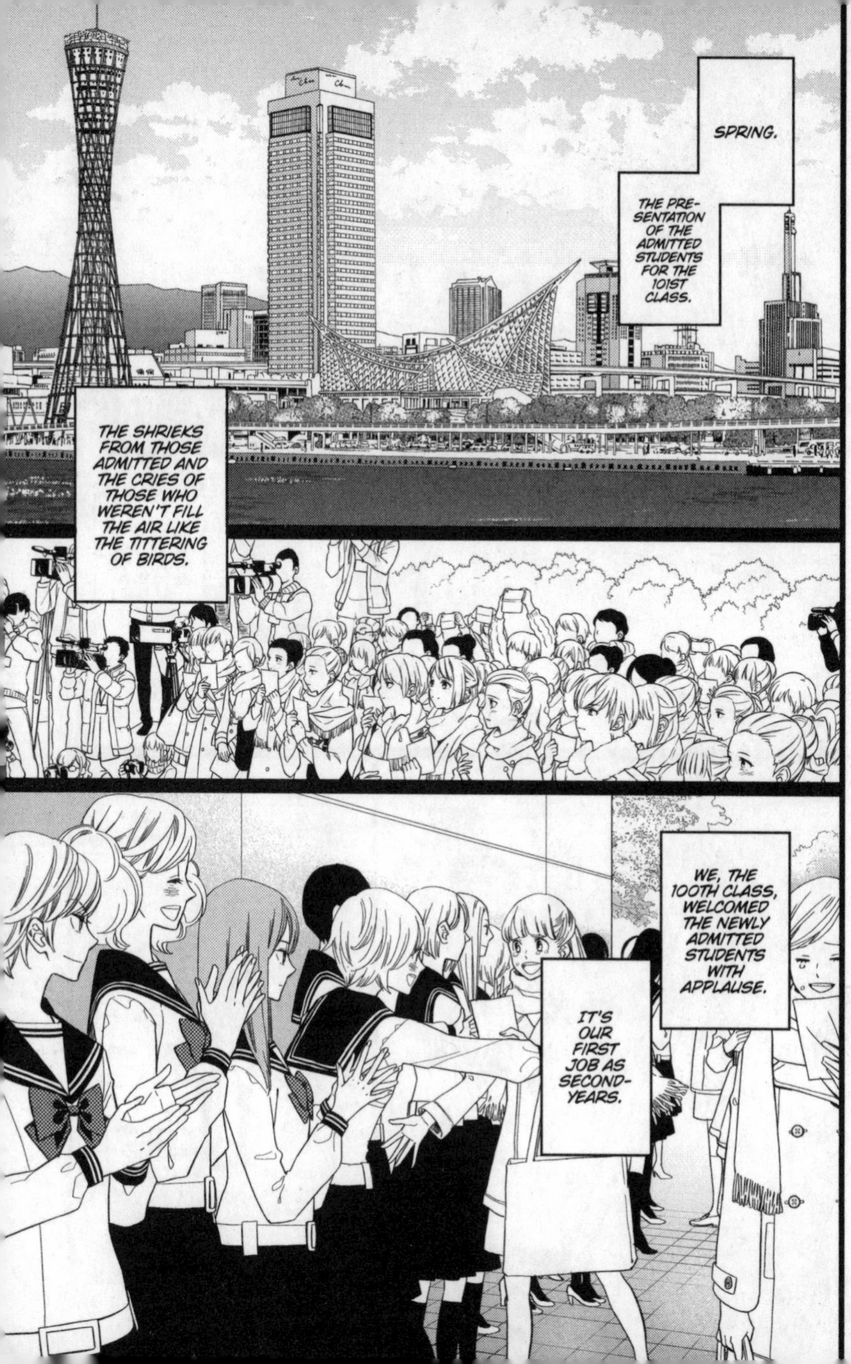
SPRING.
THE PRESENTATION OF THE ADMITTED STUDENTS FOR THE 101ST CLASS.
THE SHRIEKS FROM THOSE ADMITTED AND THE CRIES OF THOSE WHO WEREN'T FILL THE AIR LIKE THE TITTERING OF BIRDS.
WE, THE 100TH CLASS, WELCOMED THE NEWLY ADMITTED STUDENTS WITH APPLAUSE.
IT'S OUR FIRST JOB AS SECOND-YEARS.

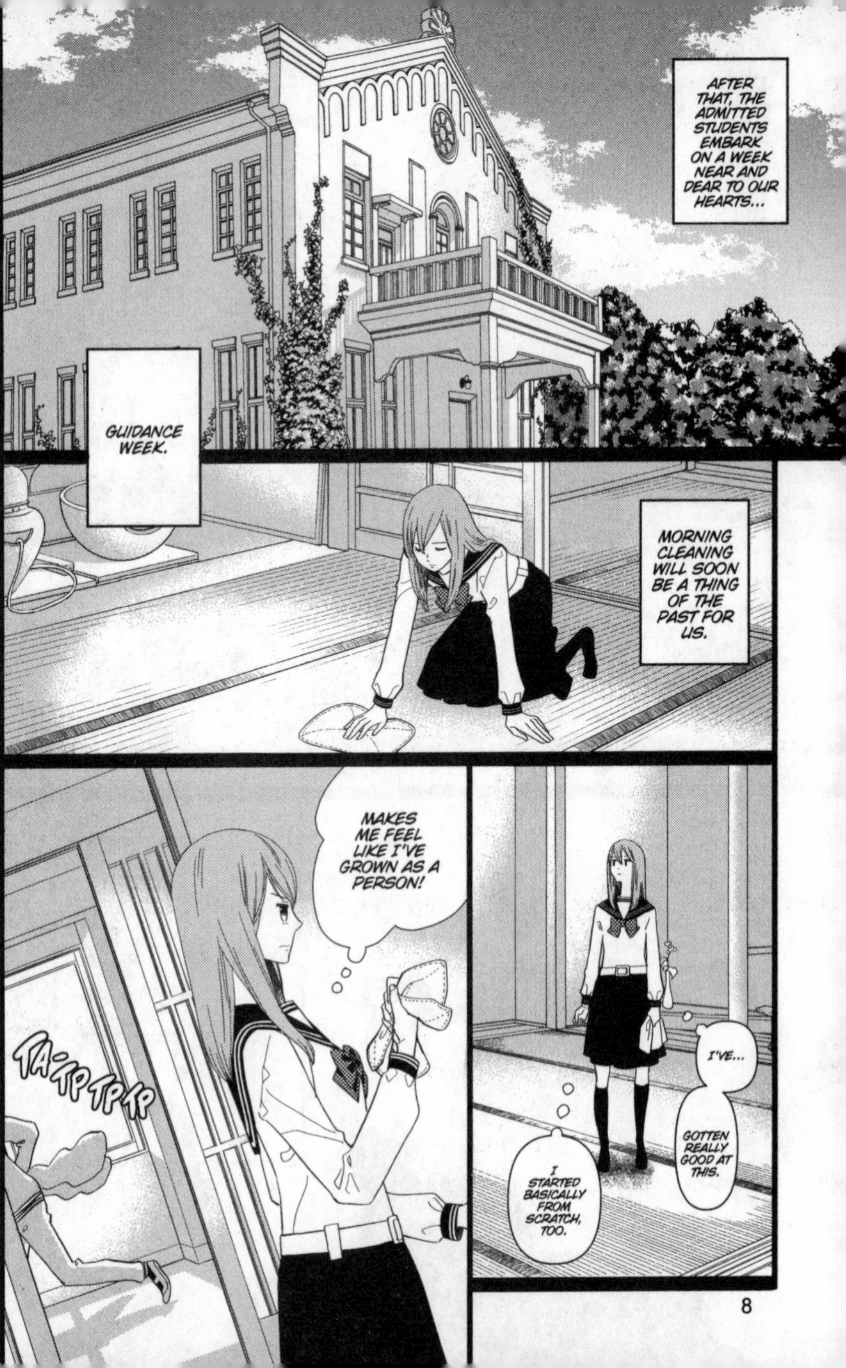
AFTER THAT, THE ADMITTED STUDENTS EMBARK ON A WEEK NEAR AND DEAR TO OUR HEARTS...
GUIDANCE WEEK.
MORNING CLEANING WILL SOON BE A THING OF THE PAST FOR US.
I'VE...
GOTTEN REALLY GOOD AT THIS.
I STARTED BASICALLY FROM SCRATCH, TOO.
MAKES ME FEEL LIKE I'VE GROWN AS A PERSON!
TA-TP TP TP

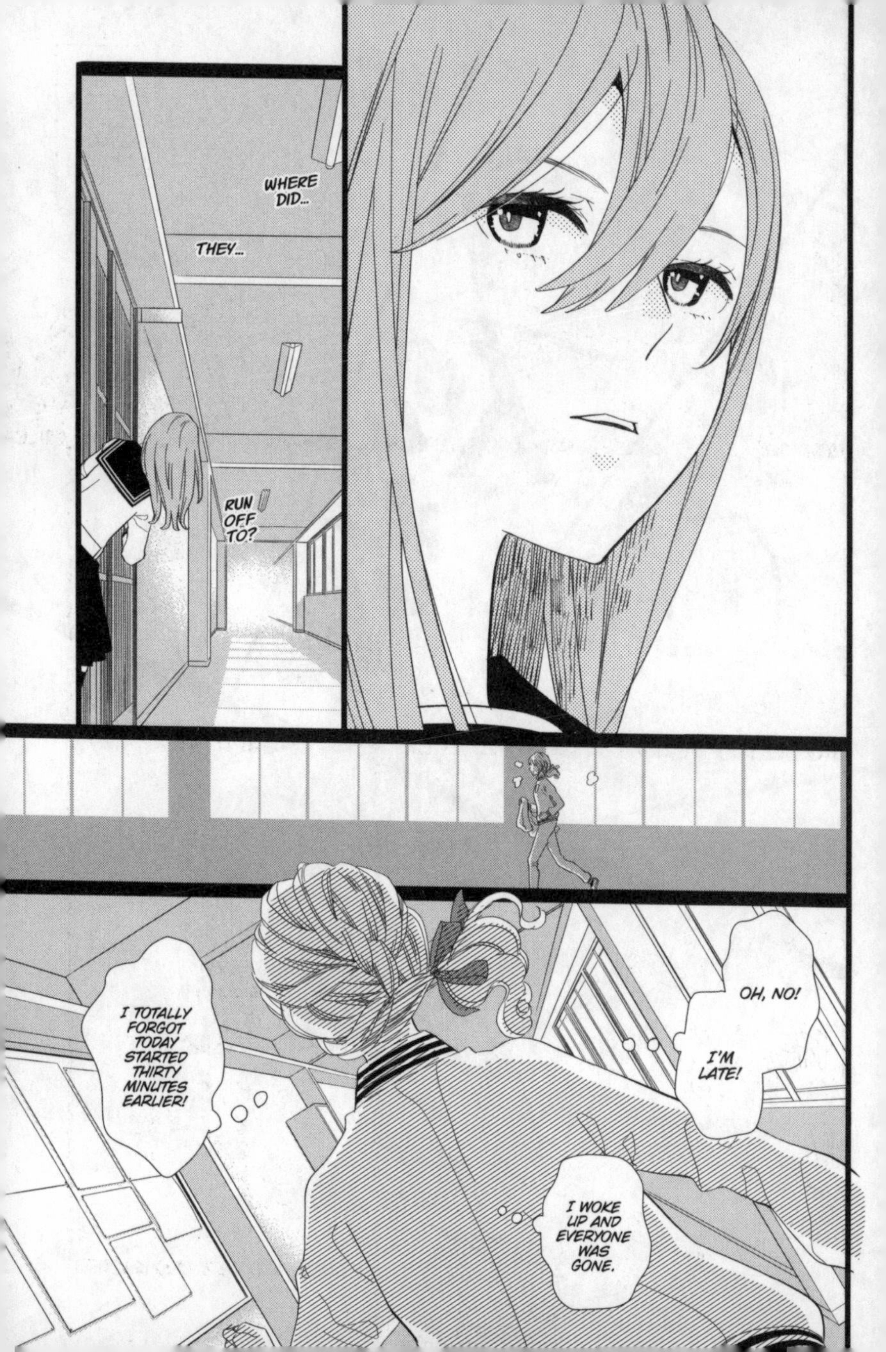
WHERE DID...
THEY...
RUN OFF TO?
OH, NO!
I'M LATE!
I WOKE UP AND EVERYONE WAS GONE.
I TOTALLY FORGOT TODAY STARTED THIRTY MINUTES EARLIER!

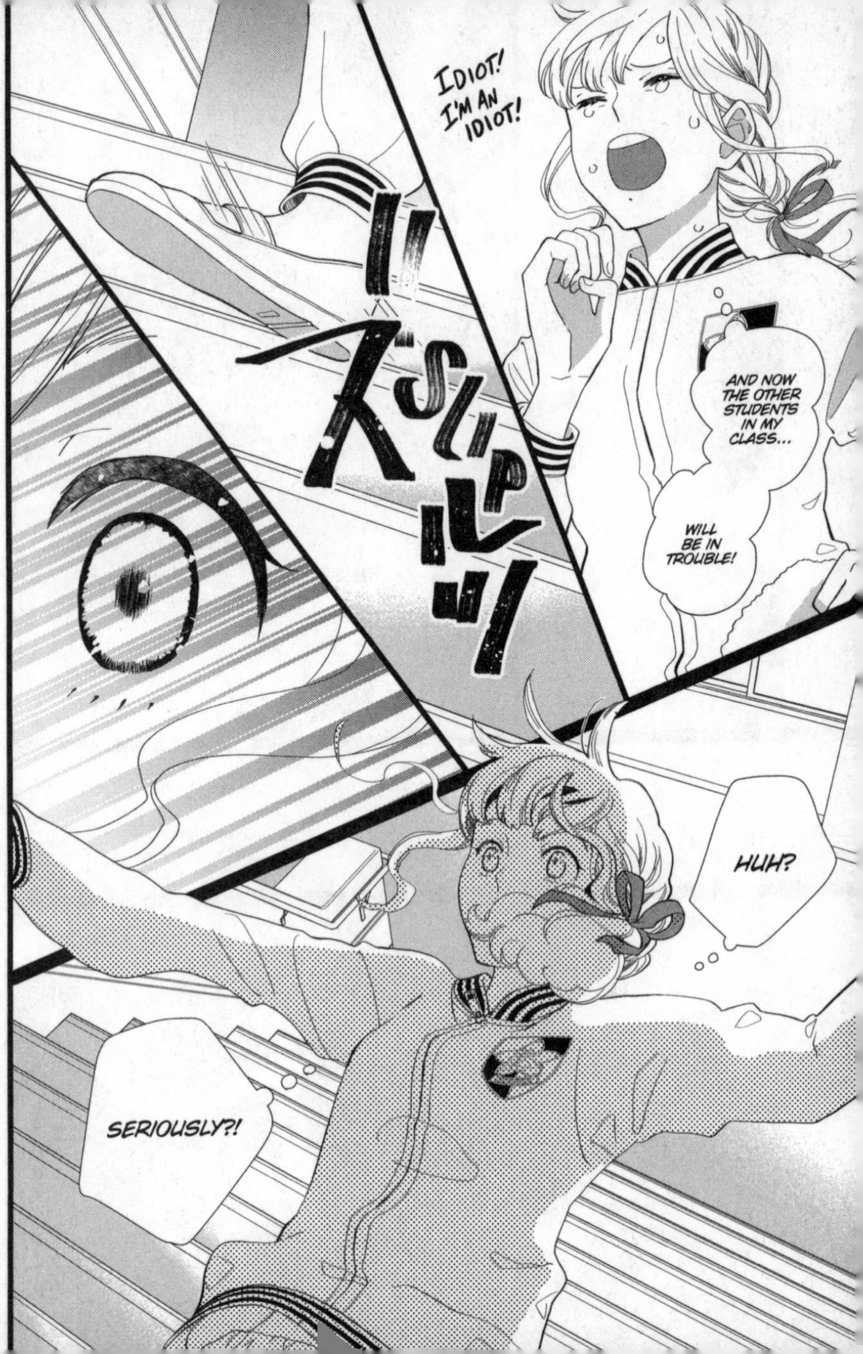
IDIOT! I'M AN IDIOT!
AND NOW THE OTHER STUDENTS IN MY CLASS...
WILL BE IN TROUBLE!
SLIP
HUH?
SERIOUSLY?!

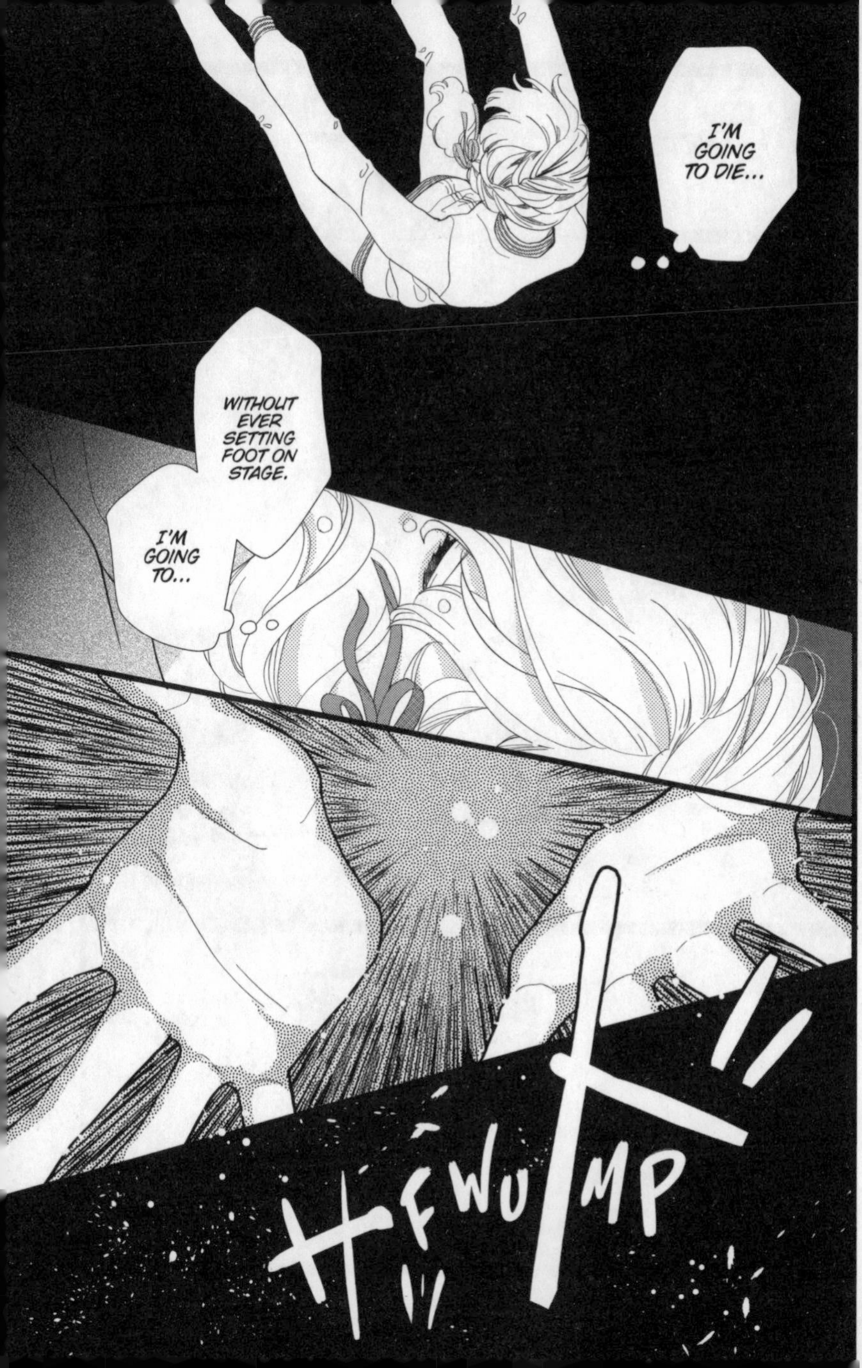
I'M GOING TO DIE...
WITHOUT EVER SETTING FOOT ON STAGE.
I'M GOING TO...
FWUMP

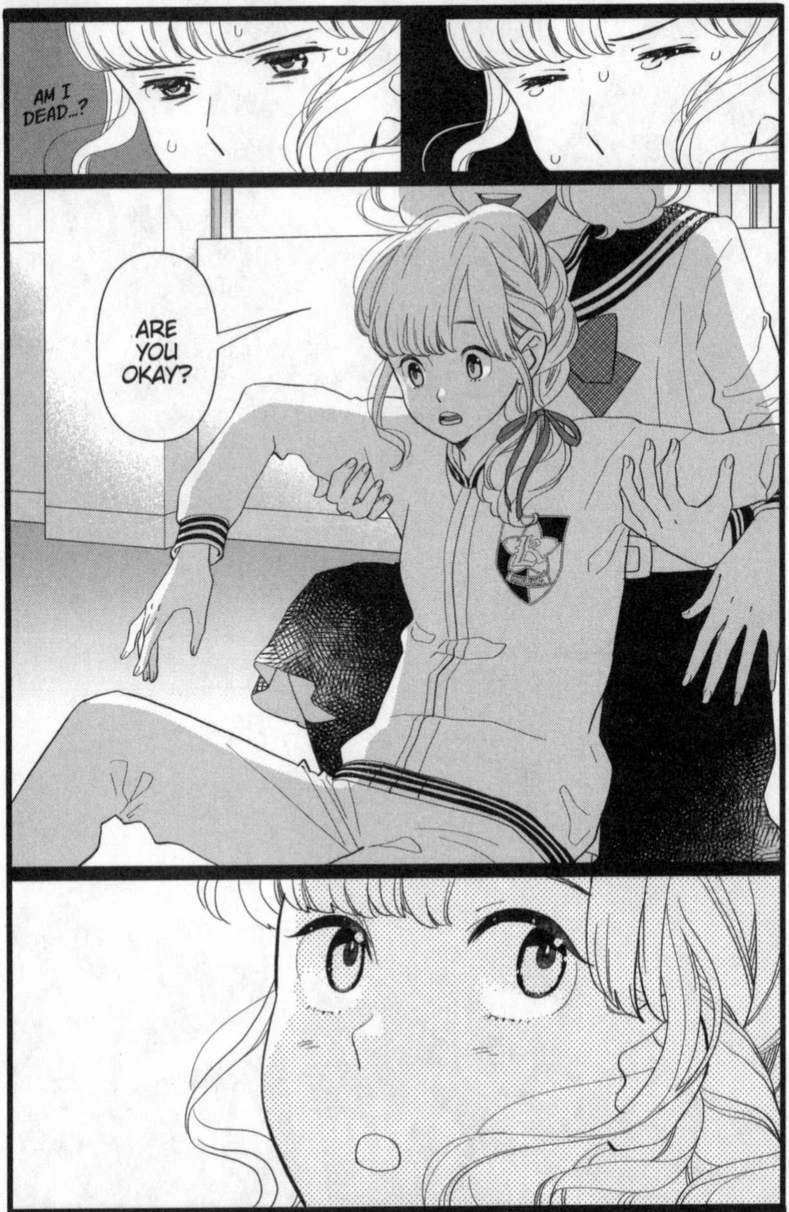
AM I DEAD...?
ARE YOU OKAY?

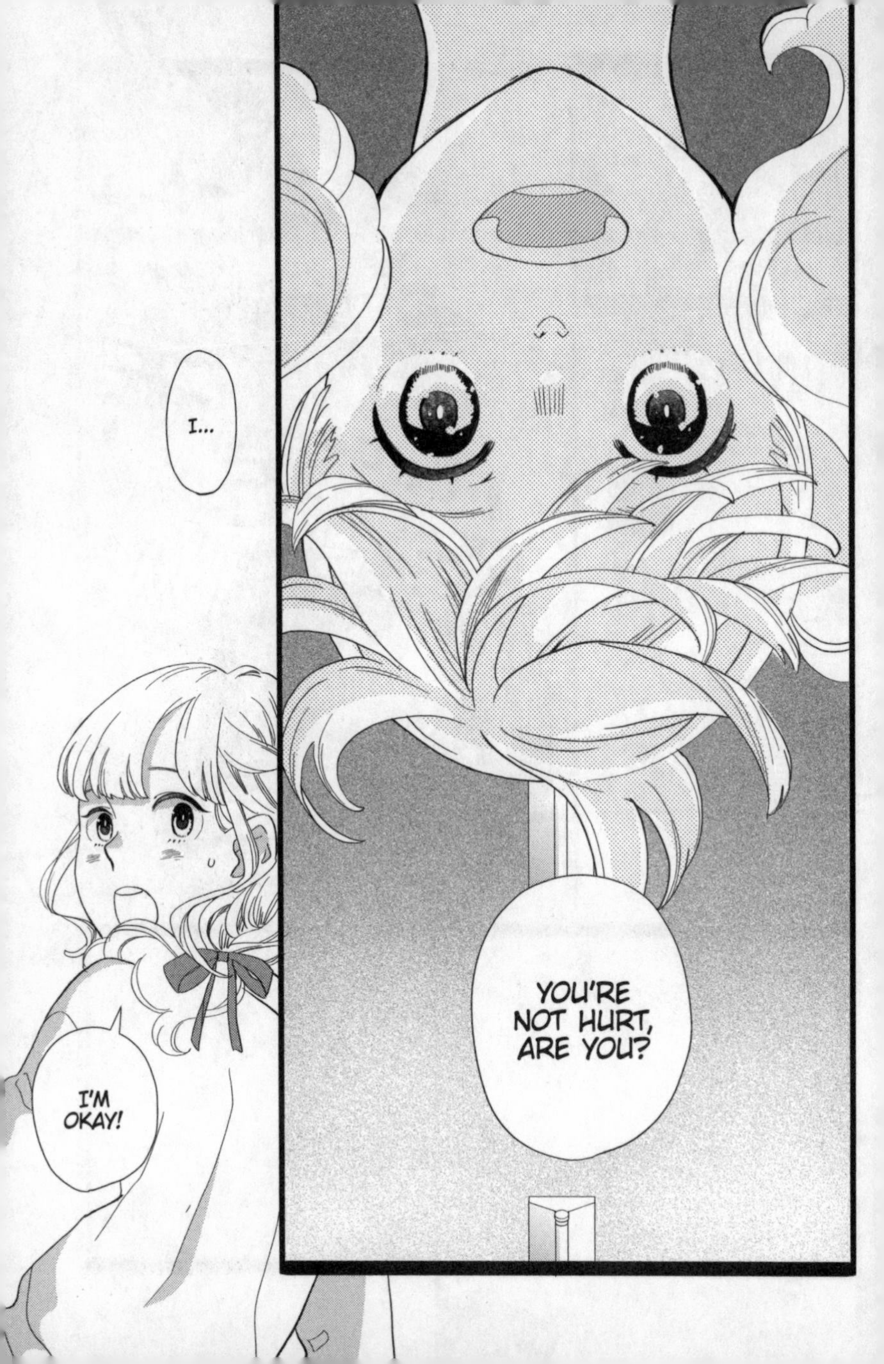
YOU'RE NOT HURT, ARE YOU?
I...
I'M OKAY!

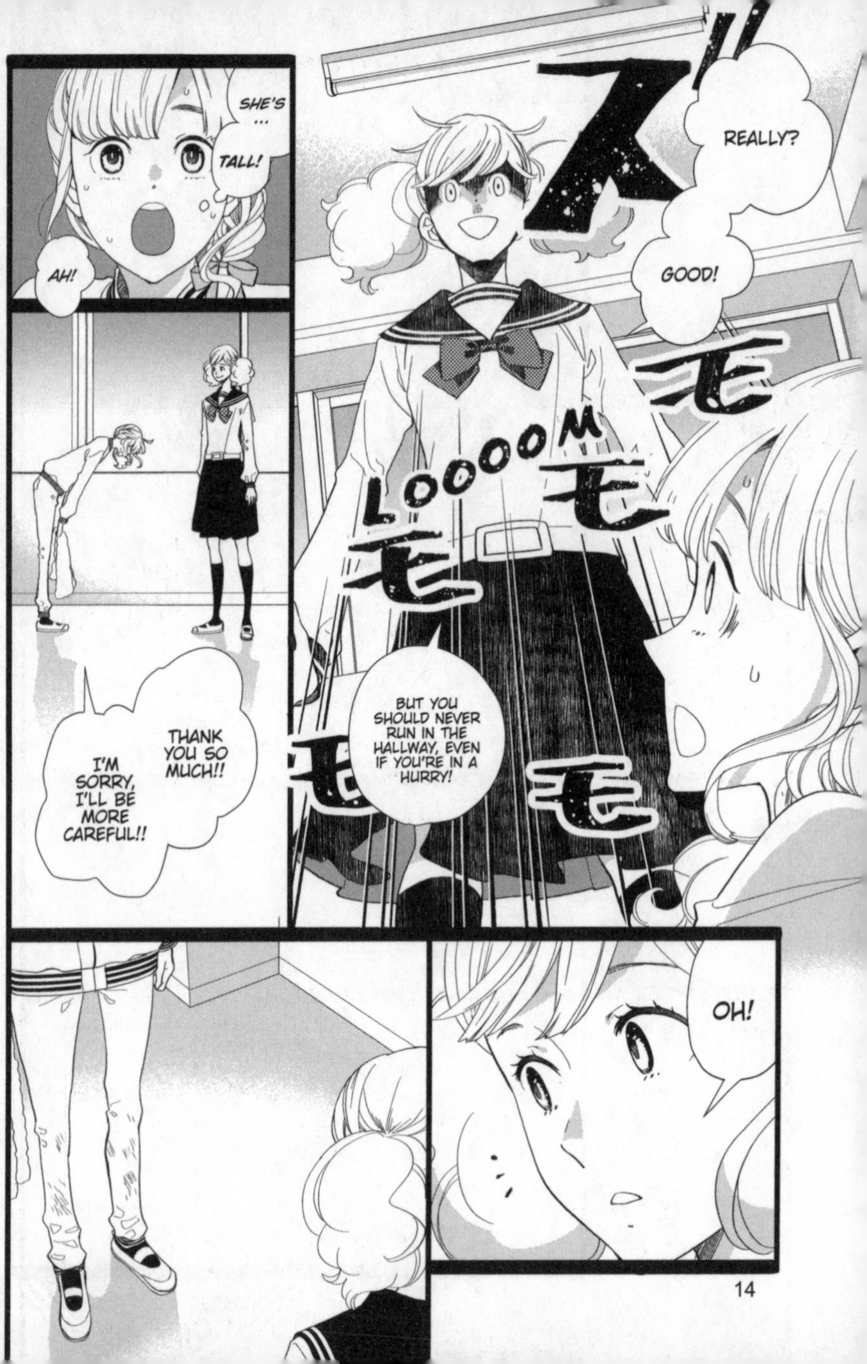
ズ
REALLY?
GOOD!
LOOOOOM
BUT YOU SHOULD NEVER RUN IN THE HALLWAY, EVEN IF YOU'RE IN A HURRY!
SHE'S ... TALL!
AH!
THANK YOU SO MUCH!!
I'M SORRY, I'LL BE MORE CAREFUL!!
OH!

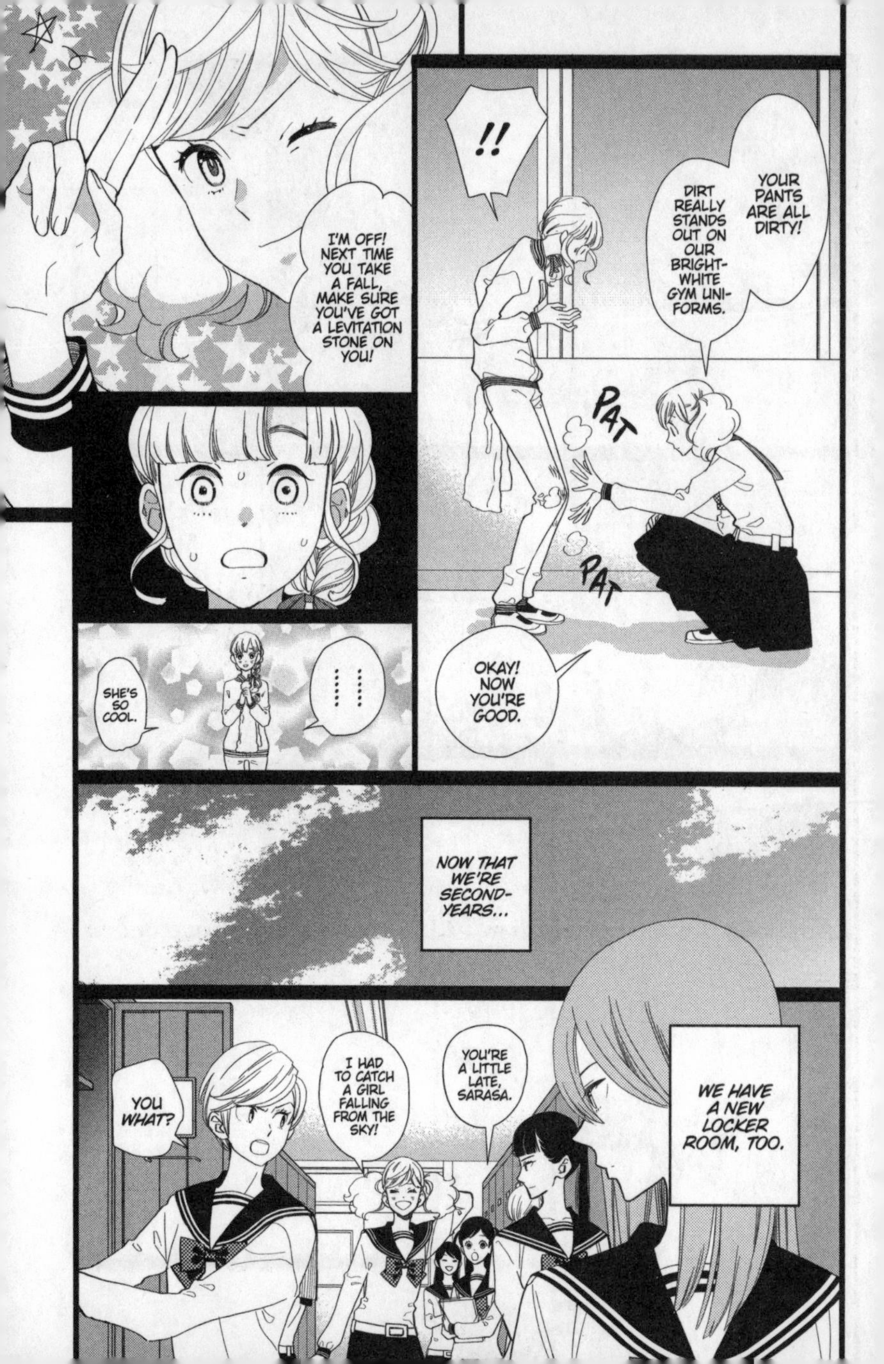
YOUR PANTS ARE ALL DIRTY!
DIRT REALLY STANDS OUT ON OUR BRIGHT-WHITE GYM UNI-FORMS.
!!
PAT
PAT
OKAY! NOW YOU'RE GOOD.
I'M OFF! NEXT TIME YOU TAKE A FALL, MAKE SURE YOU'VE GOT A LEVITATION STONE ON YOU!
......
SHE'S SO COOL.
NOW THAT WE'RE SECOND-YEARS...
WE HAVE A NEW LOCKER ROOM, TOO.
YOU'RE A LITTLE LATE, SARASA.
I HAD TO CATCH A GIRL FALLING FROM THE SKY!
YOU WHAT?

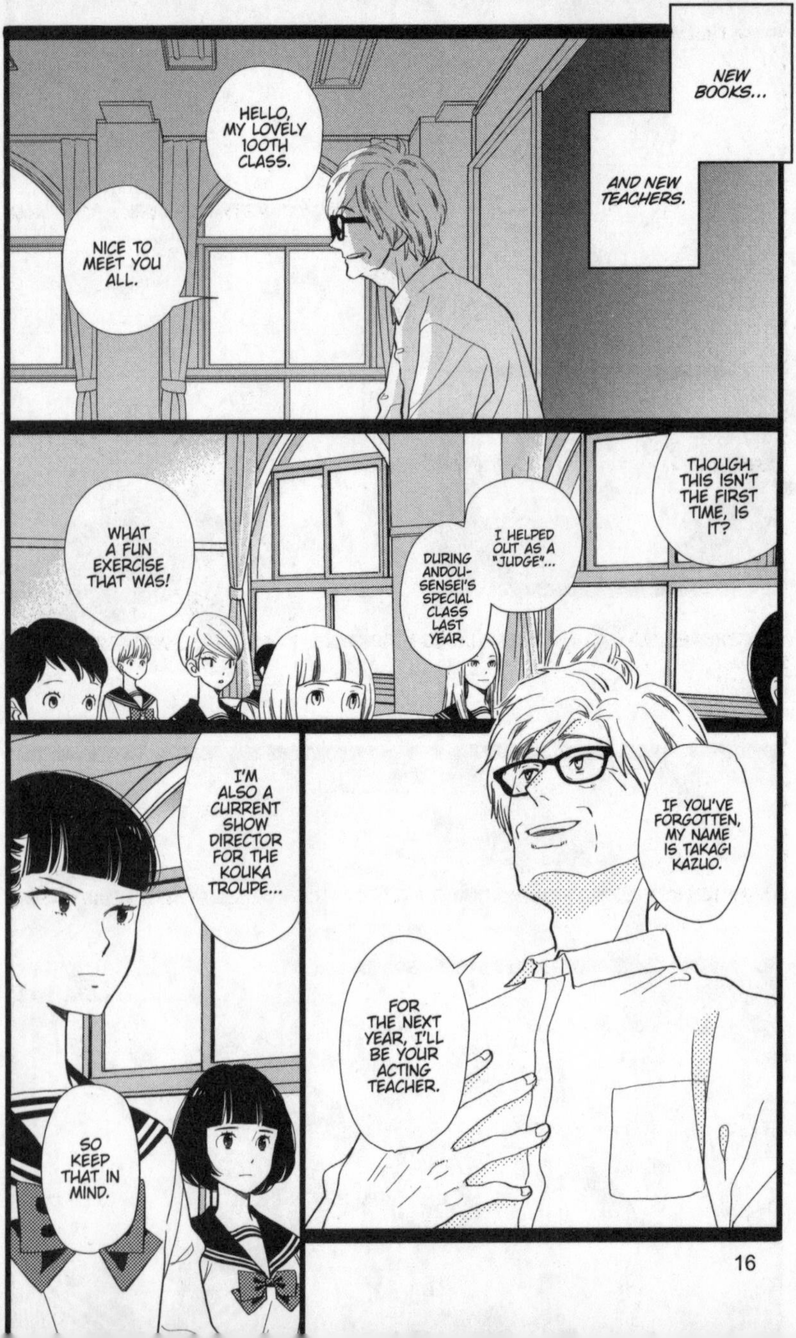
NEW BOOKS...
AND NEW TEACHERS.
HELLO, MY LOVELY 100TH CLASS.
NICE TO MEET YOU ALL.
THOUGH THIS ISN'T THE FIRST TIME, IS IT?
I HELPED OUT AS A "JUDGE"...
DURING ANDOU-SENSEI'S SPECIAL CLASS LAST YEAR.
WHAT A FUN EXERCISE THAT WAS!
IF YOU'VE FORGOTTEN, MY NAME IS TAKAGI KAZUO.
FOR THE NEXT YEAR, I'LL BE YOUR ACTING TEACHER.
I'M ALSO A CURRENT SHOW DIRECTOR FOR THE KOUKA TROUPE...
SO KEEP THAT IN MIND.

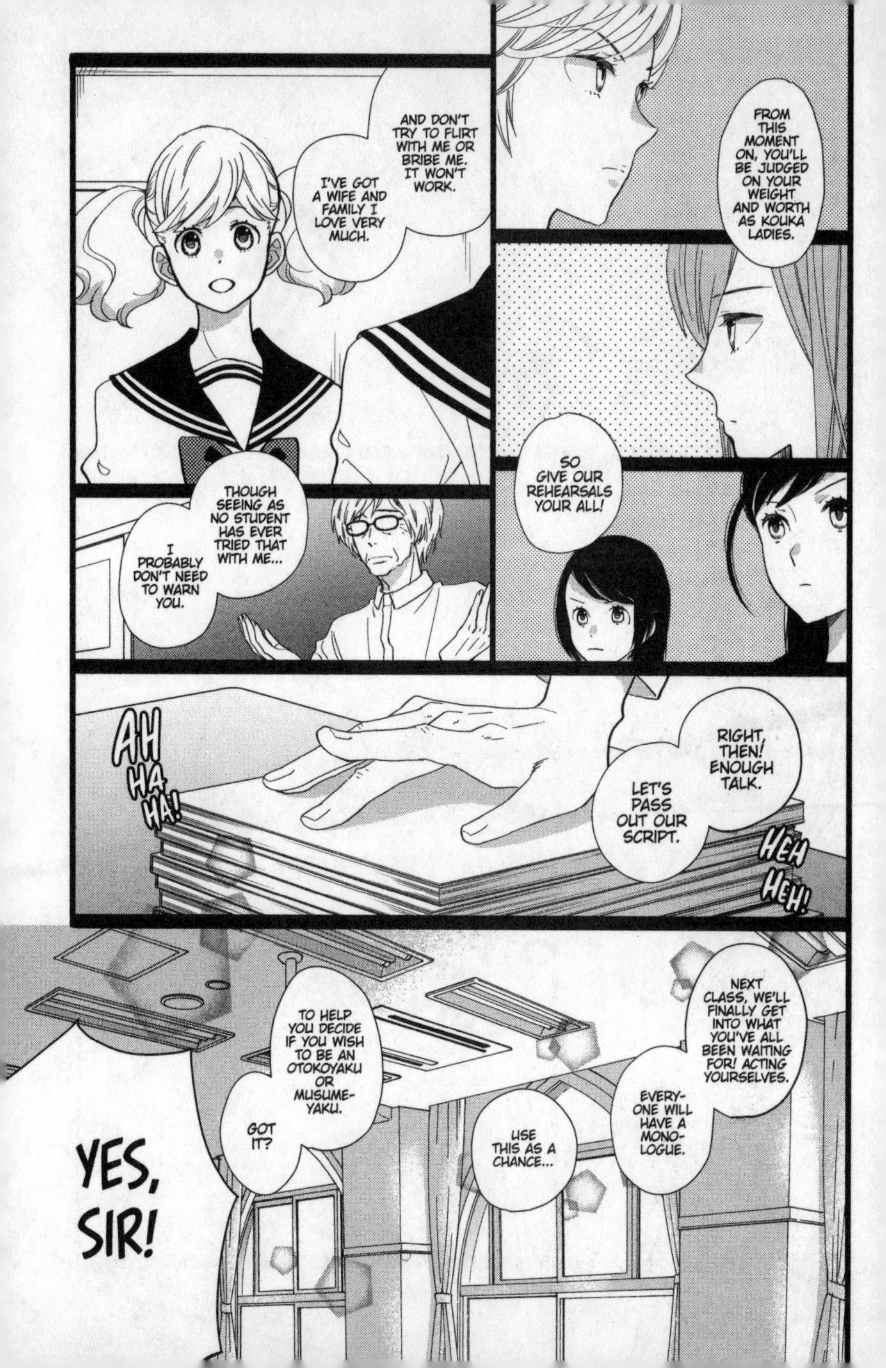
FROM THIS MOMENT ON, YOU'LL BE JUDGED ON YOUR WEIGHT AND WORTH AS KOUKA LADIES.
SO GIVE OUR REHEARSALS YOUR ALL!
AND DON'T TRY TO FLIRT WITH ME OR BRIBE ME. IT WON'T WORK.
I'VE GOT A WIFE AND FAMILY I LOVE VERY MUCH.
THOUGH SEEING AS NO STUDENT HAS EVER TRIED THAT WITH ME...
I PROBABLY DON'T NEED TO WARN YOU.
RIGHT, THEN! ENOUGH TALK.
LET'S PASS OUT OUR SCRIPT.
HEH HEH!
AH HA HA!
NEXT CLASS, WE'LL FINALLY GET INTO WHAT YOU'VE ALL BEEN WAITING FOR! ACTING YOURSELVES.
EVERY-ONE WILL HAVE A MONO-LOGUE.
USE THIS AS A CHANCE...
TO HELP YOU DECIDE IF YOU WISH TO BE AN OTOKOYAKU OR MUSUME-YAKU.
GOT IT?
YES, SIR!

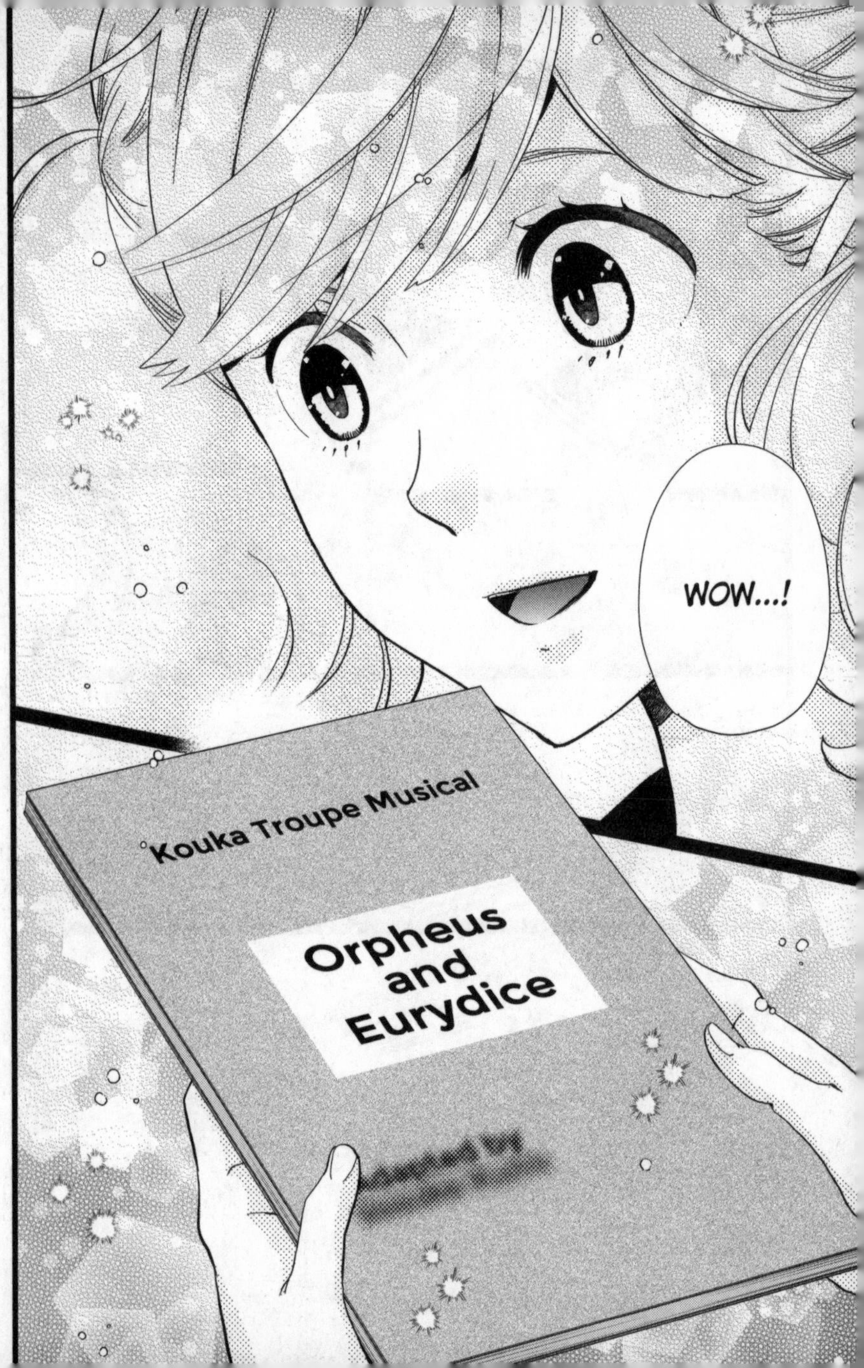
WOW...!
Kouka Troupe Musical
Orpheus and Eurydice

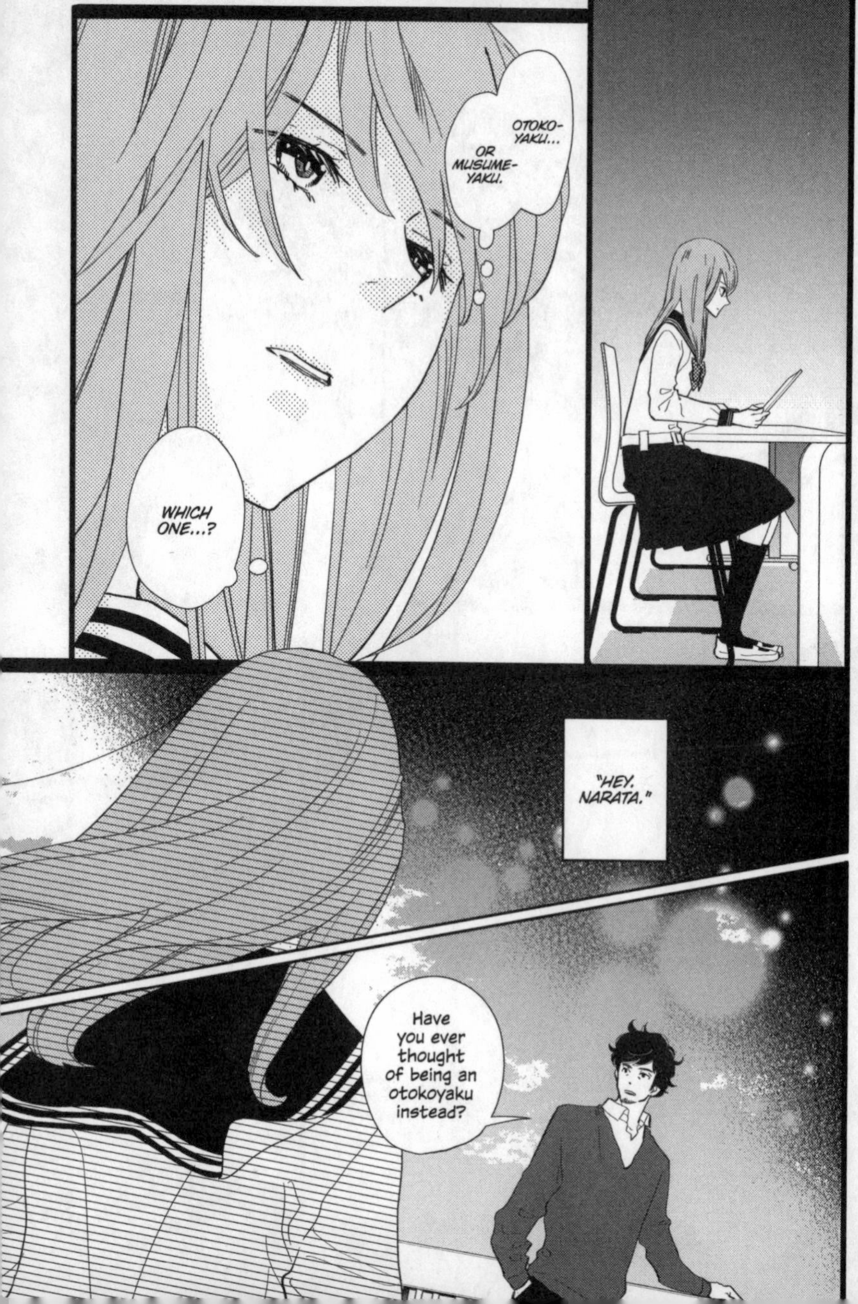
OTOKO-YAKU... OR MUSUME-YAKU.
WHICH ONE...?
"HEY. NARATA."
Have you ever thought of being an otokoyaku instead?

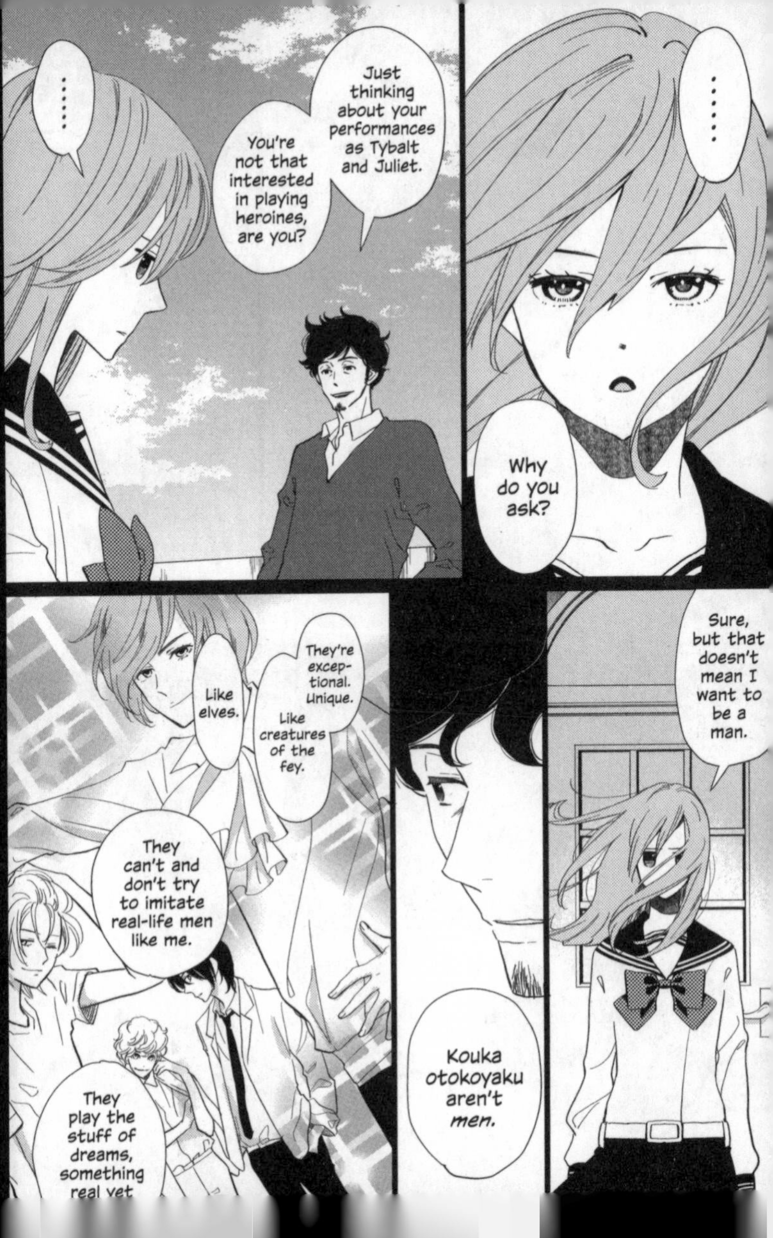
......
Why do you ask?
Just thinking about your performances as Tybalt and Juliet.
You're not that interested in playing heroines, are you?
......
Sure, but that doesn't mean I want to be a man.
Kouka otokoyaku aren't *men*.
They're excep-tional. Unique.
Like creatures of the fey.
Like elves.
They can't and don't try to imitate real-life men like me.
They play the stuff of dreams, something real yet

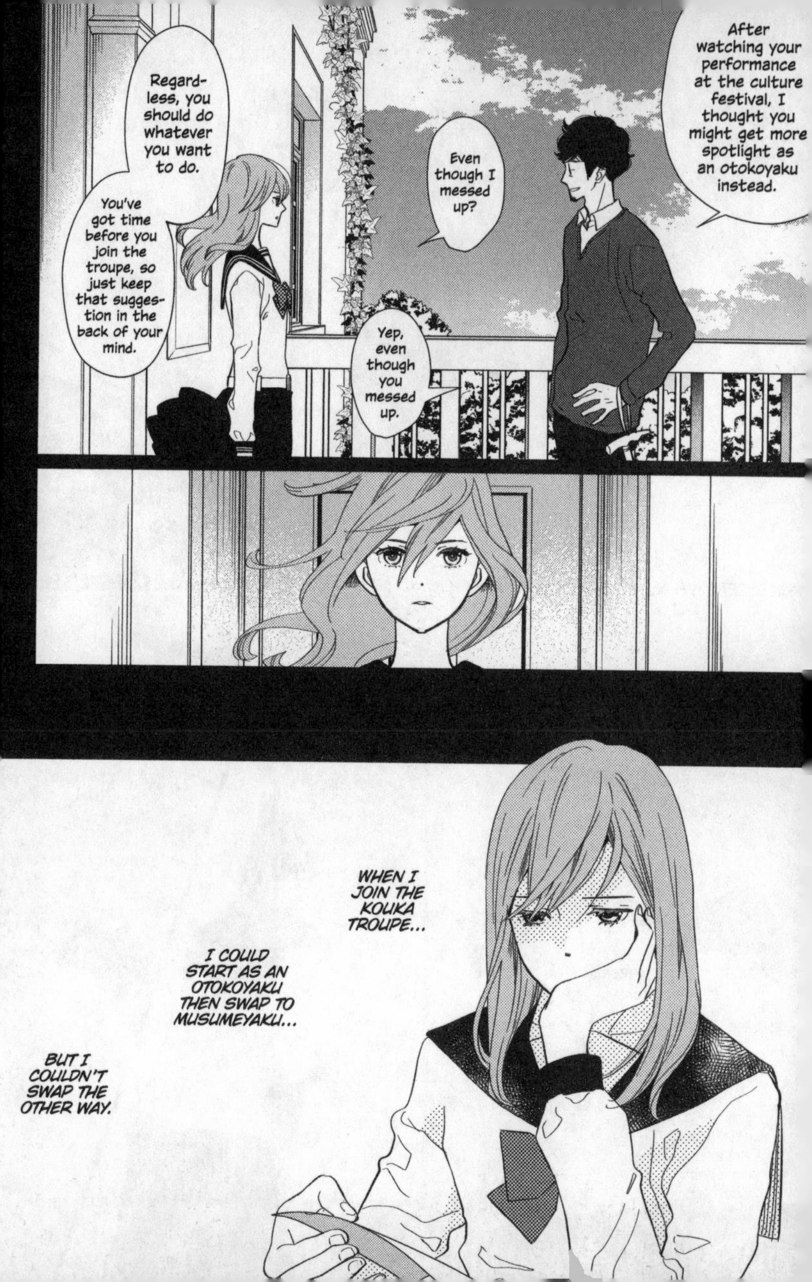
After watching your performance at the culture festival, I thought you might get more spotlight as an otokoyaku instead.
Even though I messed up?
Yep, even though you messed up.
Regardless, you should do whatever you want to do.
You've got time before you join the troupe, so just keep that suggestion in the back of your mind.
WHEN I JOIN THE KOUKA TROUPE...
I COULD START AS AN OTOKOYAKU THEN SWAP TO MUSUMEYAKU...
BUT I COULDN'T SWAP THE OTHER WAY.

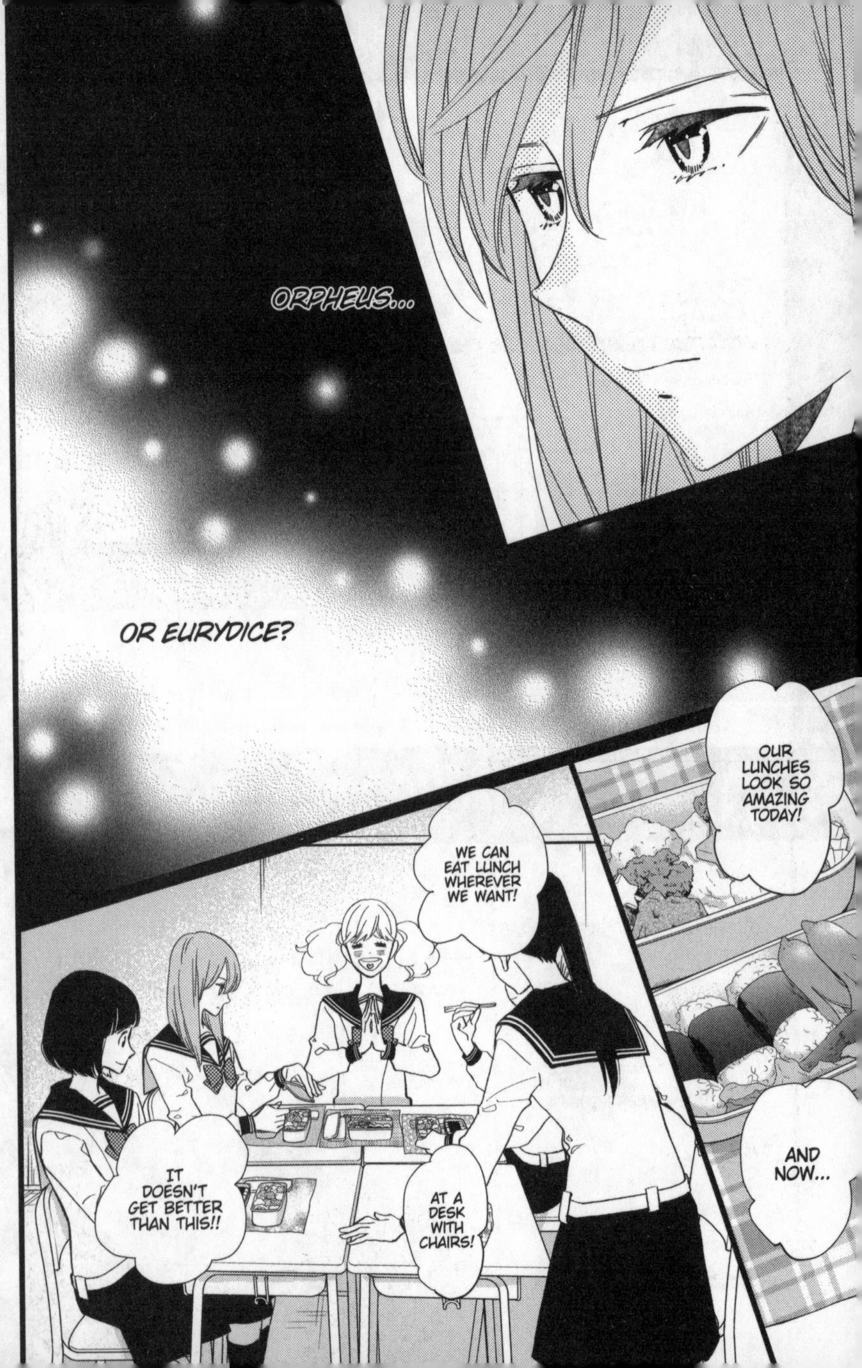
ORPHEUS...
OR EURYDICE?
OUR LUNCHES LOOK SO AMAZING TODAY!
AND NOW...
WE CAN EAT LUNCH WHEREVER WE WANT!
AT A DESK WITH CHAIRS!
IT DOESN'T GET BETTER THAN THIS!!

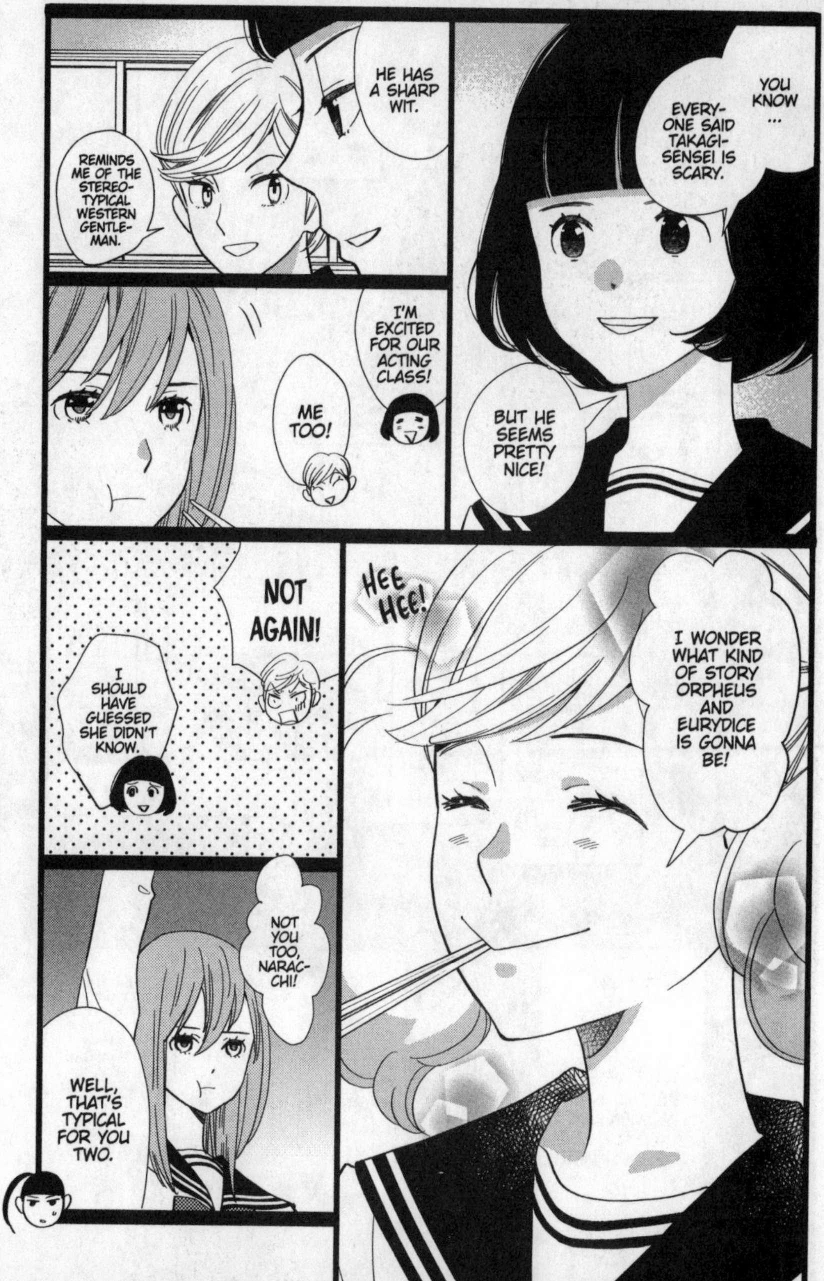
YOU KNOW ...
EVERYONE SAID TAKAGI-SENSEI IS SCARY.
BUT HE SEEMS PRETTY NICE!
HE HAS A SHARP WIT.
REMINDS ME OF THE STEREOTYPICAL WESTERN GENTLEMAN.
I'M EXCITED FOR OUR ACTING CLASS!
ME TOO!
HEE HEE!
I WONDER WHAT KIND OF STORY ORPHEUS AND EURYDICE IS GONNA BE!
NOT AGAIN!
I SHOULD HAVE GUESSED SHE DIDN'T KNOW.
NOT YOU TOO, NARACCHI!
WELL, THAT'S TYPICAL FOR YOU TWO.

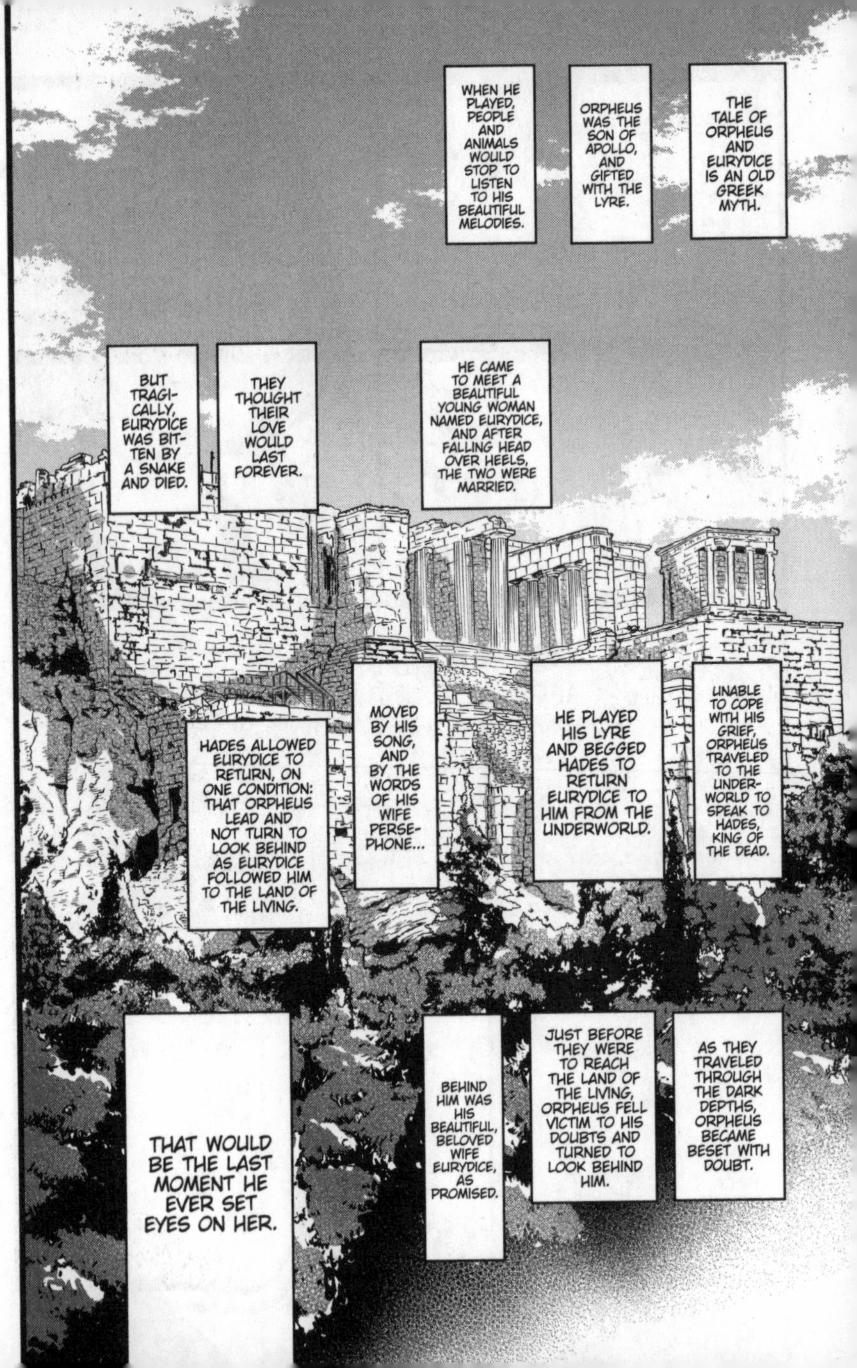
THE TALE OF ORPHEUS AND EURYDICE IS AN OLD GREEK MYTH.
ORPHEUS WAS THE SON OF APOLLO, AND GIFTED WITH THE LYRE.
WHEN HE PLAYED, PEOPLE AND ANIMALS WOULD STOP TO LISTEN TO HIS BEAUTIFUL MELODIES.
HE CAME TO MEET A BEAUTIFUL YOUNG WOMAN NAMED EURYDICE, AND AFTER FALLING HEAD OVER HEELS, THE TWO WERE MARRIED.
THEY THOUGHT THEIR LOVE WOULD LAST FOREVER.
BUT TRAGI-CALLY, EURYDICE WAS BIT-TEN BY A SNAKE AND DIED.
UNABLE TO COPE WITH HIS GRIEF, ORPHEUS TRAVELED TO THE UNDER-WORLD TO SPEAK TO HADES, KING OF THE DEAD.
HE PLAYED HIS LYRE AND BEGGED HADES TO RETURN EURYDICE TO HIM FROM THE UNDERWORLD.
MOVED BY HIS SONG, AND BY THE WORDS OF HIS WIFE PERSE-PHONE...
HADES ALLOWED EURYDICE TO RETURN, ON ONE CONDITION: THAT ORPHEUS LEAD AND NOT TURN TO LOOK BEHIND AS EURYDICE FOLLOWED HIM TO THE LAND OF THE LIVING.
AS THEY TRAVELED THROUGH THE DARK DEPTHS, ORPHEUS BECAME BESET WITH DOUBT.
JUST BEFORE THEY WERE TO REACH THE LAND OF THE LIVING, ORPHEUS FELL VICTIM TO HIS DOUBTS AND TURNED TO LOOK BEHIND HIM.
BEHIND HIM WAS HIS BEAUTIFUL, BELOVED WIFE EURYDICE, AS PROMISED.
THAT WOULD BE THE LAST MOMENT HE EVER SET EYES ON HER.

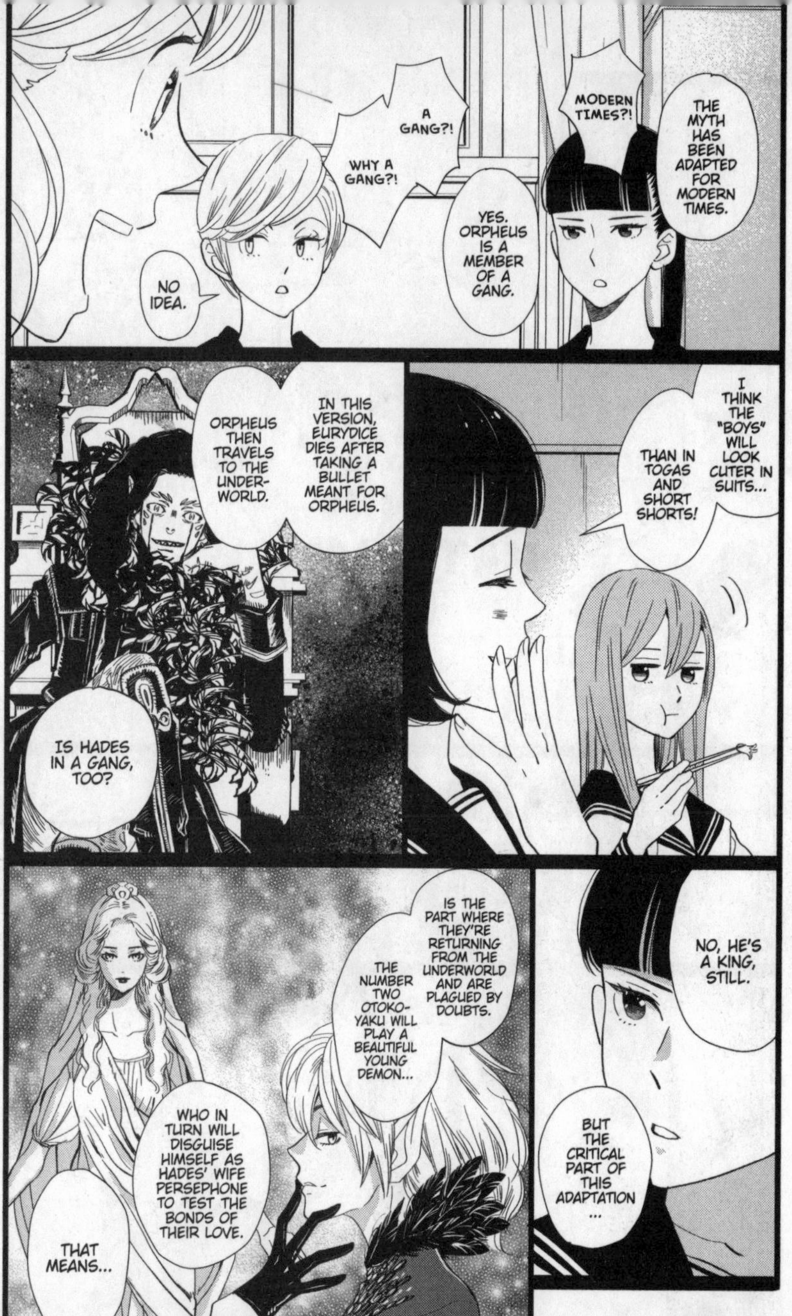
THE MYTH HAS BEEN ADAPTED FOR MODERN TIMES.
MODERN TIMES?!
YES. ORPHEUS IS A MEMBER OF A GANG.
A GANG?!
WHY A GANG?!
NO IDEA.
I THINK THE "BOYS" WILL LOOK CUTER IN SUITS...
THAN IN TOGAS AND SHORT SHORTS!
IN THIS VERSION, EURYDICE DIES AFTER TAKING A BULLET MEANT FOR ORPHEUS.
ORPHEUS THEN TRAVELS TO THE UNDER-WORLD.
IS HADES IN A GANG, TOO?
NO, HE'S A KING, STILL.
BUT THE CRITICAL PART OF THIS ADAPTATION ...
IS THE PART WHERE THEY'RE RETURNING FROM THE UNDERWORLD AND ARE PLAGUED BY DOUBTS.
THE NUMBER TWO OTOKO-YAKU WILL PLAY A BEAUTIFUL YOUNG DEMON...
WHO IN TURN WILL DISGUISE HIMSELF AS HADES' WIFE PERSEPHONE TO TEST THE BONDS OF THEIR LOVE.
THAT MEANS...

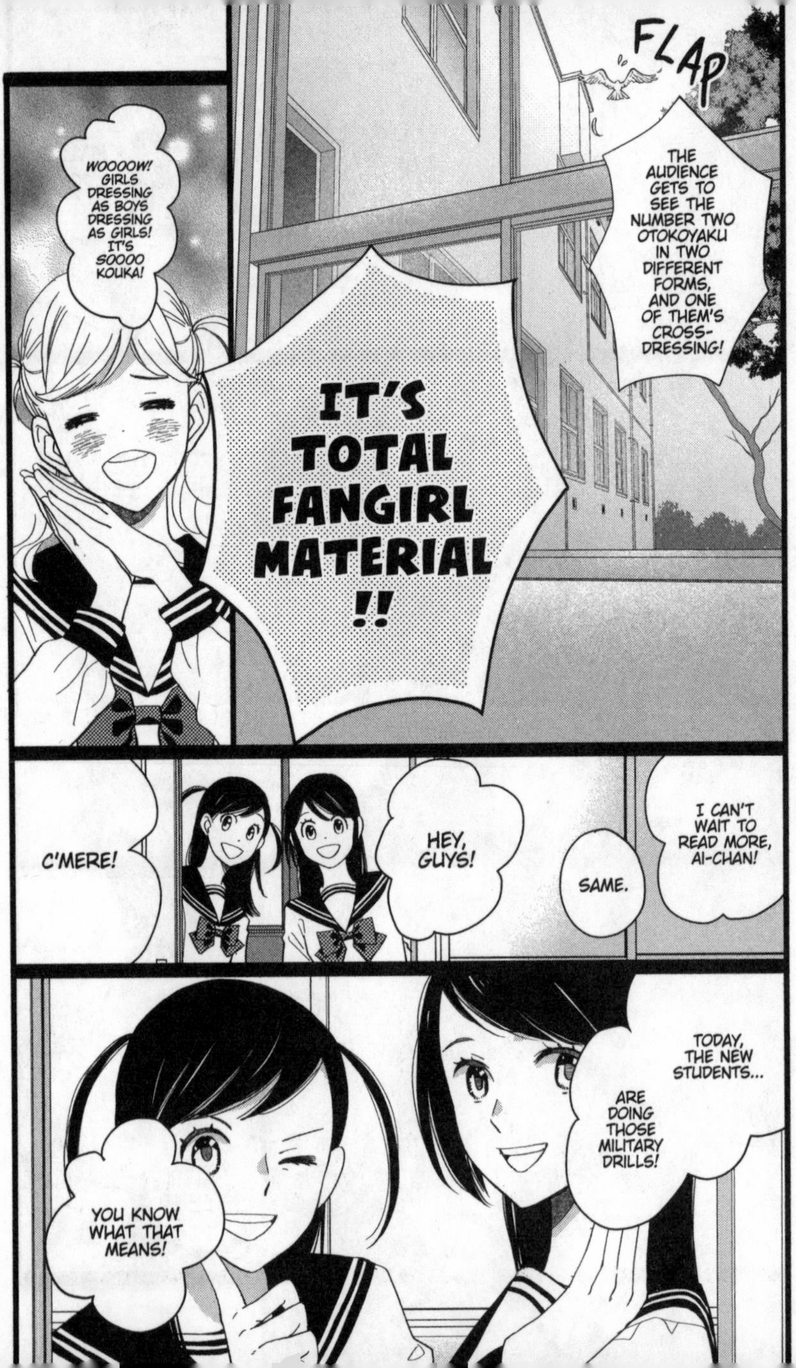
FLAP
THE AUDIENCE GETS TO SEE THE NUMBER TWO OTOKOYAKU IN TWO DIFFERENT FORMS, AND ONE OF THEM'S CROSS-DRESSING!
WOOOOW! GIRLS DRESSING AS BOYS DRESSING AS GIRLS! IT'S SOOOO KOUKA!
IT'S TOTAL FANGIRL MATERIAL!!
I CAN'T WAIT TO READ MORE, AI-CHAN!
SAME.
HEY, GUYS!
C'MERE!
TODAY, THE NEW STUDENTS...
ARE DOING THOSE MILITARY DRILLS!
YOU KNOW WHAT THAT MEANS!

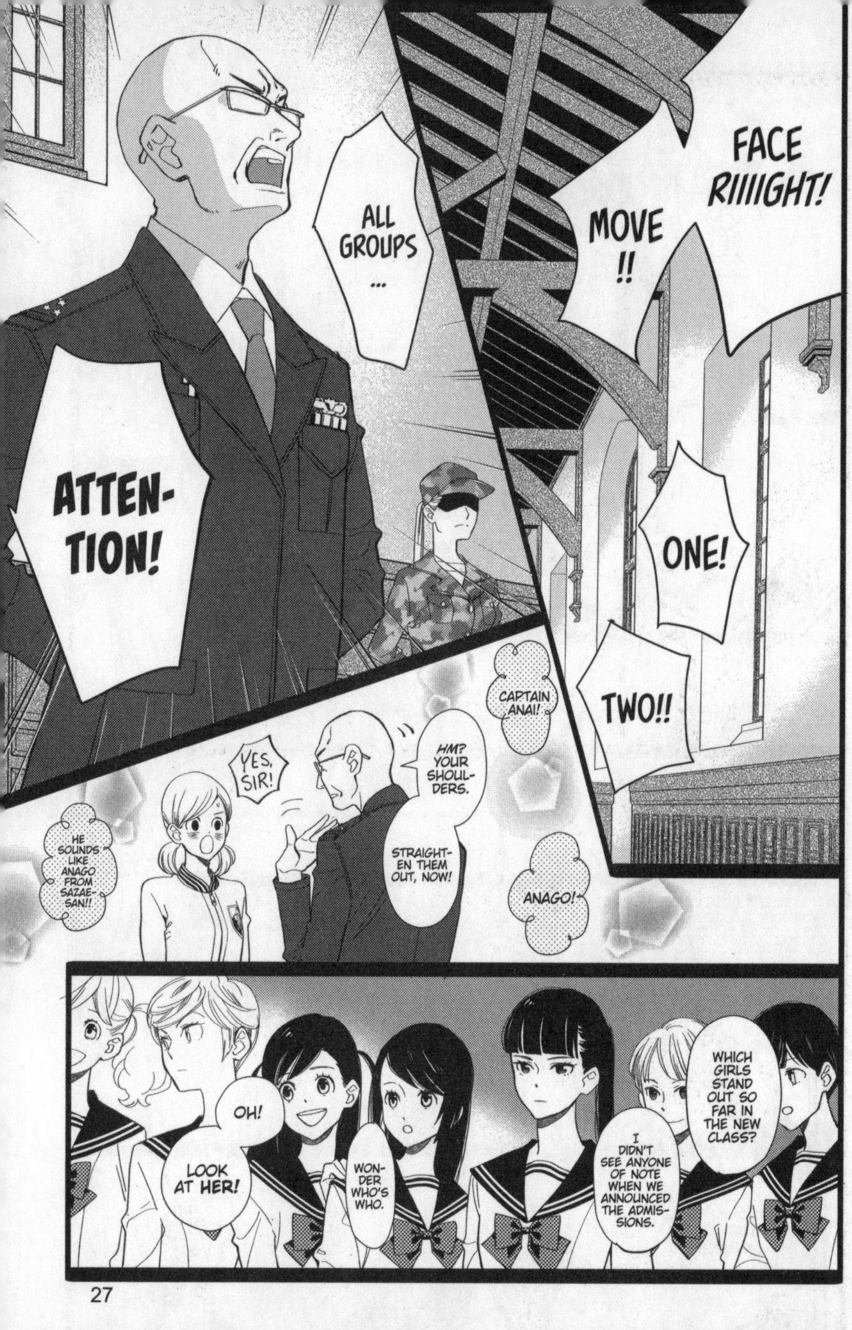
FACE RIIIIGHT!
MOVE!!
ONE!
TWO!!
ALL GROUPS...
ATTENTION!
CAPTAIN ANAI!
HM? YOUR SHOULDERS.
YES, SIR!
STRAIGHTEN THEM OUT, NOW!
ANAGO!
HE SOUNDS LIKE ANAGO FROM SAZAE-SAN!!
WHICH GIRLS STAND OUT SO FAR IN THE NEW CLASS?
I DIDN'T SEE ANYONE OF NOTE WHEN WE ANNOUNCED THE ADMISSIONS.
WONDER WHO'S WHO.
OH!
LOOK AT HER!

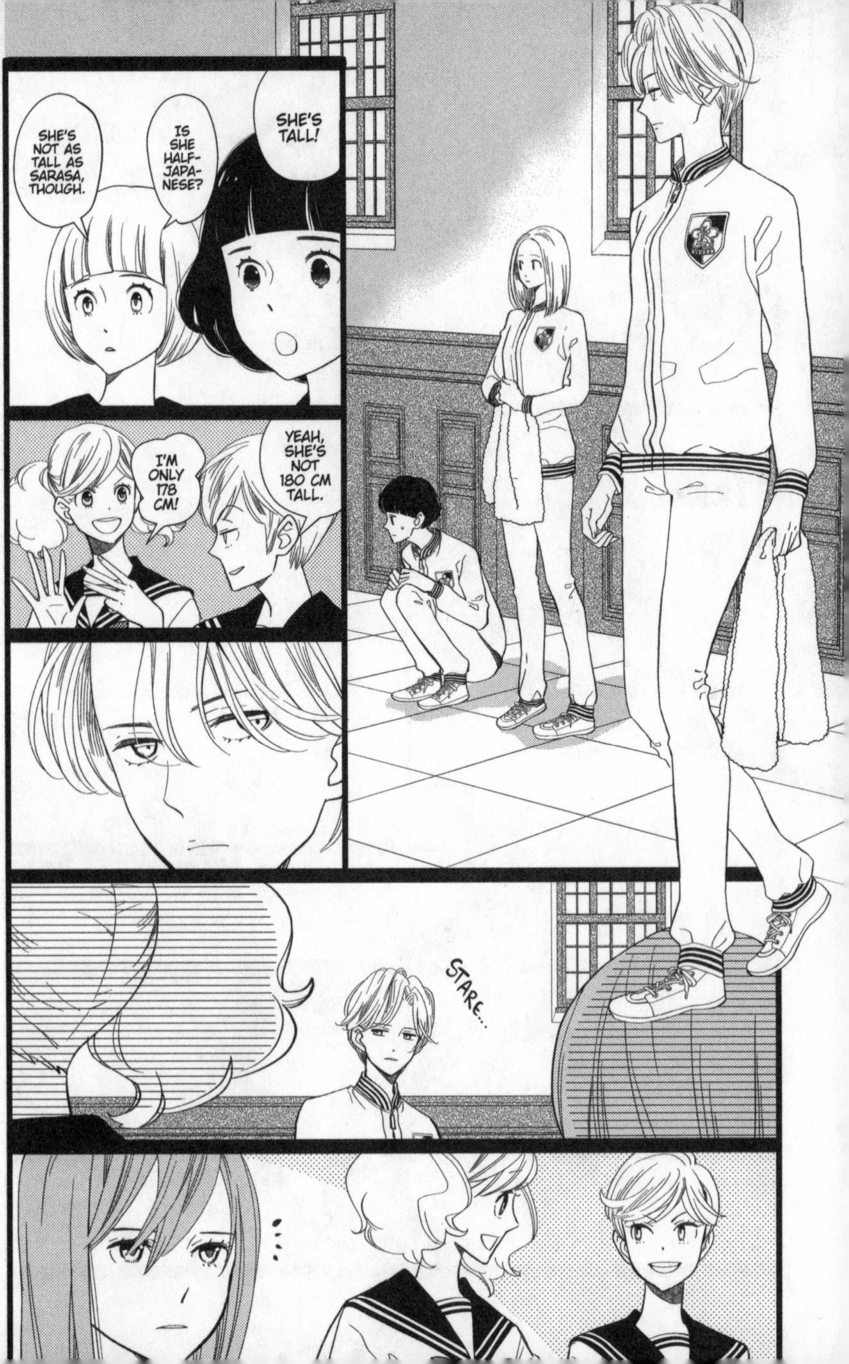
SHE'S TALL!
IS SHE HALF-JAPANESE?
SHE'S NOT AS TALL AS SARASA, THOUGH.
YEAH, SHE'S NOT 180 CM TALL.
I'M ONLY 178 CM!
STARE...
...

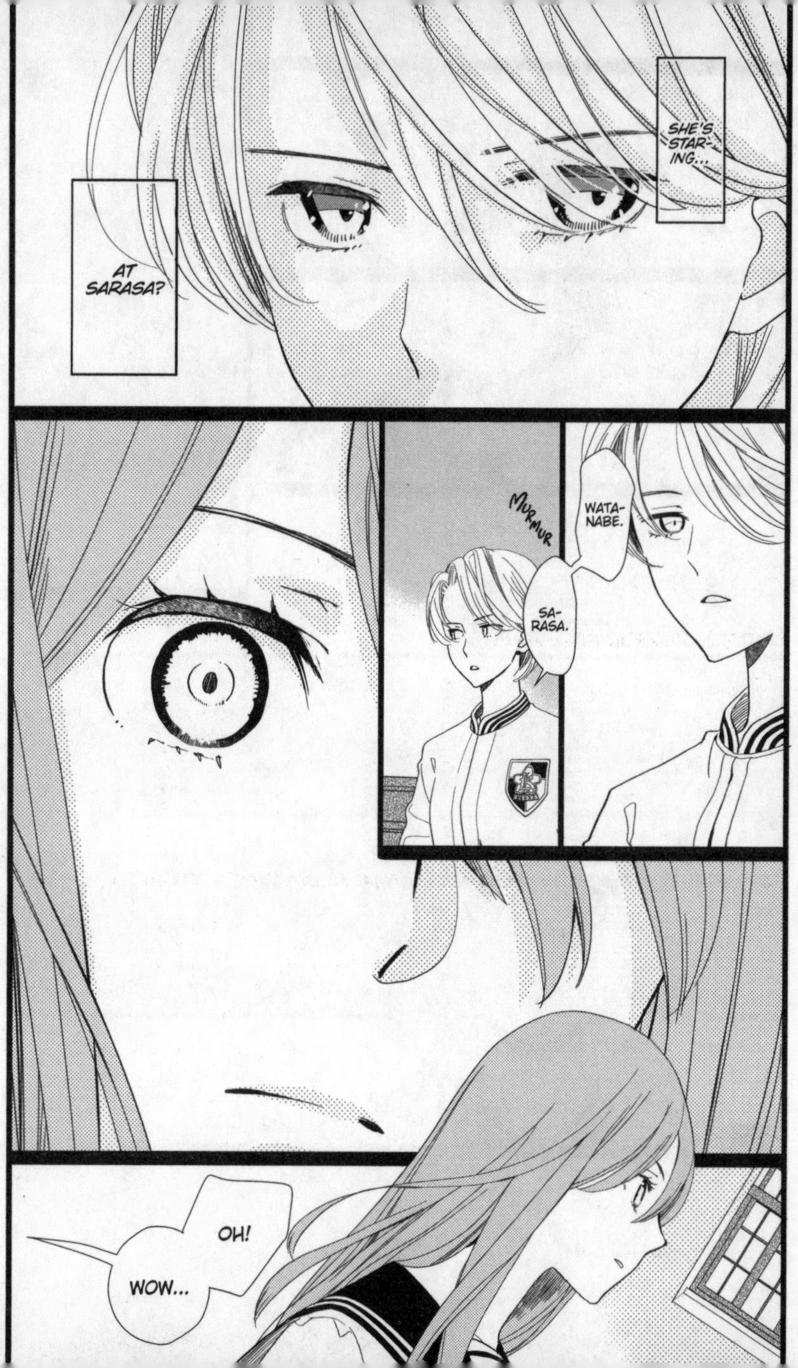
SHE'S STARING...
AT SARASA?
WATANABE.
SARASA.
MURMUR
OH!
WOW...

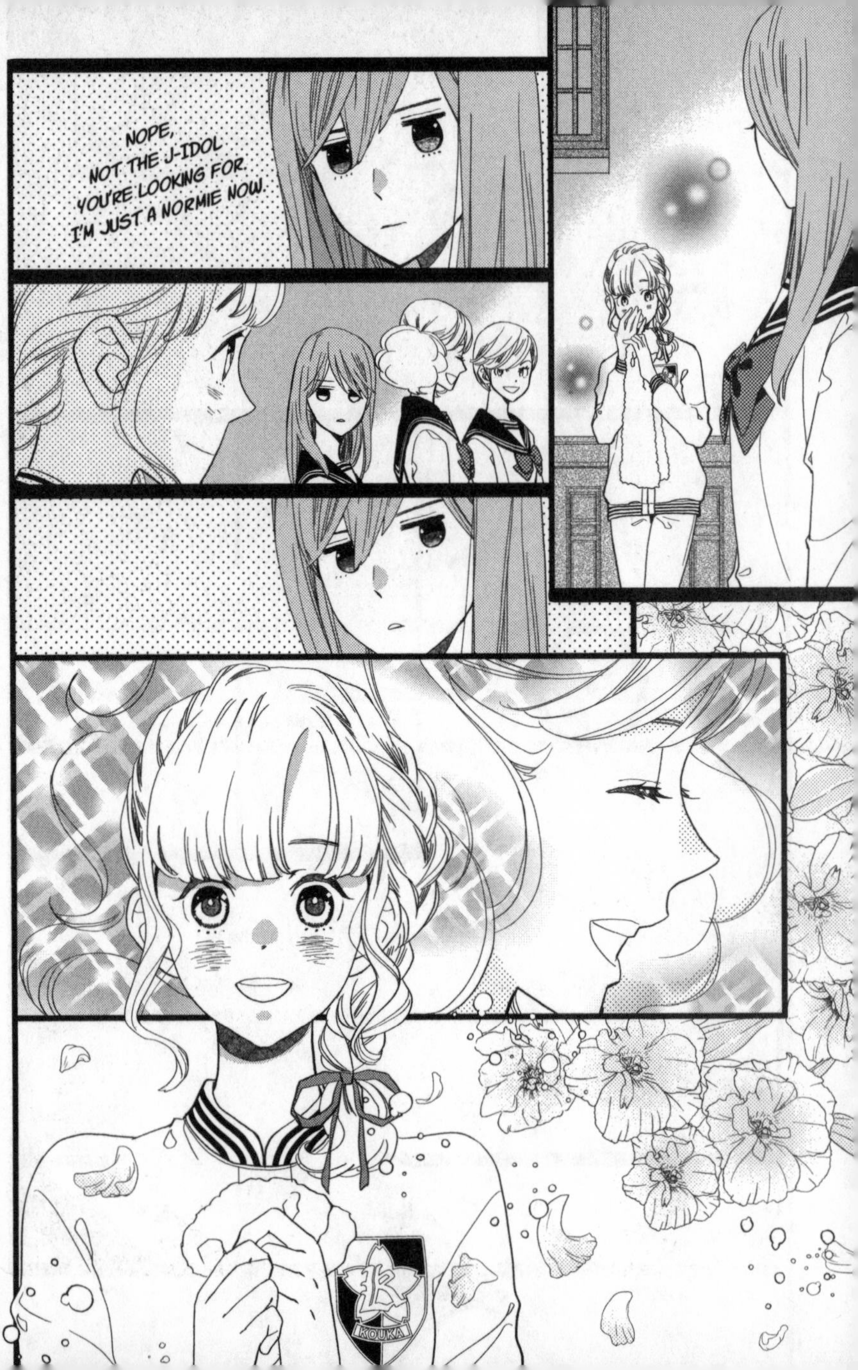
NOPE, NOT THE J-IDOL YOU'RE LOOKING FOR. I'M JUST A NORMIE NOW.
KOUKA

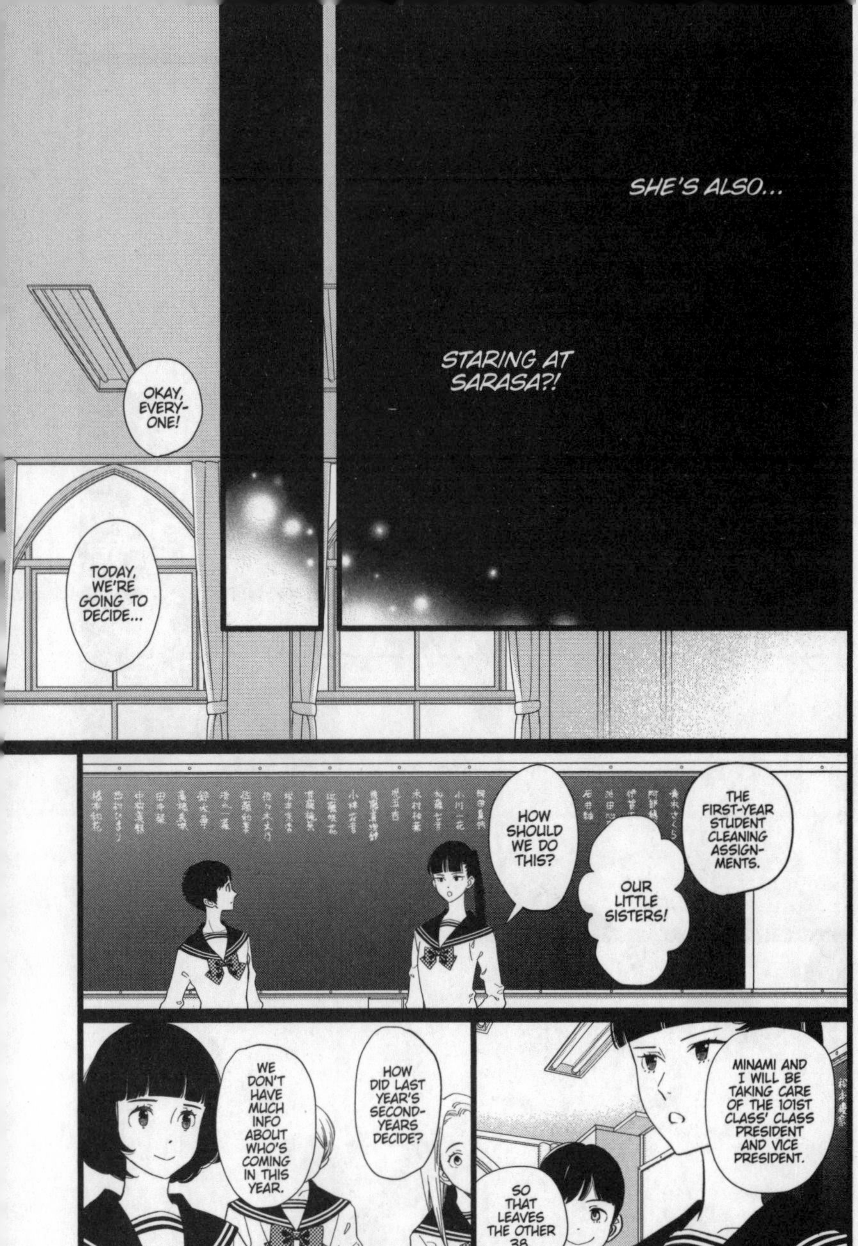
SHE'S ALSO...
STARING AT SARASA?!
OKAY, EVERY-ONE!
TODAY, WE'RE GOING TO DECIDE...
THE FIRST-YEAR STUDENT CLEANING ASSIGN-MENTS.
OUR LITTLE SISTERS!
HOW SHOULD WE DO THIS?
MINAMI AND I WILL BE TAKING CARE OF THE 101ST CLASS' CLASS PRESIDENT AND VICE PRESIDENT.
SO THAT LEAVES THE OTHER 38.
HOW DID LAST YEAR'S SECOND-YEARS DECIDE?
WE DON'T HAVE MUCH INFO ABOUT WHO'S COMING IN THIS YEAR.

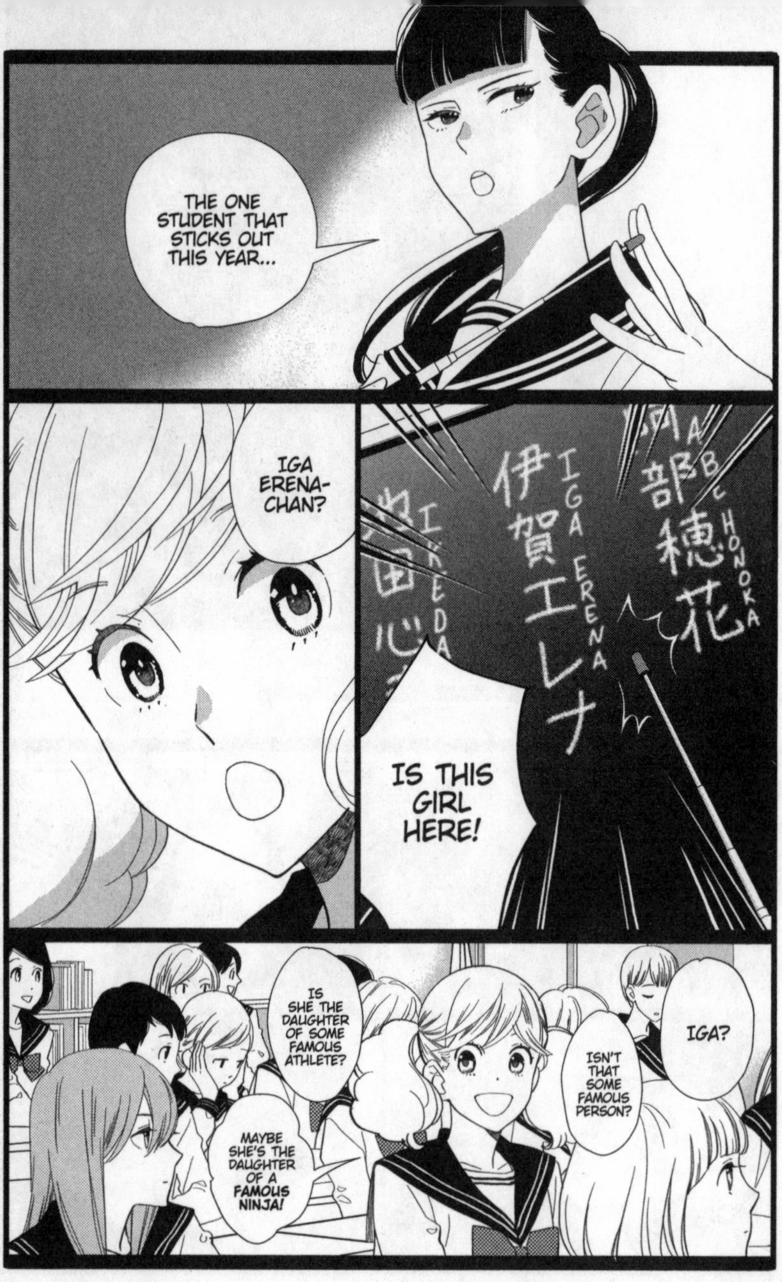
THE ONE STUDENT THAT STICKS OUT THIS YEAR...
部穂花
HONOKA
伊賀エレナ
IGA ERENA
IS THIS GIRL HERE!
IGA ERENA-CHAN?
IGA?
ISN'T THAT SOME FAMOUS PERSON?
IS SHE THE DAUGHTER OF SOME FAMOUS ATHLETE?
MAYBE SHE'S THE DAUGHTER OF A FAMOUS NINJA!

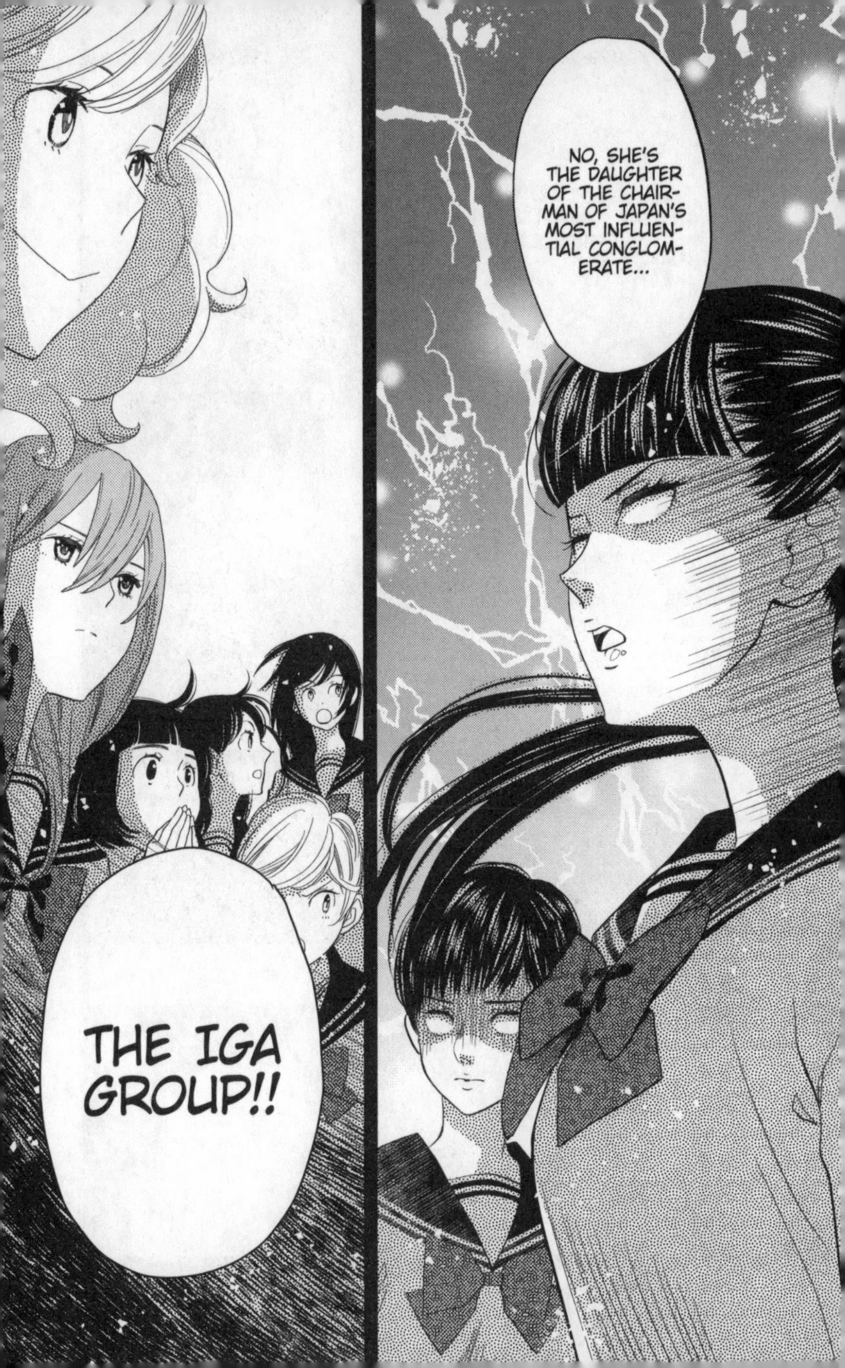
NO, SHE'S THE DAUGHTER OF THE CHAIR-MAN OF JAPAN'S MOST INFLUEN-TIAL CONGLOM-ERATE...
THE IGA GROUP!!

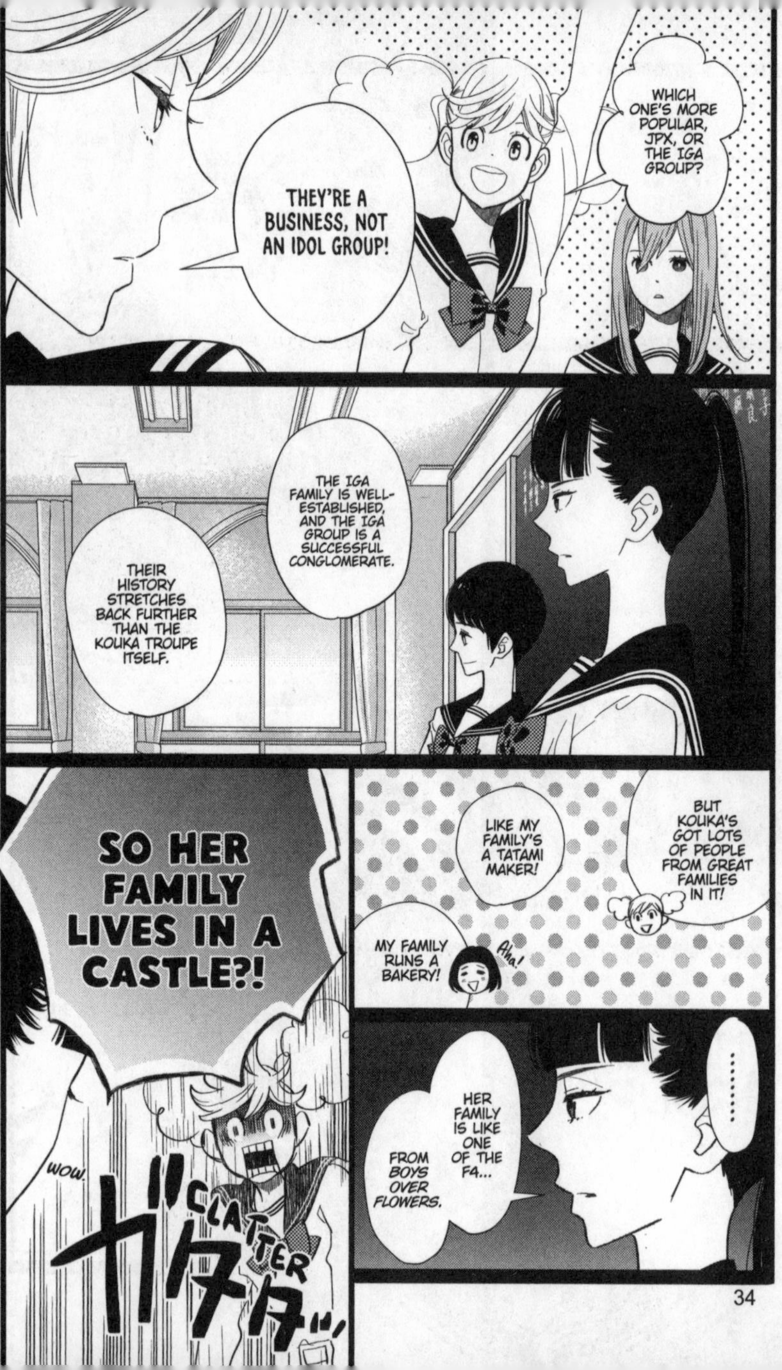
WHICH ONE'S MORE POPULAR, JPX, OR THE IGA GROUP?
THEY'RE A BUSINESS, NOT AN IDOL GROUP!
THE IGA FAMILY IS WELL-ESTABLISHED, AND THE IGA GROUP IS A SUCCESSFUL CONGLOMERATE.
THEIR HISTORY STRETCHES BACK FURTHER THAN THE KOUKA TROUPE ITSELF.
BUT KOUKA'S GOT LOTS OF PEOPLE FROM GREAT FAMILIES IN IT!
LIKE MY FAMILY'S A TATAMI MAKER!
Aha!
MY FAMILY RUNS A BAKERY!
......
HER FAMILY IS LIKE ONE OF THE F4...
FROM BOYS OVER FLOWERS.
SO HER FAMILY LIVES IN A CASTLE?!
WOW.
CLATTER

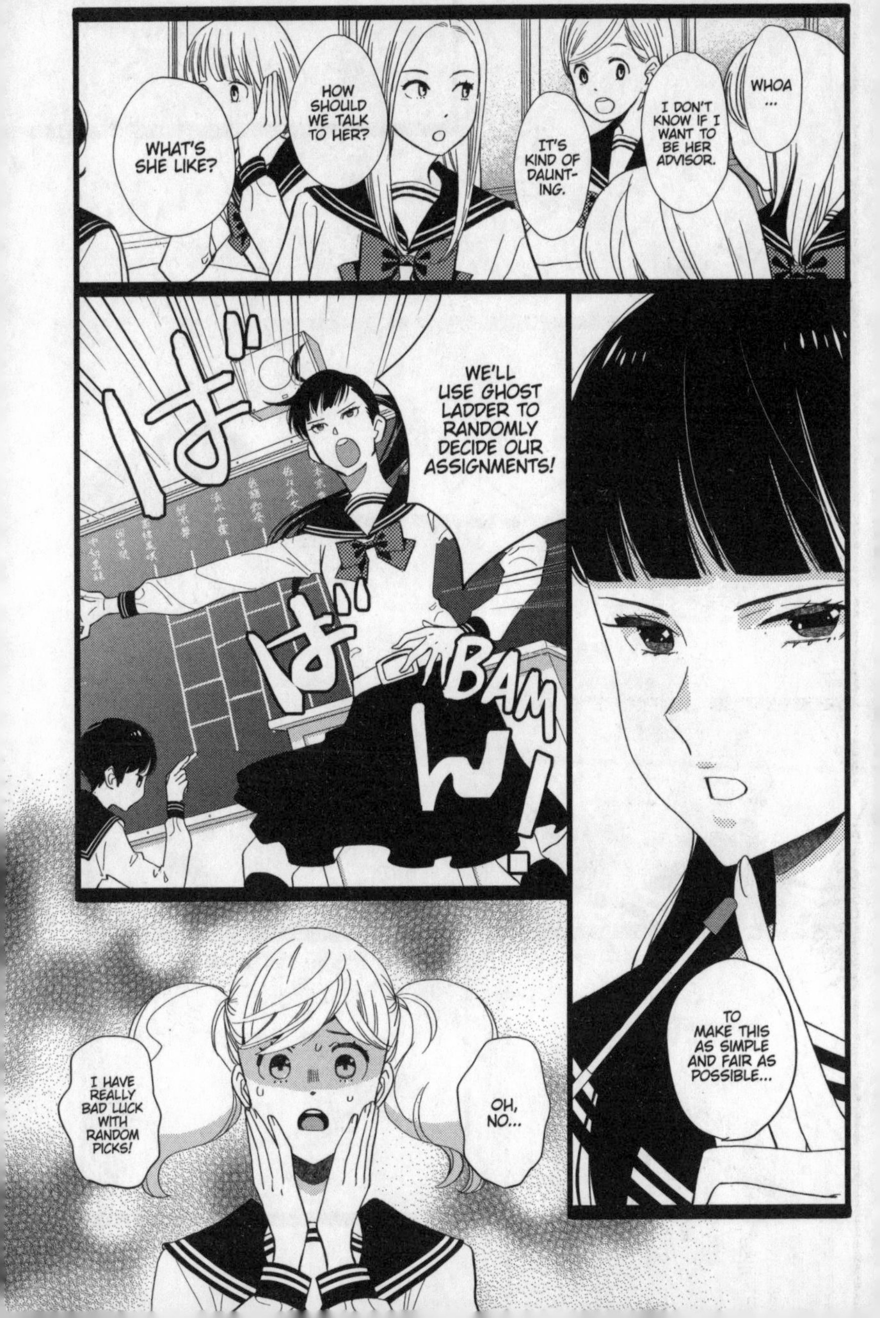
WHOA ...
I DON'T KNOW IF I WANT TO BE HER ADVISOR.
IT'S KIND OF DAUNT-ING.
HOW SHOULD WE TALK TO HER?
WHAT'S SHE LIKE?
TO MAKE THIS AS SIMPLE AND FAIR AS POSSIBLE...
WE'LL USE GHOST LADDER TO RANDOMLY DECIDE OUR ASSIGNMENTS!
BAM
OH, NO...
I HAVE REALLY BAD LUCK WITH RANDOM PICKS!

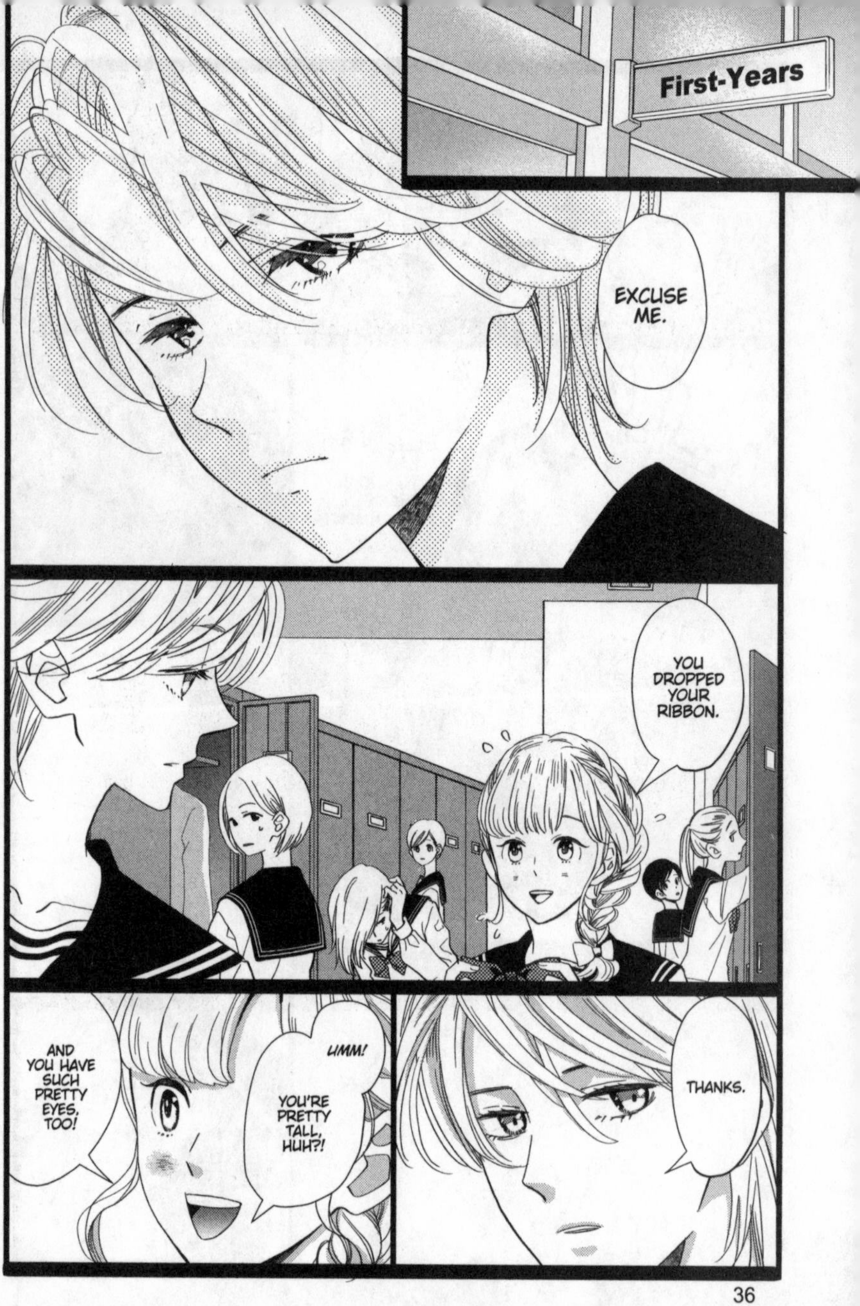
First-Years
EXCUSE ME.
YOU DROPPED YOUR RIBBON.
THANKS.
UMM!
YOU'RE PRETTY TALL, HUH?!
AND YOU HAVE SUCH PRETTY EYES, TOO!

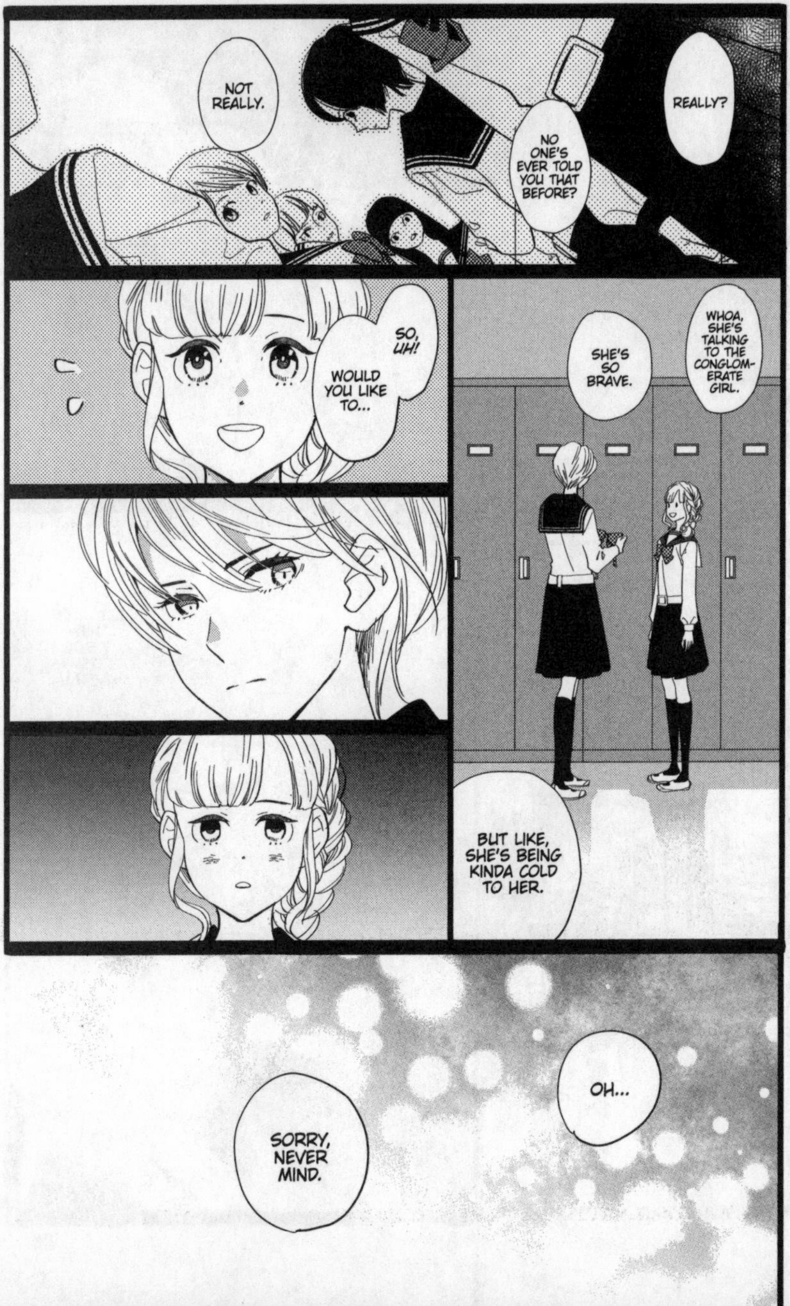
REALLY?
NO ONE'S EVER TOLD YOU THAT BEFORE?
NOT REALLY.
WHOA, SHE'S TALKING TO THE CONGLOM-ERATE GIRL.
SHE'S SO BRAVE.
BUT LIKE, SHE'S BEING KINDA COLD TO HER.
SO, UH!
WOULD YOU LIKE TO...
OH...
SORRY, NEVER MIND.

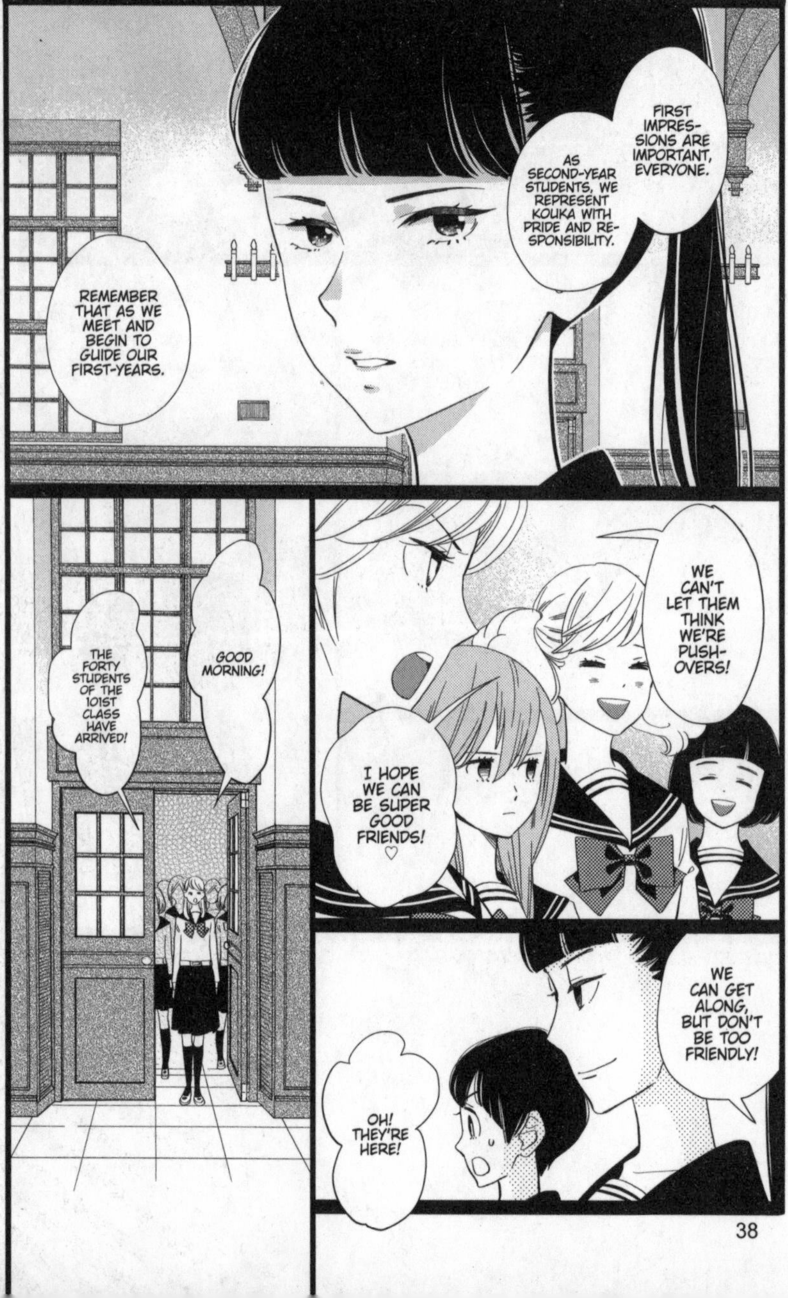
FIRST IMPRESSIONS ARE IMPORTANT, EVERYONE.
AS SECOND-YEAR STUDENTS, WE REPRESENT KOUKA WITH PRIDE AND RESPONSIBILITY.
REMEMBER THAT AS WE MEET AND BEGIN TO GUIDE OUR FIRST-YEARS.
WE CAN'T LET THEM THINK WE'RE PUSHOVERS!
I HOPE WE CAN BE SUPER GOOD FRIENDS! ♡
WE CAN GET ALONG, BUT DON'T BE TOO FRIENDLY!
OH! THEY'RE HERE!
GOOD MORNING!
THE FORTY STUDENTS OF THE 101ST CLASS HAVE ARRIVED!

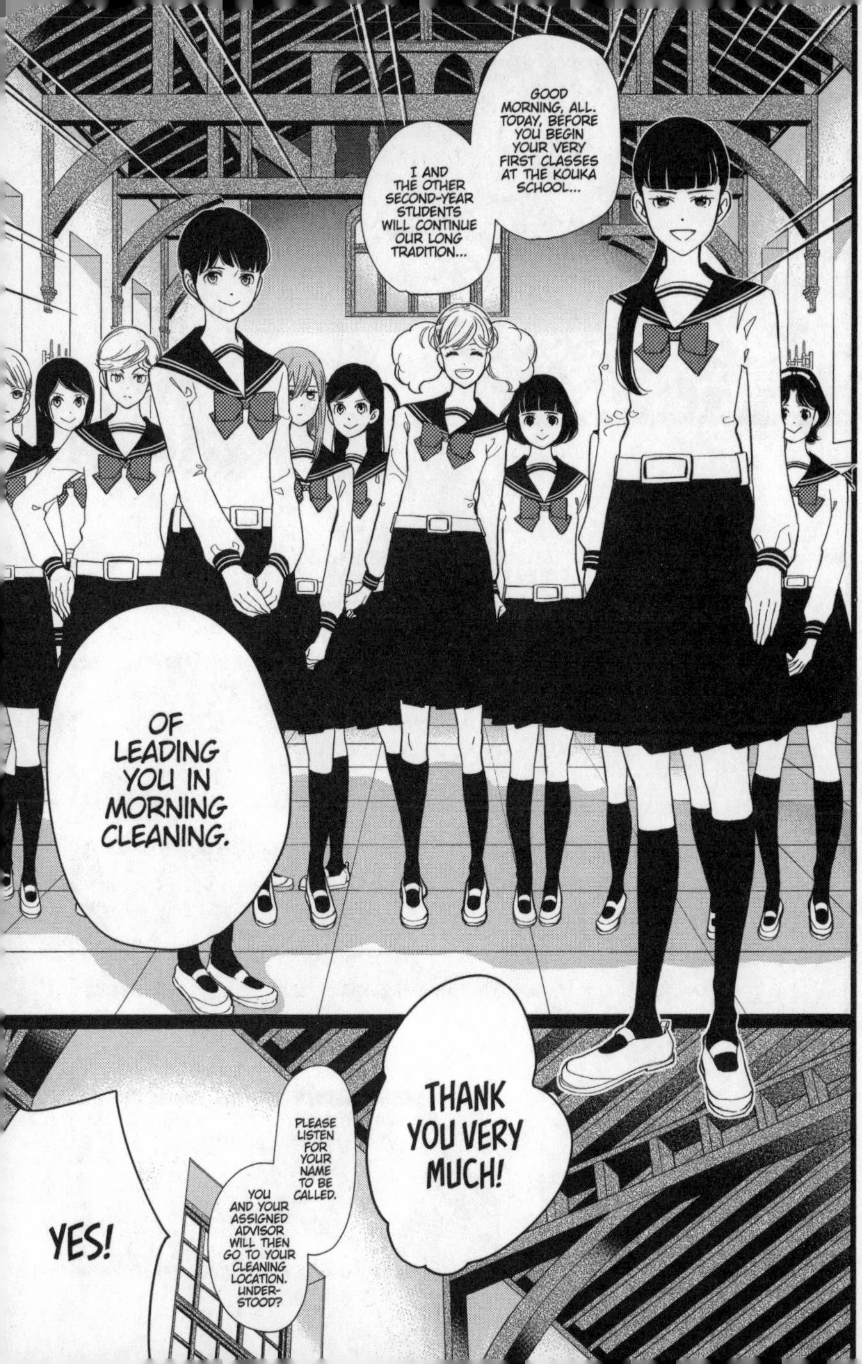
GOOD MORNING, ALL. TODAY, BEFORE YOU BEGIN YOUR VERY FIRST CLASSES AT THE KOUKA SCHOOL...
I AND THE OTHER SECOND-YEAR STUDENTS WILL CONTINUE OUR LONG TRADITION...
OF LEADING YOU IN MORNING CLEANING.
THANK YOU VERY MUCH!
PLEASE LISTEN FOR YOUR NAME TO BE CALLED.
YOU AND YOUR ASSIGNED ADVISOR WILL THEN GO TO YOUR CLEANING LOCATION. UNDER-STOOD?
YES!

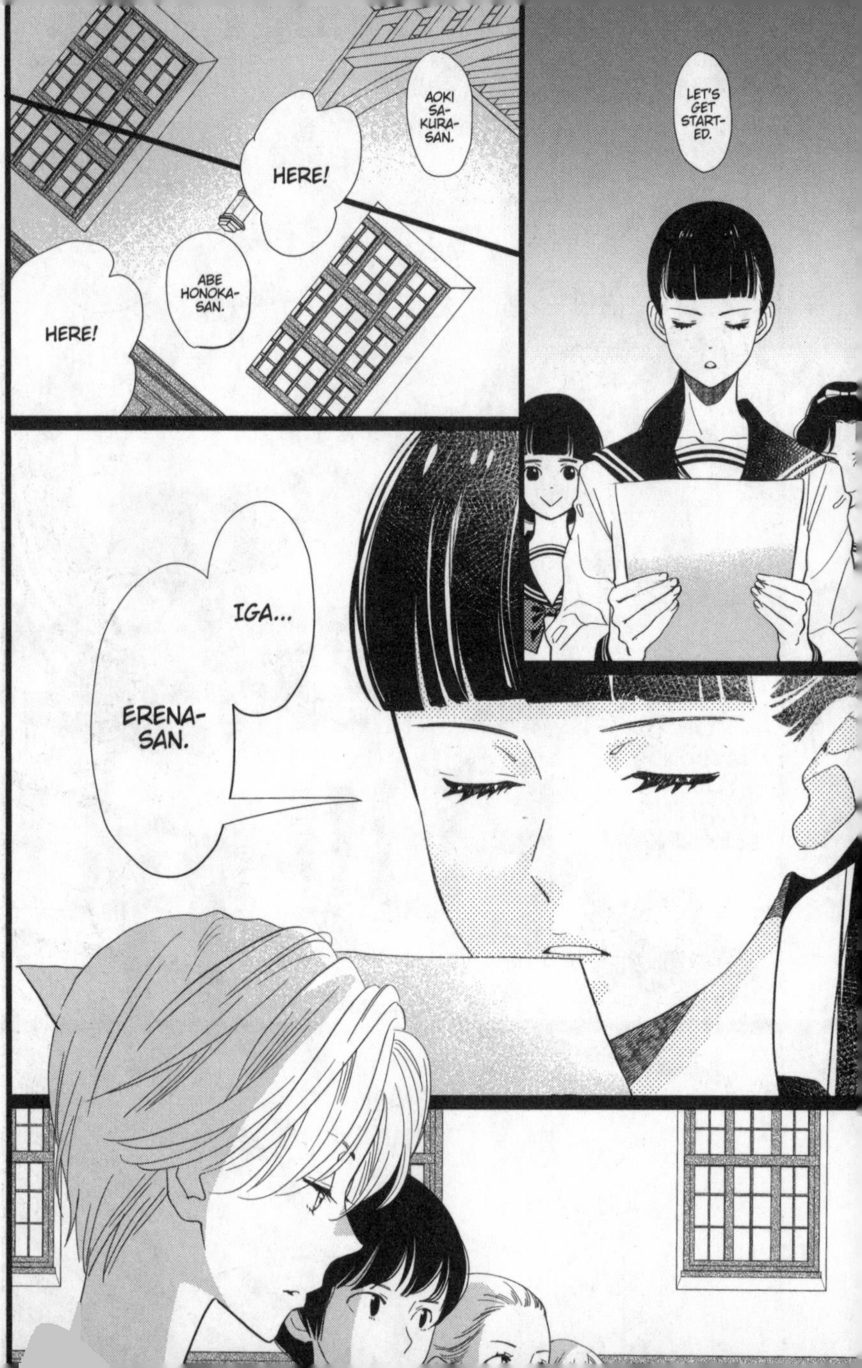
LET'S GET START-ED.
AOKI SA-KURA-SAN.
HERE!
ABE HONOKA-SAN.
HERE!
IGA...
ERENA-SAN.

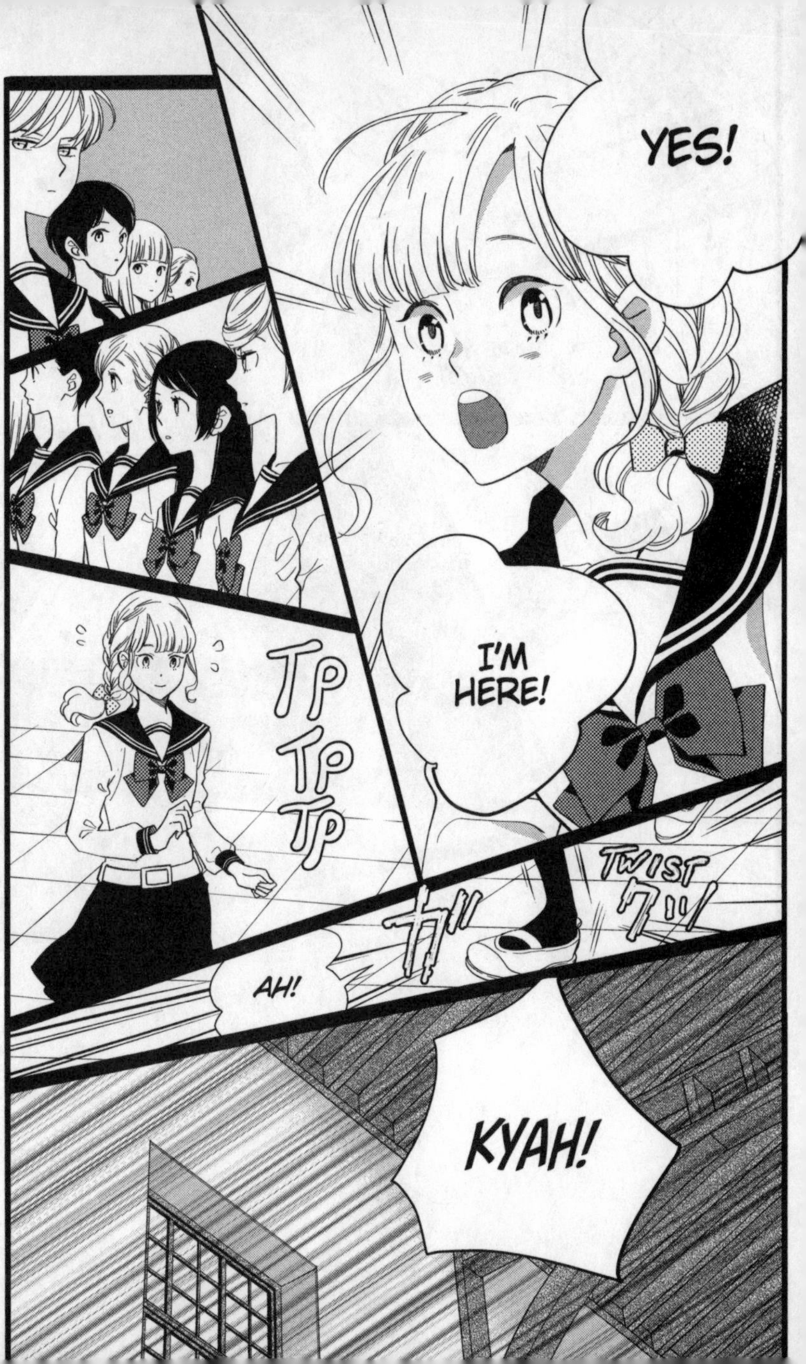
YES!
I'M HERE!
Tp Tp Tp
TWIST
AH!
KYAH!

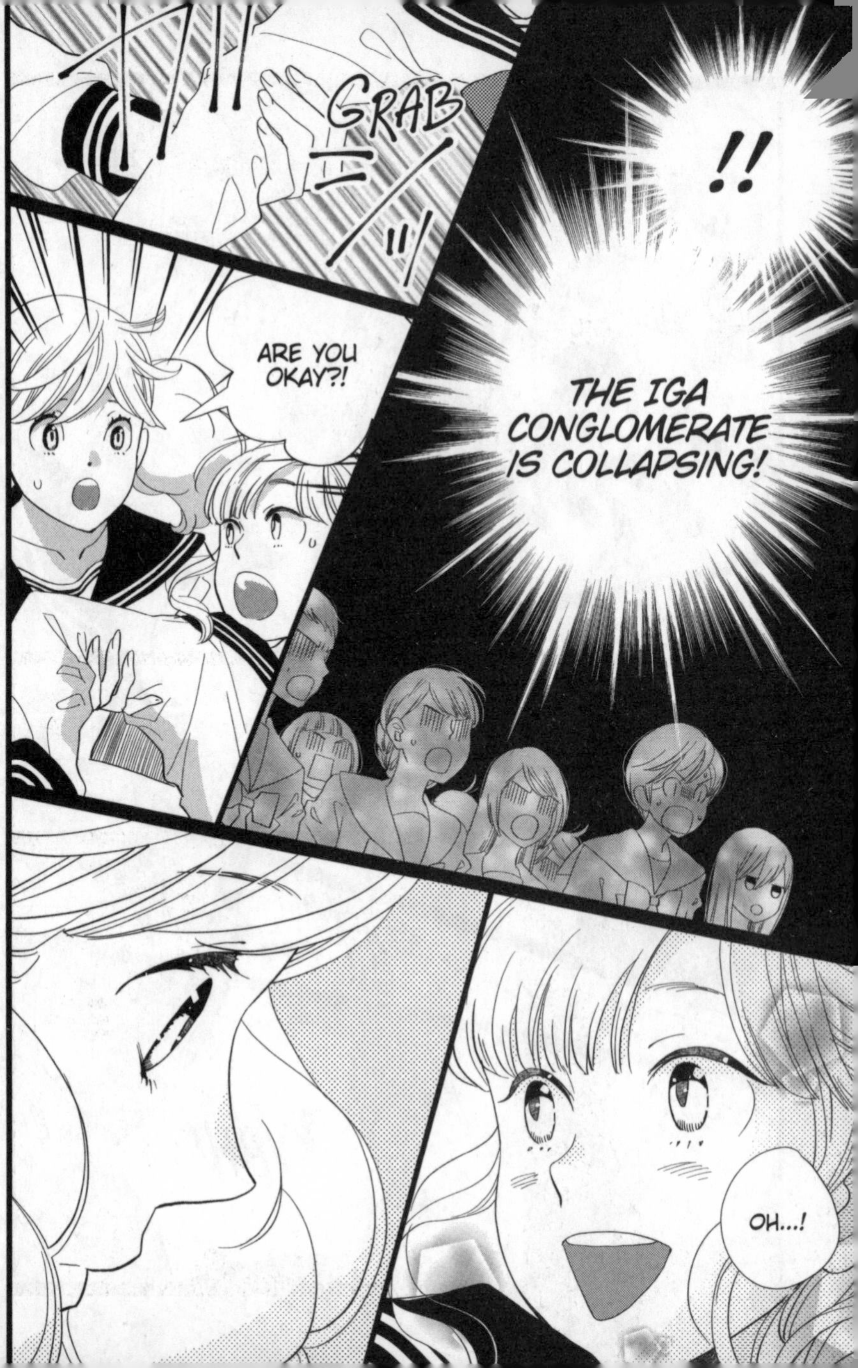
!!
THE IGA CONGLOMERATE IS COLLAPSING!
GRAB
ARE YOU OKAY?!
OH...!

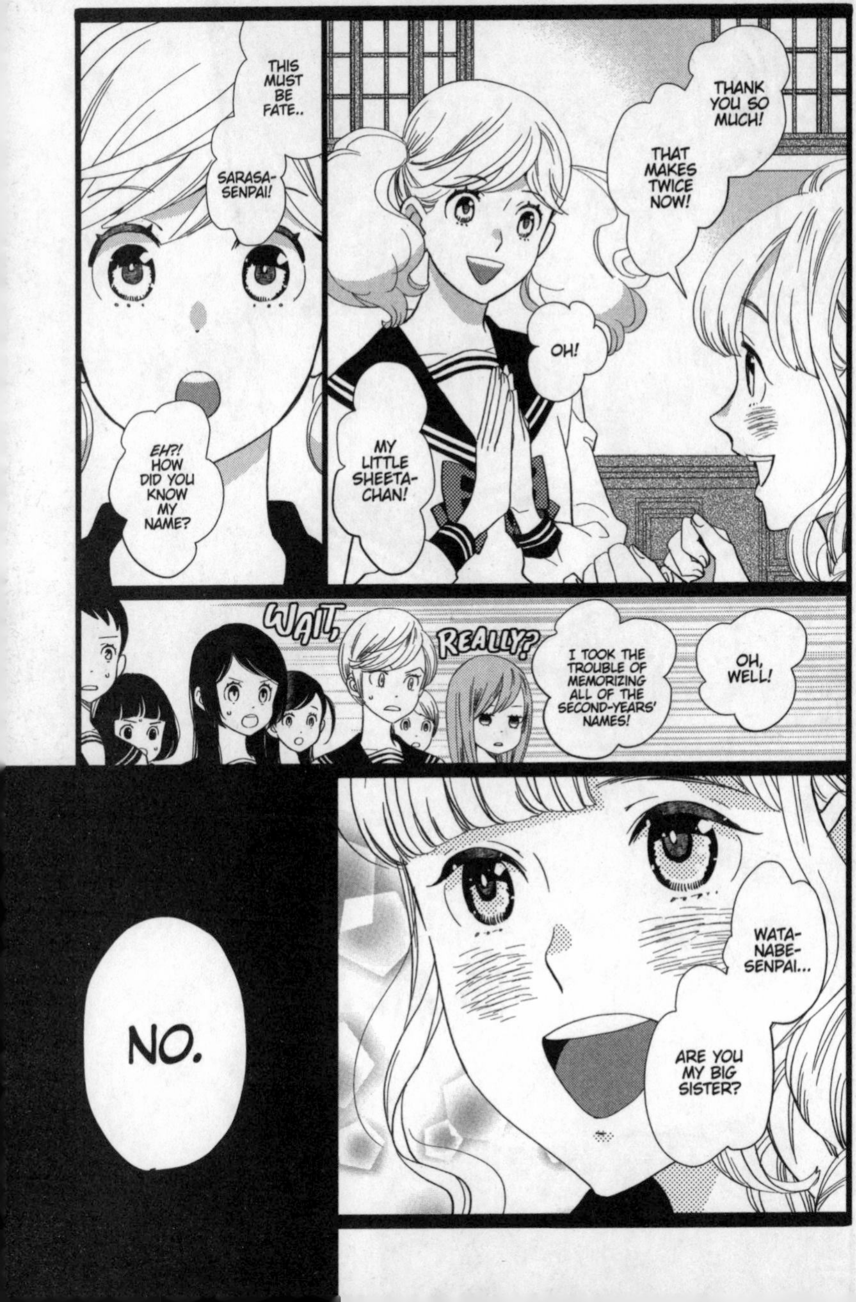
THANK YOU SO MUCH!
THAT MAKES TWICE NOW!
OH!
MY LITTLE SHEETA-CHAN!
THIS MUST BE FATE..
SARASA-SENPAI!
EH?! HOW DID YOU KNOW MY NAME?
OH, WELL!
I TOOK THE TROUBLE OF MEMORIZING ALL OF THE SECOND-YEARS' NAMES!
WAIT, REALLY?
WATA-NABE-SENPAI...
ARE YOU MY BIG SISTER?
NO.

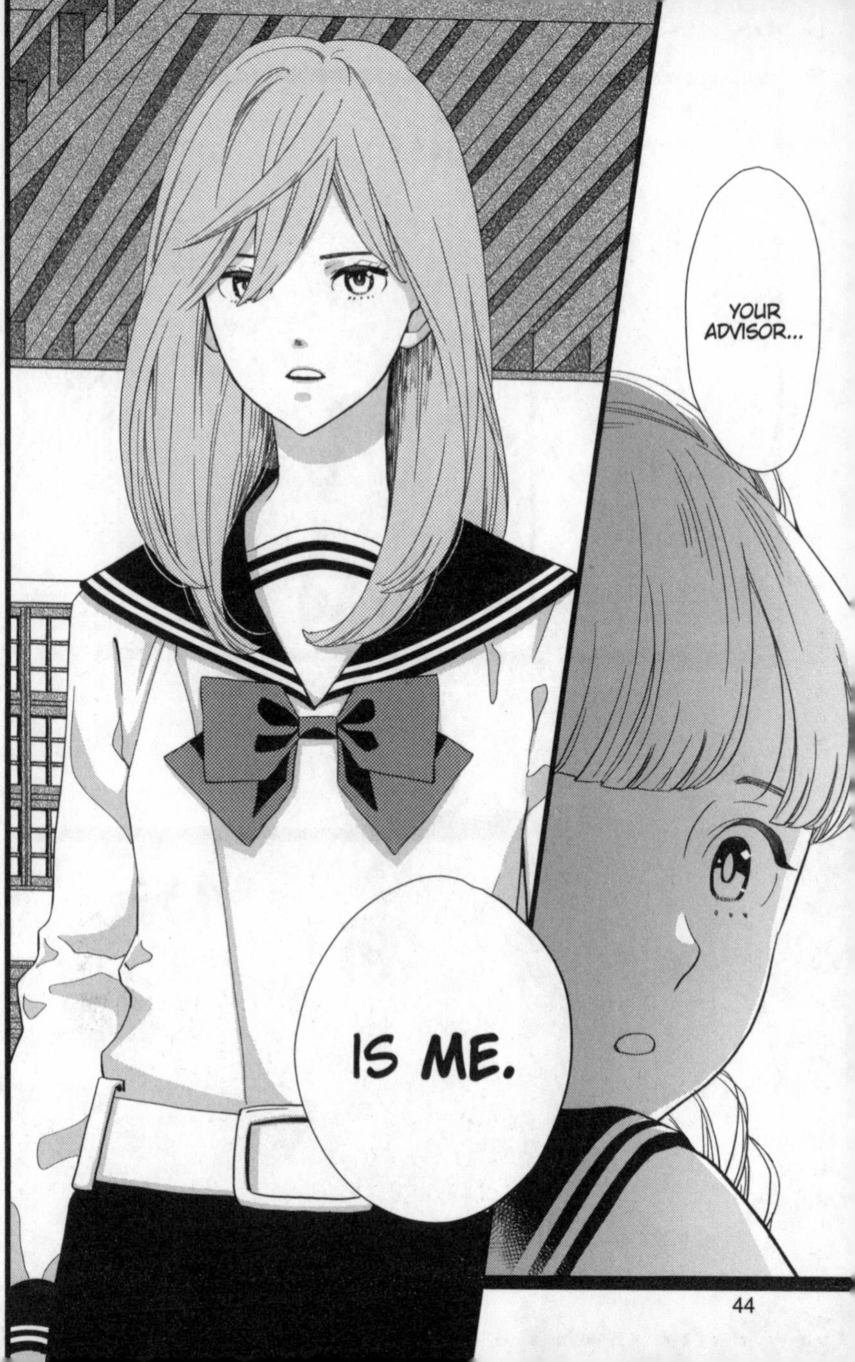
YOUR ADVISOR...
IS ME.

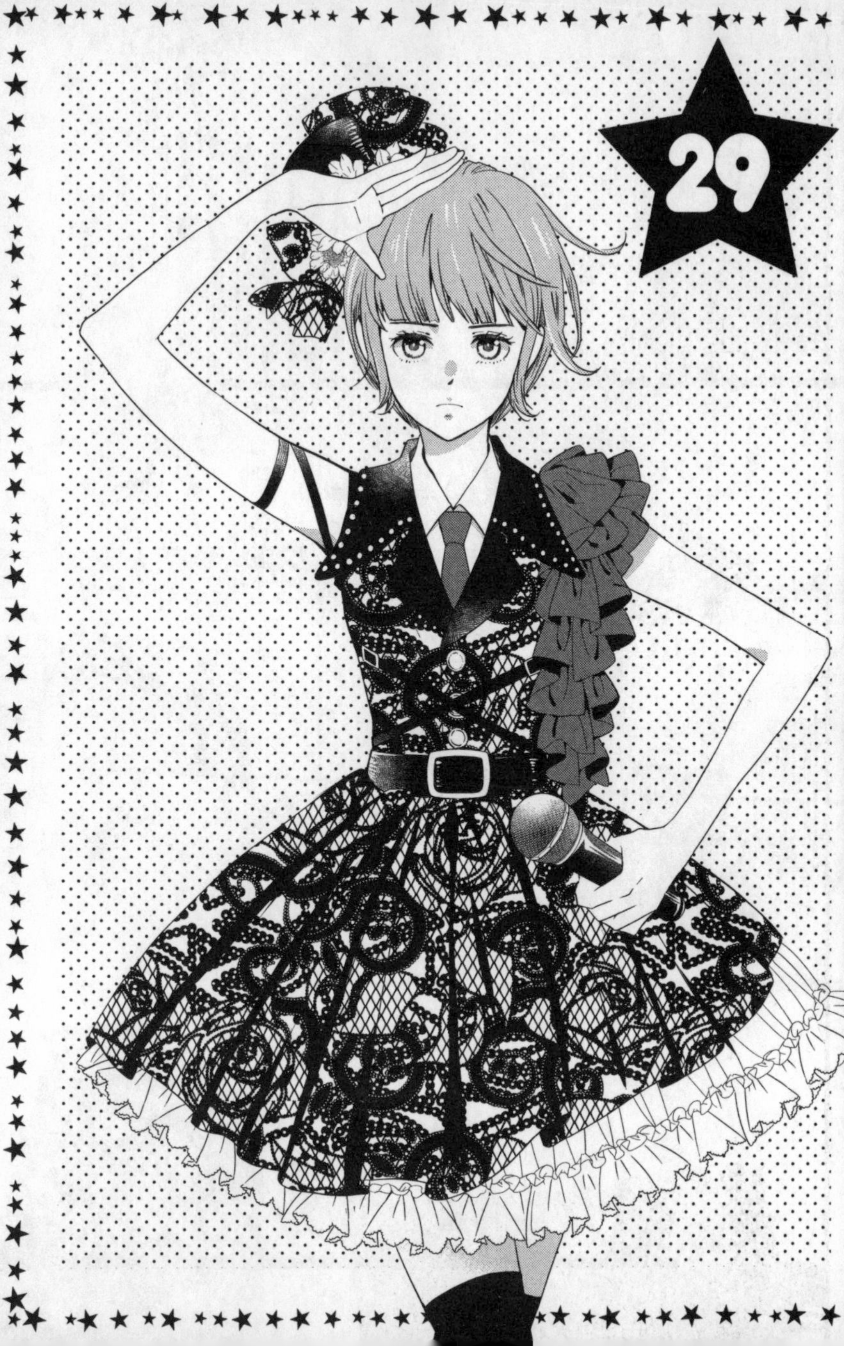
29

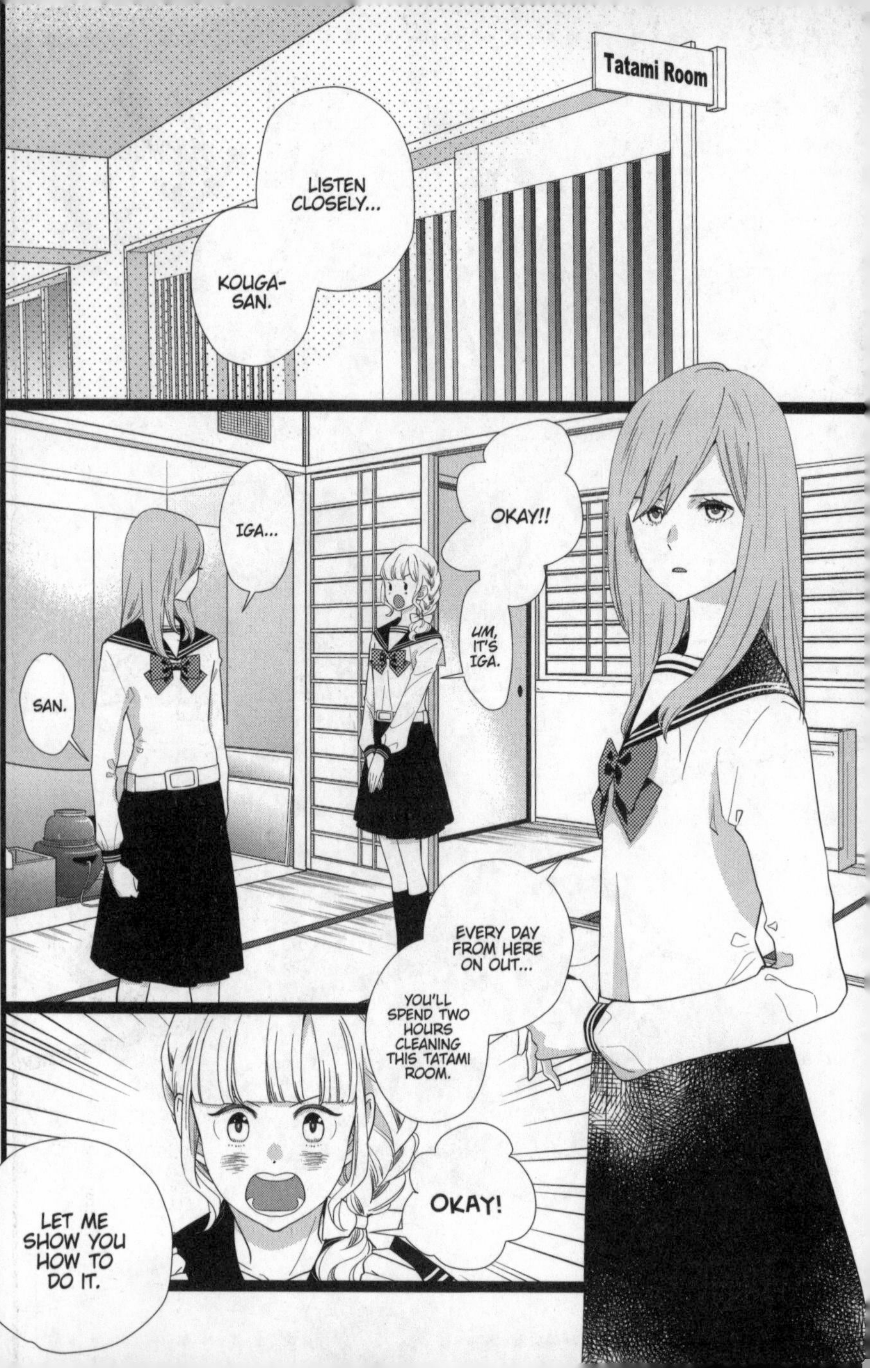
Tatami Room
LISTEN CLOSELY...
KOUGA-SAN.
OKAY!!
UM, IT'S IGA.
IGA...
SAN.
EVERY DAY FROM HERE ON OUT...
YOU'LL SPEND TWO HOURS CLEANING THIS TATAMI ROOM.
OKAY!
LET ME SHOW YOU HOW TO DO IT.

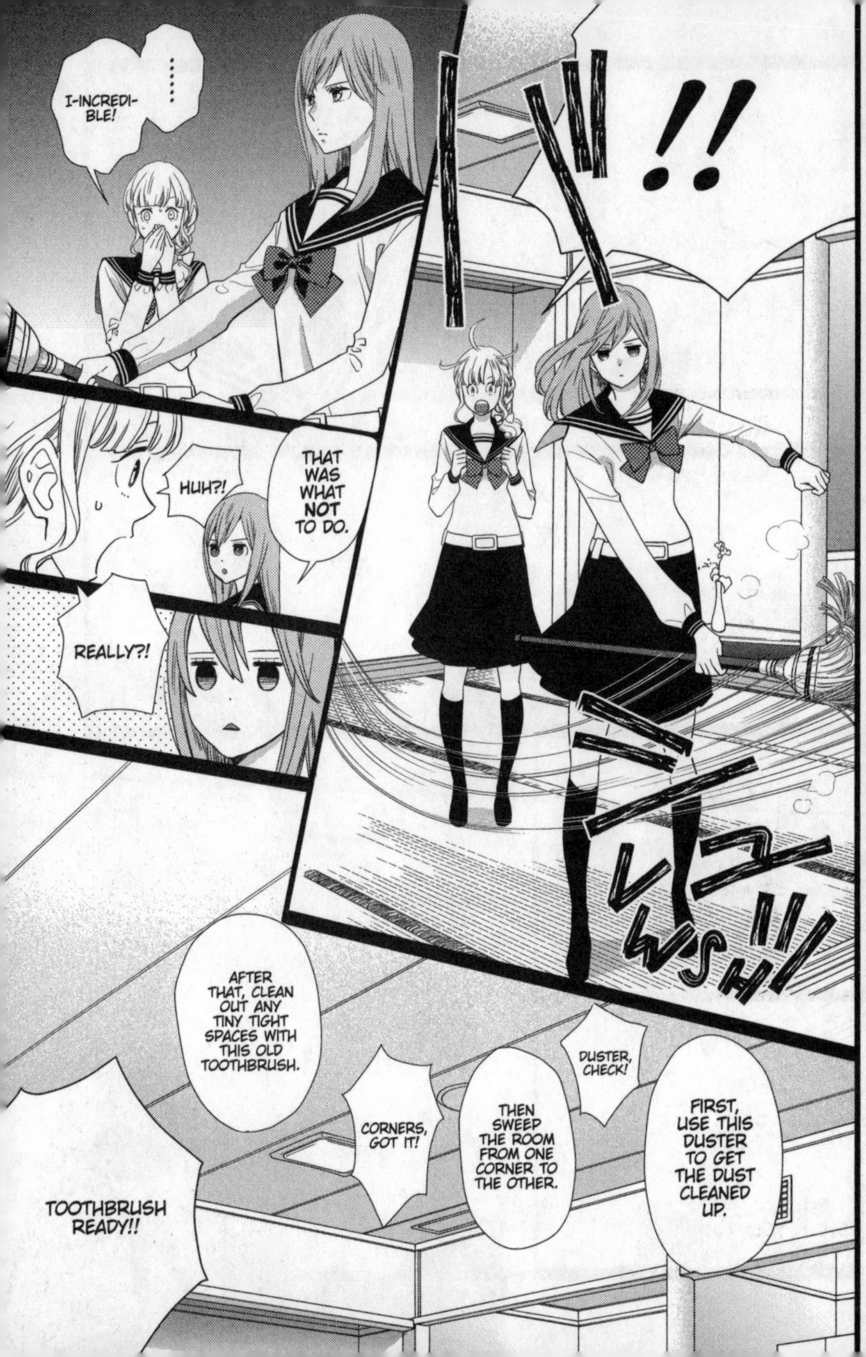
!!
WSH!!
……
I-INCREDIBLE!
THAT WAS WHAT NOT TO DO.
HUH?!
REALLY?!
FIRST, USE THIS DUSTER TO GET THE DUST CLEANED UP.
DUSTER, CHECK!
THEN SWEEP THE ROOM FROM ONE CORNER TO THE OTHER.
CORNERS, GOT IT!
AFTER THAT, CLEAN OUT ANY TINY TIGHT SPACES WITH THIS OLD TOOTHBRUSH.
TOOTHBRUSH READY!!

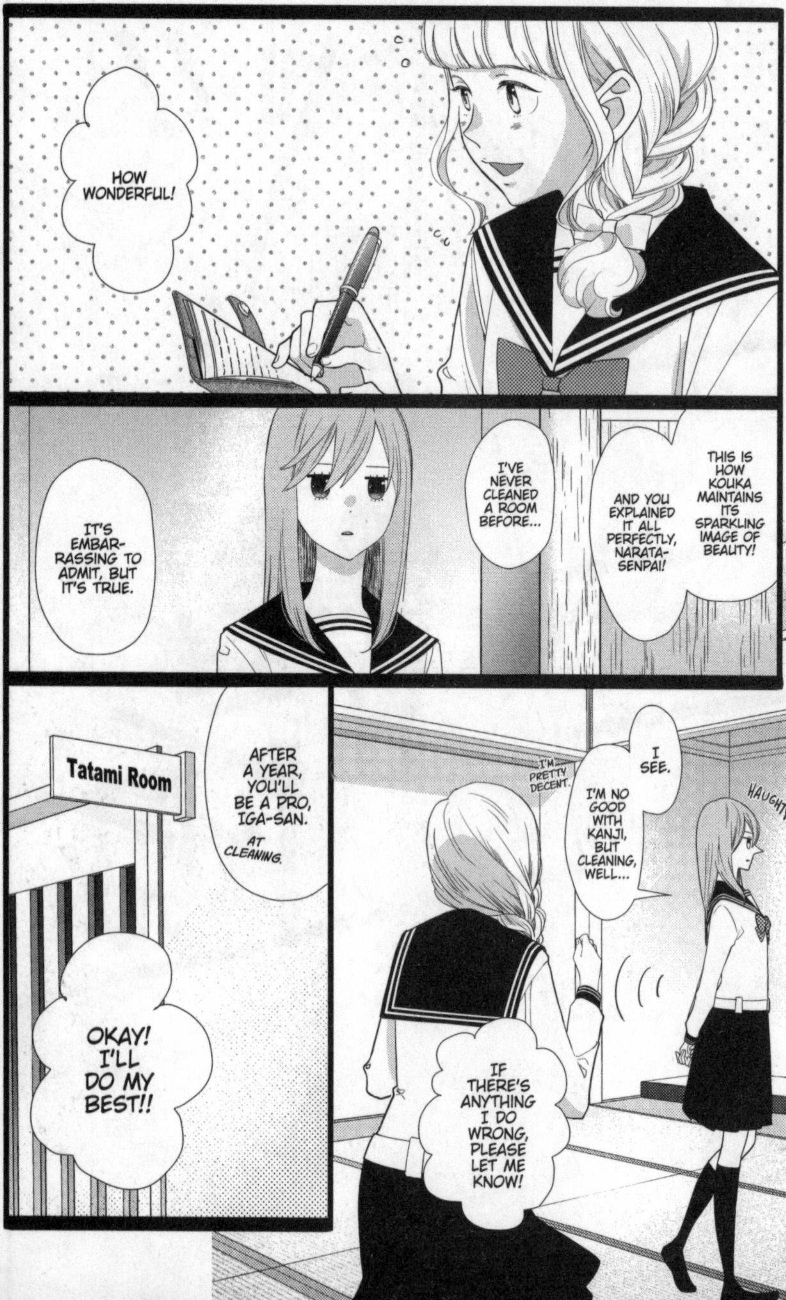
HOW WONDERFUL!
THIS IS HOW KOUKA MAINTAINS ITS SPARKLING IMAGE OF BEAUTY!
AND YOU EXPLAINED IT ALL PERFECTLY, NARATA-SENPAI!
I'VE NEVER CLEANED A ROOM BEFORE...
IT'S EMBAR-RASSING TO ADMIT, BUT IT'S TRUE.
HAUGHTY
I SEE.
I'M NO GOOD WITH KANJI, BUT CLEANING, WELL...
I'M PRETTY DECENT.
IF THERE'S ANYTHING I DO WRONG, PLEASE LET ME KNOW!
Tatami Room
AFTER A YEAR, YOU'LL BE A PRO, IGA-SAN.
AT CLEANING.
OKAY! I'LL DO MY BEST!!

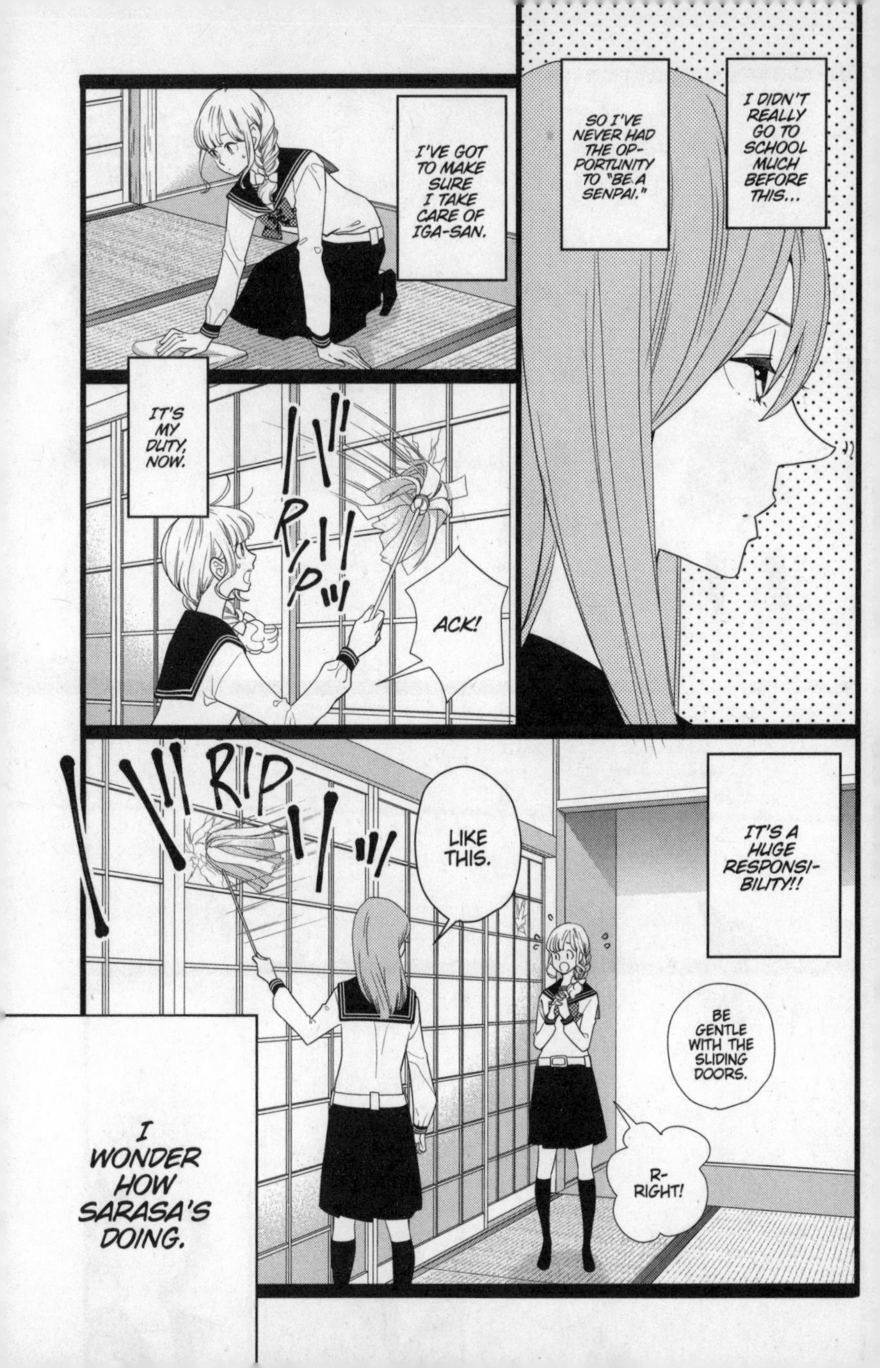
I DIDN'T REALLY GO TO SCHOOL MUCH BEFORE THIS...
SO I'VE NEVER HAD THE OP-PORTUNITY TO "BE A SENPAI."
I'VE GOT TO MAKE SURE I TAKE CARE OF IGA-SAN.
IT'S MY DUTY, NOW.
RIP
ACK!
IT'S A HUGE RESPONSI-BILITY!!
LIKE THIS.
RIP
BE GENTLE WITH THE SLIDING DOORS.
R-RIGHT!
I WONDER HOW SARASA'S DOING.

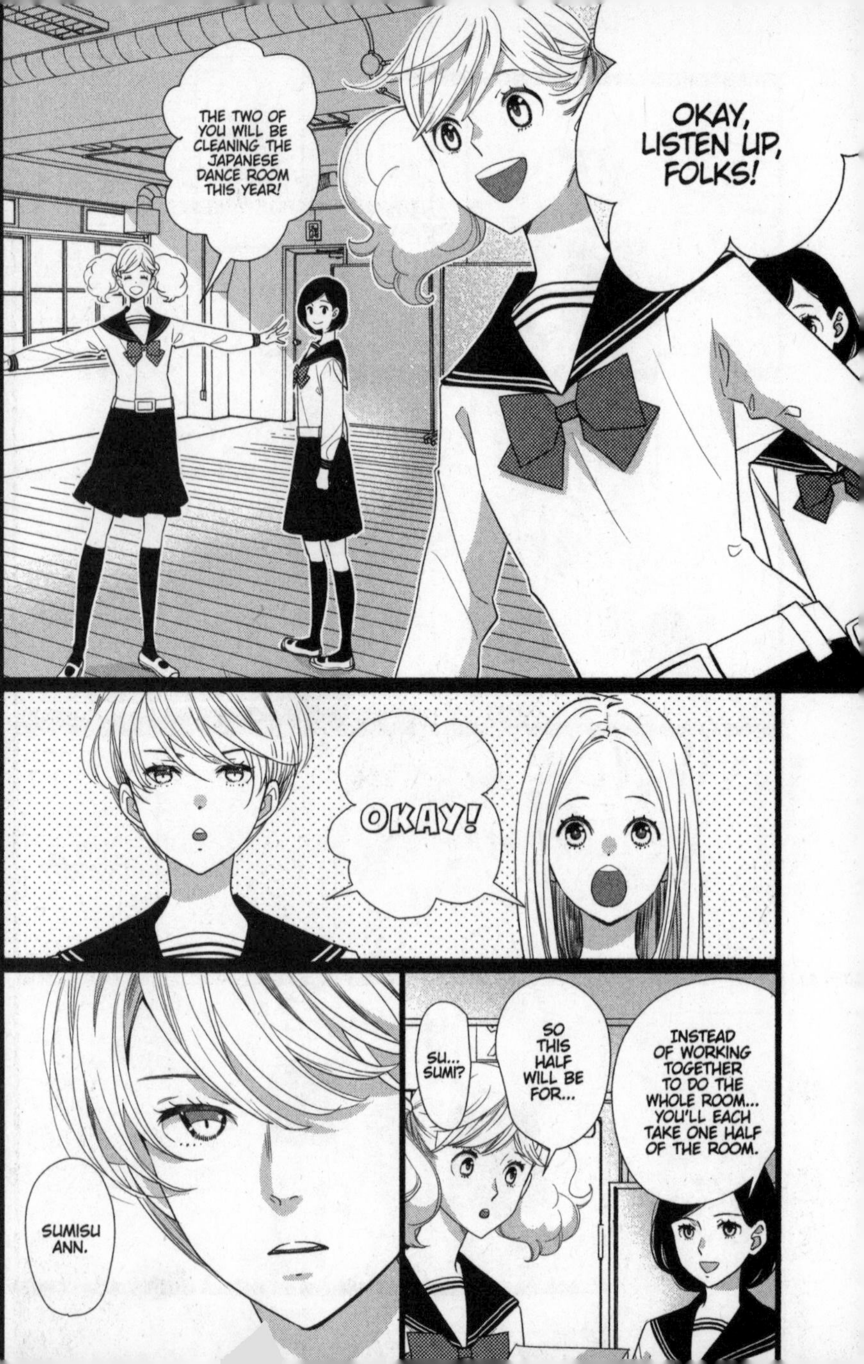
OKAY, LISTEN UP, FOLKS!
THE TWO OF YOU WILL BE CLEANING THE JAPANESE DANCE ROOM THIS YEAR!
OKAY!
INSTEAD OF WORKING TOGETHER TO DO THE WHOLE ROOM... YOU'LL EACH TAKE ONE HALF OF THE ROOM.
SO THIS HALF WILL BE FOR...
SU... SUMI?
SUMISU ANN.

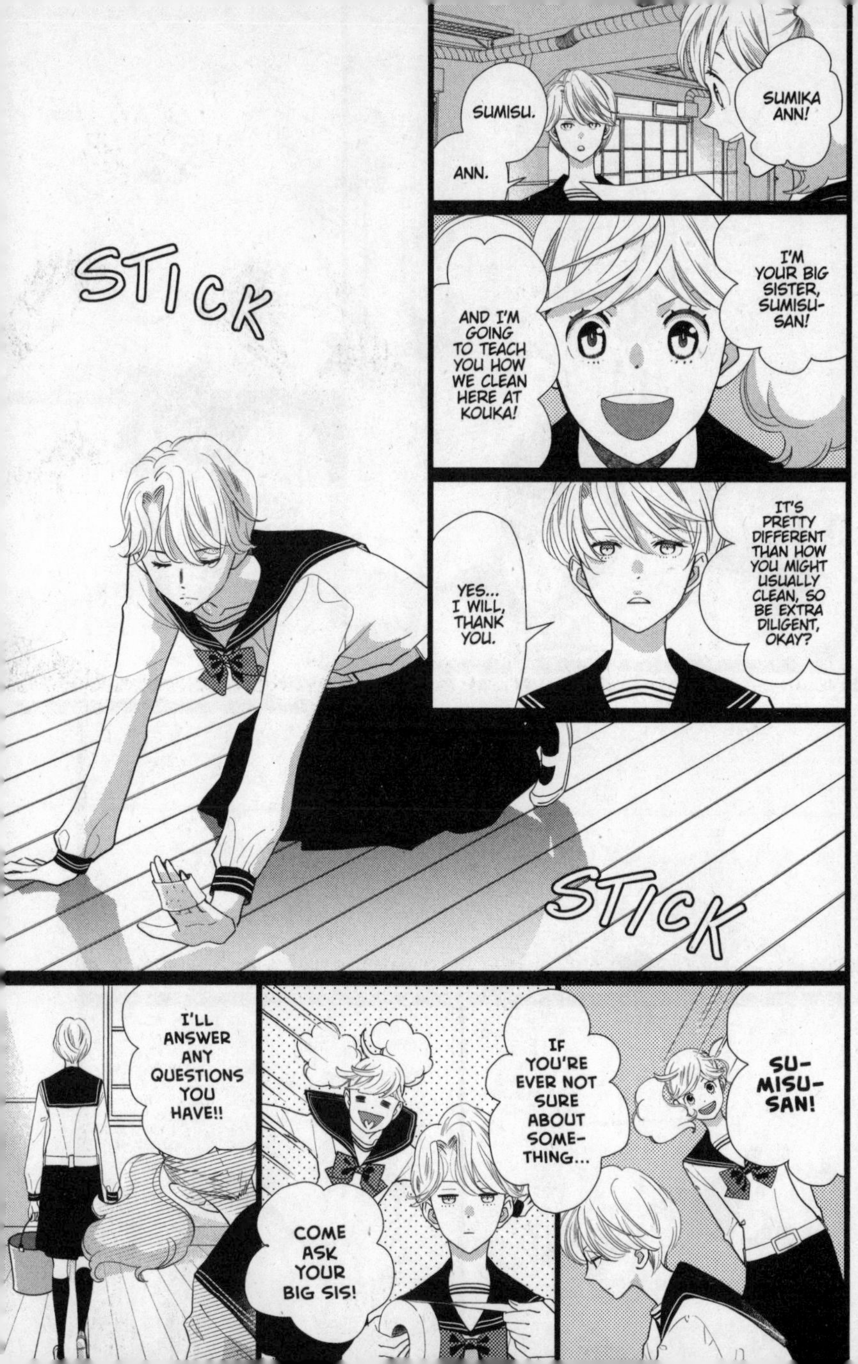
SUMIKA ANN!
SUMISU.
ANN.
I'M YOUR BIG SISTER, SUMISU-SAN!
AND I'M GOING TO TEACH YOU HOW WE CLEAN HERE AT KOUKA!
IT'S PRETTY DIFFERENT THAN HOW YOU MIGHT USUALLY CLEAN, SO BE EXTRA DILIGENT, OKAY?
YES... I WILL, THANK YOU.
STICK
STICK
SU-MISU-SAN!
IF YOU'RE EVER NOT SURE ABOUT SOME-THING...
COME ASK YOUR BIG SIS!
I'LL ANSWER ANY QUESTIONS YOU HAVE!!

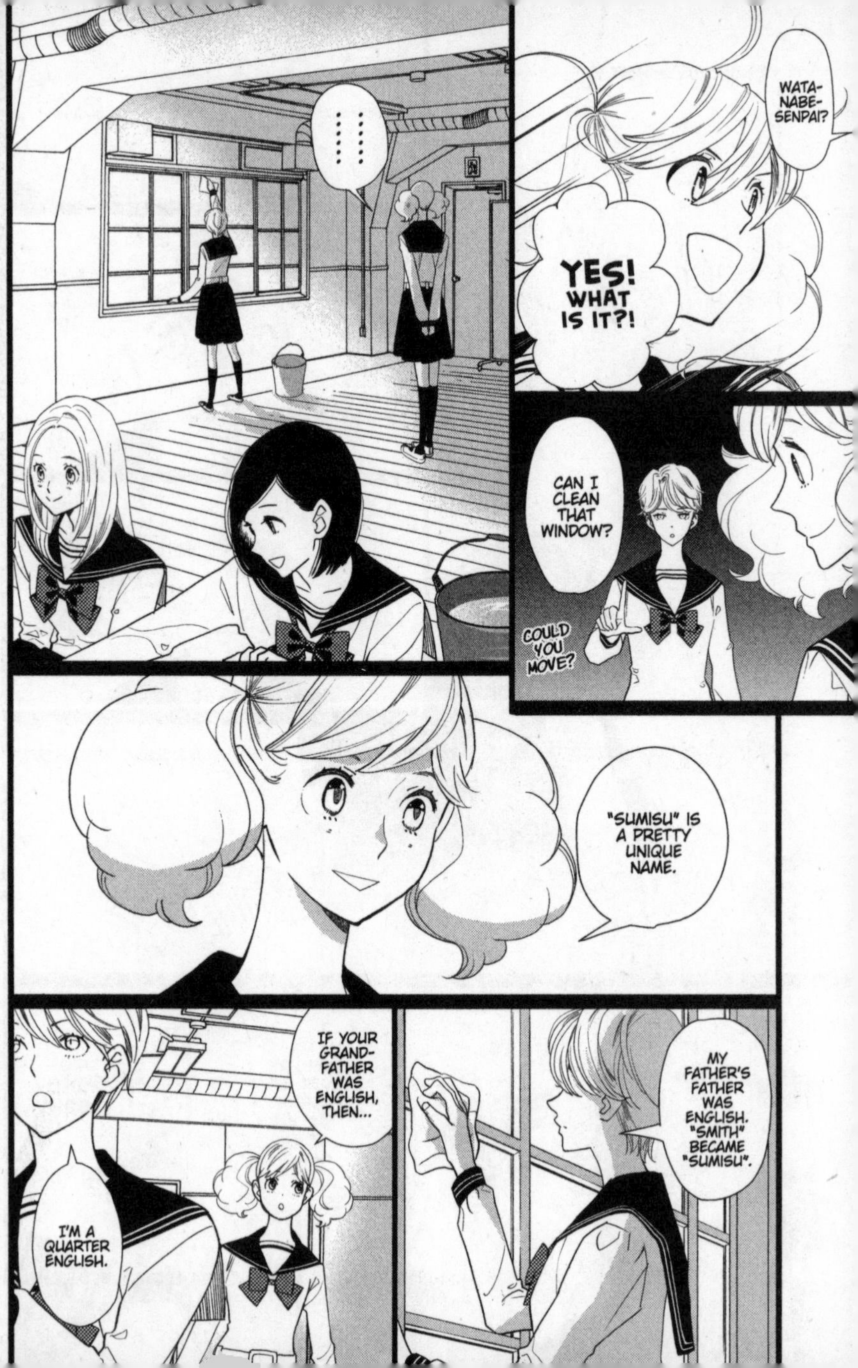
WATA-NABE-SENPAI?
YES! WHAT IS IT?!
CAN I CLEAN THAT WINDOW?
COULD YOU MOVE?
......
"SUMISU" IS A PRETTY UNIQUE NAME.
MY FATHER'S FATHER WAS ENGLISH. "SMITH" BECAME "SUMISU".
IF YOUR GRAND-FATHER WAS ENGLISH, THEN...
I'M A QUARTER ENGLISH.

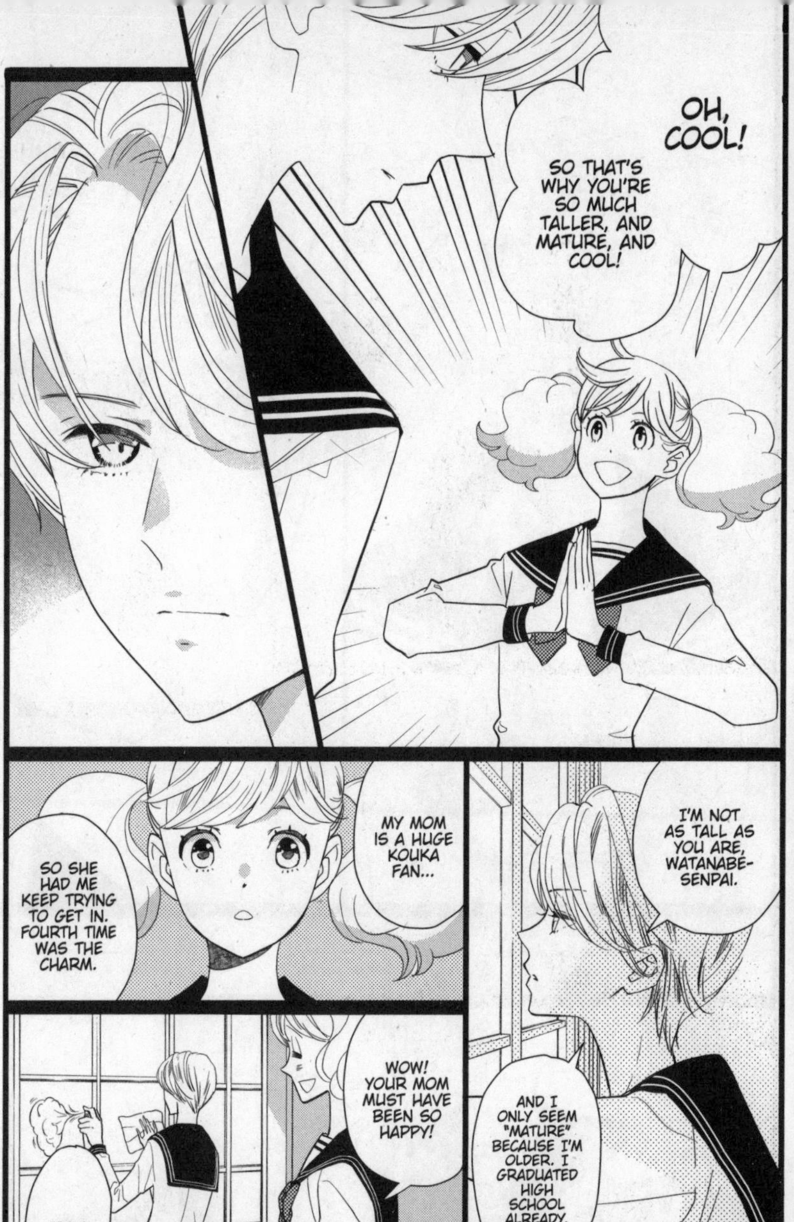
OH, COOL!
SO THAT'S WHY YOU'RE SO MUCH TALLER, AND MATURE, AND COOL!
I'M NOT AS TALL AS YOU ARE, WATANABE-SENPAI.
AND I ONLY SEEM "MATURE" BECAUSE I'M OLDER. I GRADUATED HIGH SCHOOL ALREADY.
MY MOM IS A HUGE KOUKA FAN...
SO SHE HAD ME KEEP TRYING TO GET IN. FOURTH TIME WAS THE CHARM.
WOW! YOUR MOM MUST HAVE BEEN SO HAPPY!
YEAH.

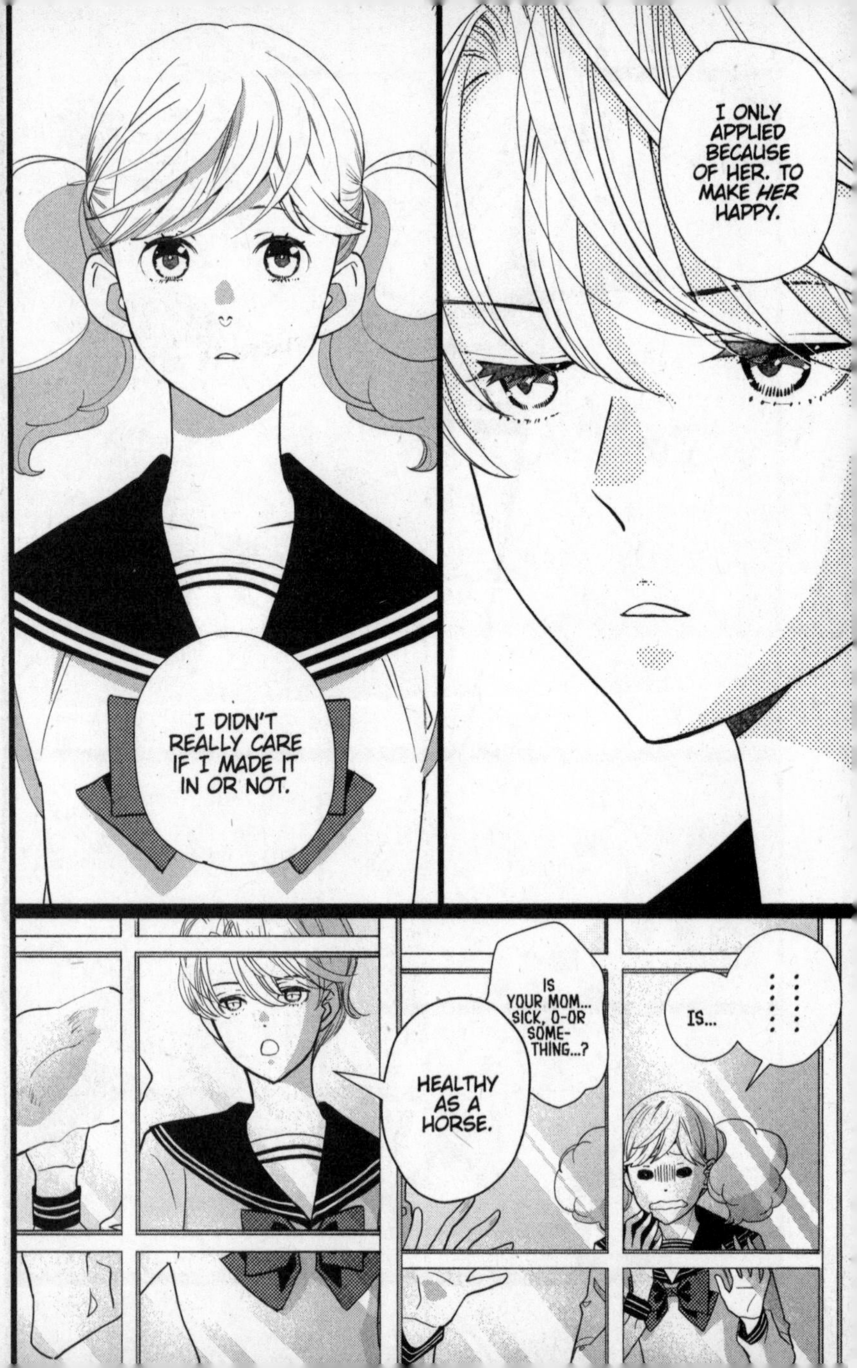
I ONLY APPLIED BECAUSE OF HER. TO MAKE *HER* HAPPY.
I DIDN'T REALLY CARE IF I MADE IT IN OR NOT.
IS...
IS YOUR MOM... SICK, O-OR SOME-THING...?
HEALTHY AS A HORSE.

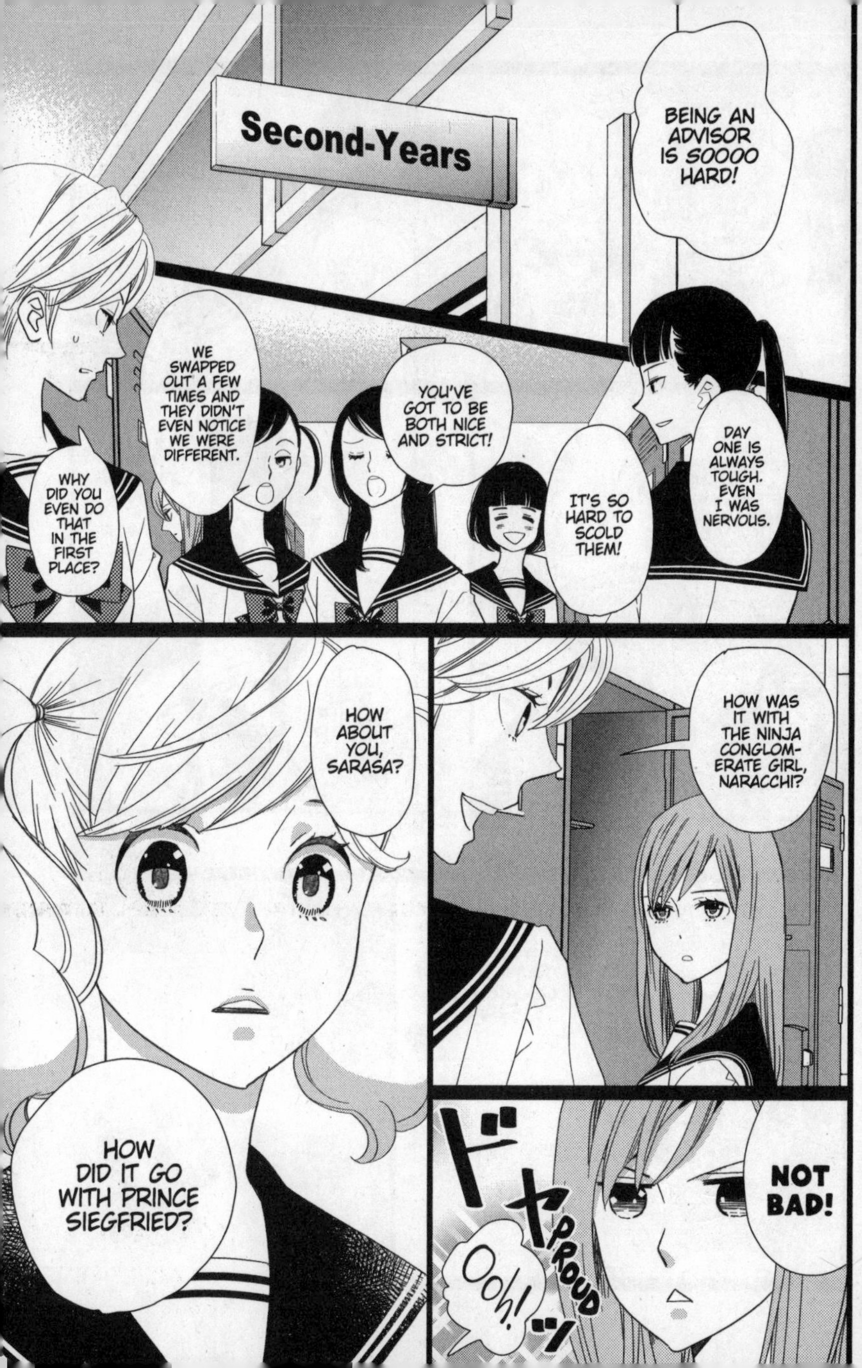

Second-Years
BEING AN ADVISOR IS *SOOOO* HARD!
DAY ONE IS ALWAYS TOUGH. EVEN I WAS NERVOUS.
IT'S SO HARD TO SCOLD THEM!
YOU'VE GOT TO BE BOTH NICE AND STRICT!
WE SWAPPED OUT A FEW TIMES AND THEY DIDN'T EVEN NOTICE WE WERE DIFFERENT.
WHY DID YOU EVEN DO THAT IN THE FIRST PLACE?
HOW WAS IT WITH THE NINJA CONGLOM-ERATE GIRL, NARACCHI?
NOT BAD!
ドヤ
PROUD
Ooh!
HOW ABOUT YOU, SARASA?
HOW DID IT GO WITH PRINCE SIEGFRIED?

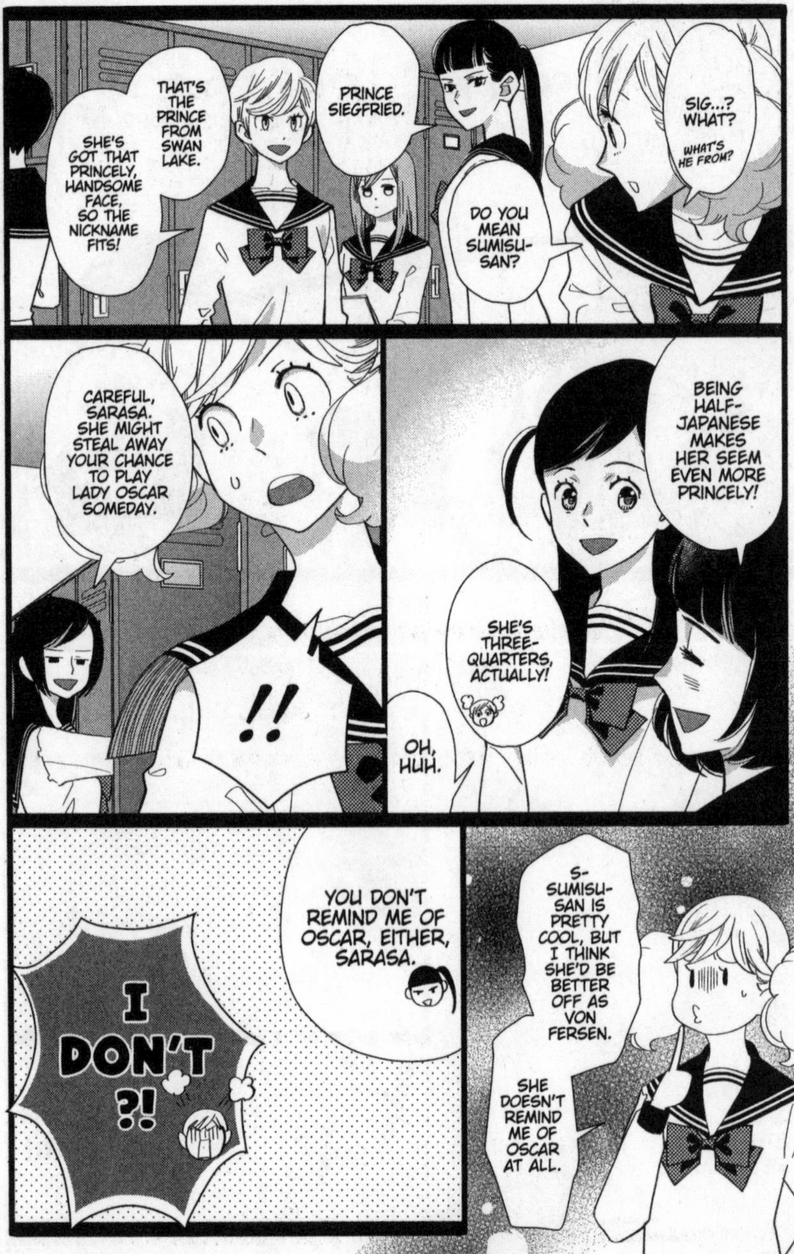
SIG...? WHAT?
WHAT'S HE FROM?
PRINCE SIEGFRIED.
DO YOU MEAN SUMISU-SAN?
THAT'S THE PRINCE FROM SWAN LAKE.
SHE'S GOT THAT PRINCELY, HANDSOME FACE, SO THE NICKNAME FITS!
BEING HALF-JAPANESE MAKES HER SEEM EVEN MORE PRINCELY!
SHE'S THREE-QUARTERS, ACTUALLY!
OH, HUH.
CAREFUL, SARASA. SHE MIGHT STEAL AWAY YOUR CHANCE TO PLAY LADY OSCAR SOMEDAY.
!!
S-SUMISU-SAN IS PRETTY COOL, BUT I THINK SHE'D BE BETTER OFF AS VON FERSEN.
SHE DOESN'T REMIND ME OF OSCAR AT ALL.
YOU DON'T REMIND ME OF OSCAR, EITHER, SARASA.
I DON'T ?!

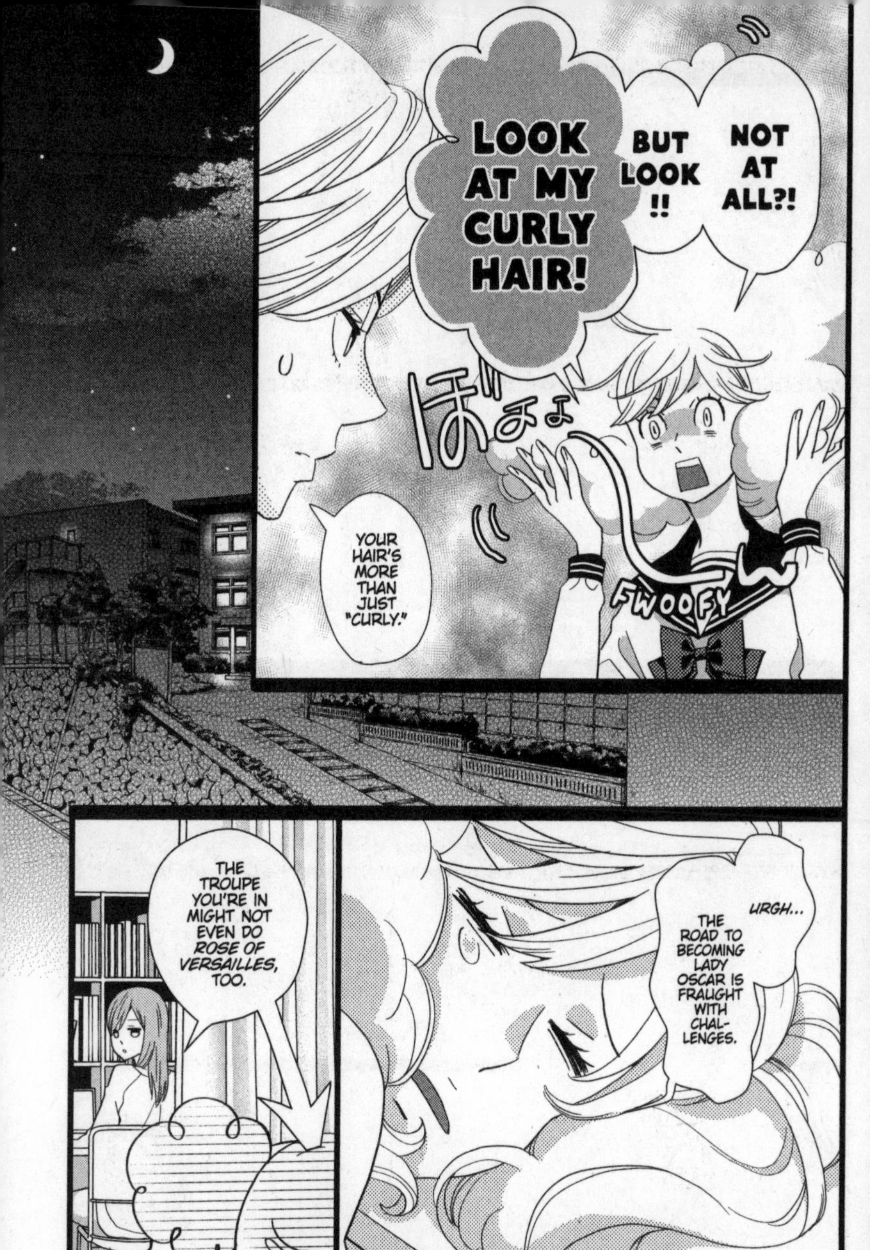
NOT AT ALL?!
BUT LOOK !!
LOOK AT MY CURLY HAIR!
FWOOFY
YOUR HAIR'S MORE THAN JUST "CURLY."
URGH...
THE ROAD TO BECOMING LADY OSCAR IS FRAUGHT WITH CHAL-LENGES.
THE TROUPE YOU'RE IN MIGHT NOT EVEN DO *ROSE OF VERSAILLES*, TOO.

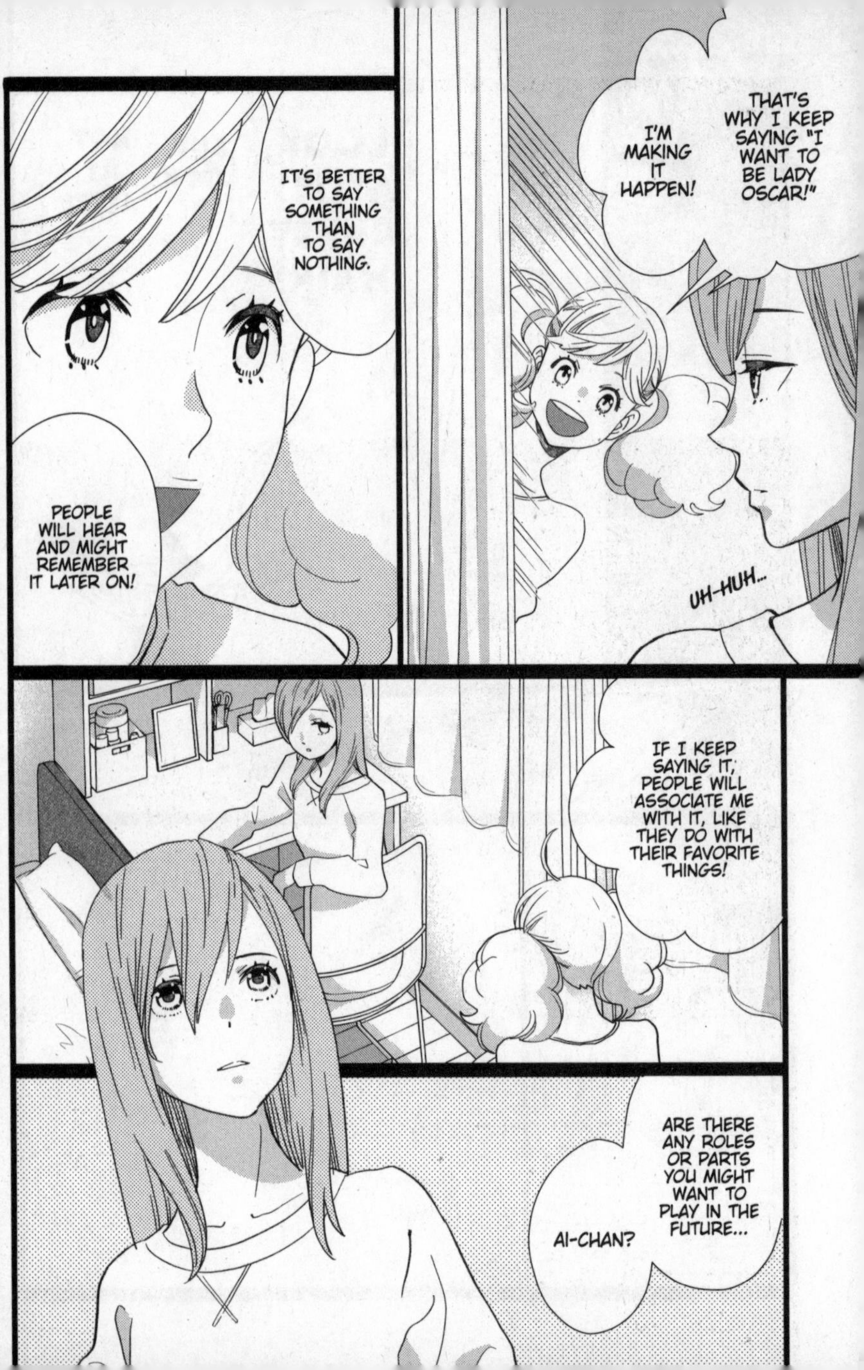

THAT'S WHY I KEEP SAYING "I WANT TO BE LADY OSCAR!"
I'M MAKING IT HAPPEN!
UH-HUH...
IT'S BETTER TO SAY SOMETHING THAN TO SAY NOTHING.
PEOPLE WILL HEAR AND MIGHT REMEMBER IT LATER ON!
IF I KEEP SAYING IT, PEOPLE WILL ASSOCIATE ME WITH IT, LIKE THEY DO WITH THEIR FAVORITE THINGS!
ARE THERE ANY ROLES OR PARTS YOU MIGHT WANT TO PLAY IN THE FUTURE...
AI-CHAN?

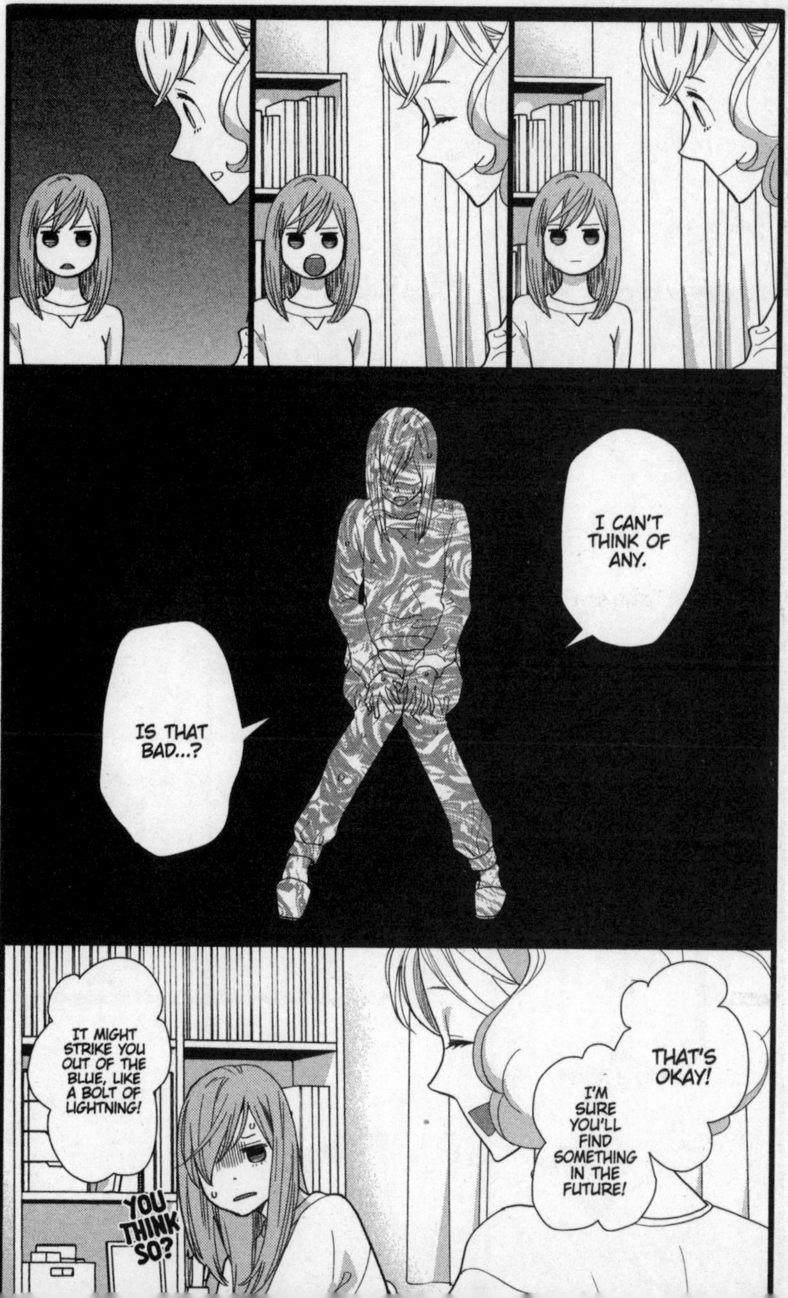
I CAN'T THINK OF ANY.
IS THAT BAD...?
THAT'S OKAY!
I'M SURE YOU'LL FIND SOMETHING IN THE FUTURE!
IT MIGHT STRIKE YOU OUT OF THE BLUE, LIKE A BOLT OF LIGHTNING!
YOU THINK SO?

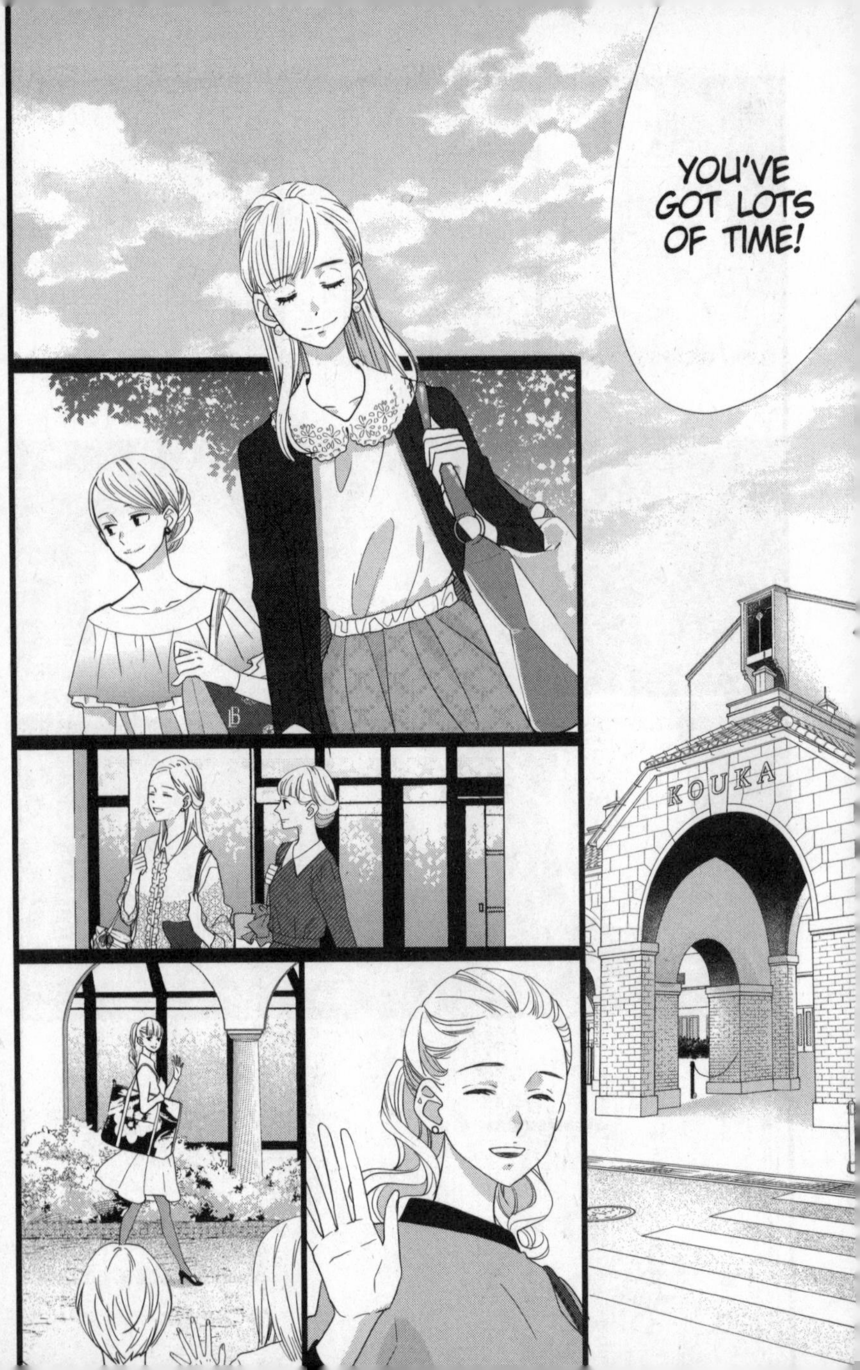
YOU'VE GOT LOTS OF TIME!
KOUKA

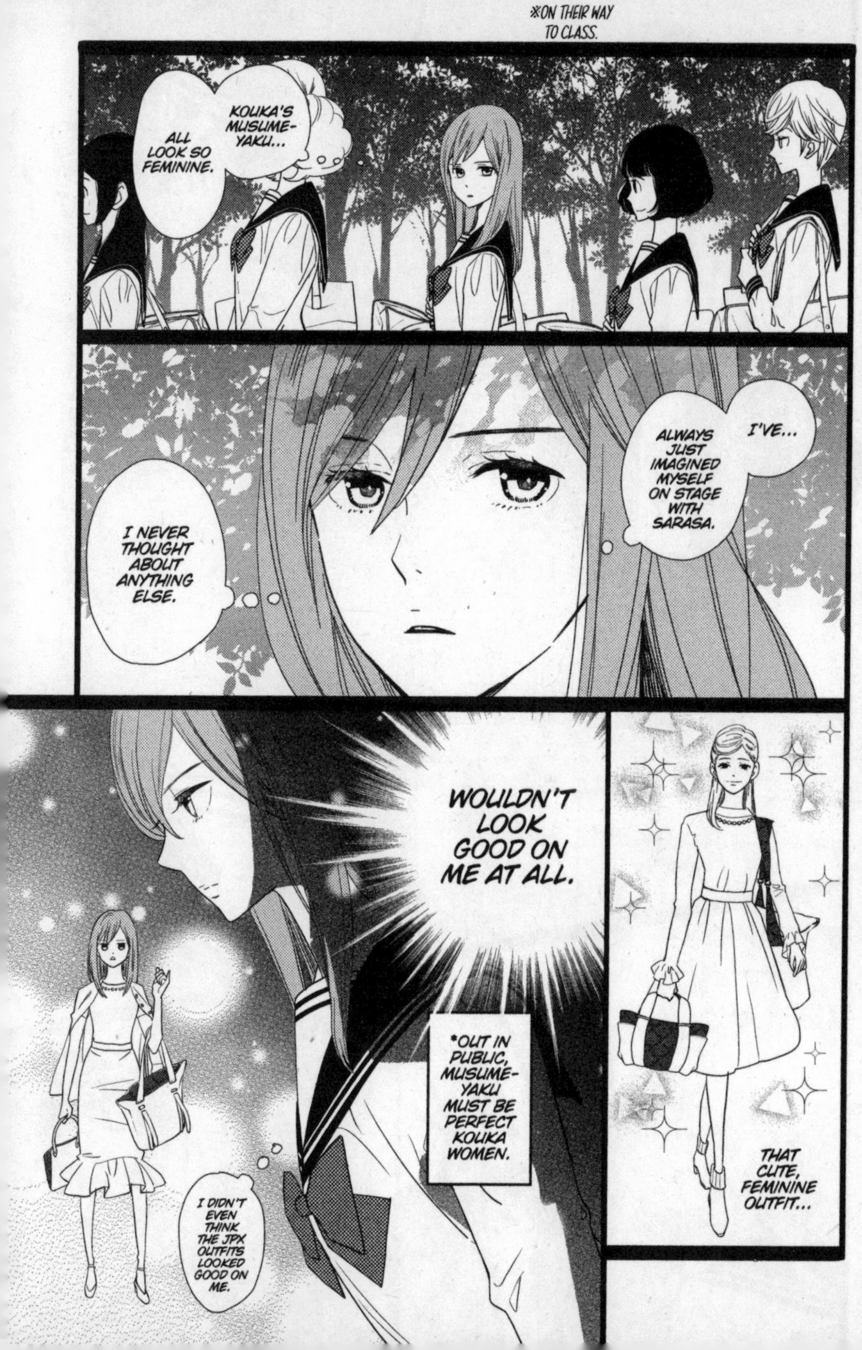
※ON THEIR WAY TO CLASS.
KOUKA'S MUSUME-YAKU...
ALL LOOK SO FEMININE.
I'VE...
ALWAYS JUST IMAGINED MYSELF ON STAGE WITH SARASA.
I NEVER THOUGHT ABOUT ANYTHING ELSE.
THAT CUTE, FEMININE OUTFIT...
WOULDN'T LOOK GOOD ON ME AT ALL.
*OUT IN PUBLIC, MUSUME-YAKU MUST BE PERFECT KOUKA WOMEN.
I DIDN'T EVEN THINK THE JPX OUTFITS LOOKED GOOD ON ME.

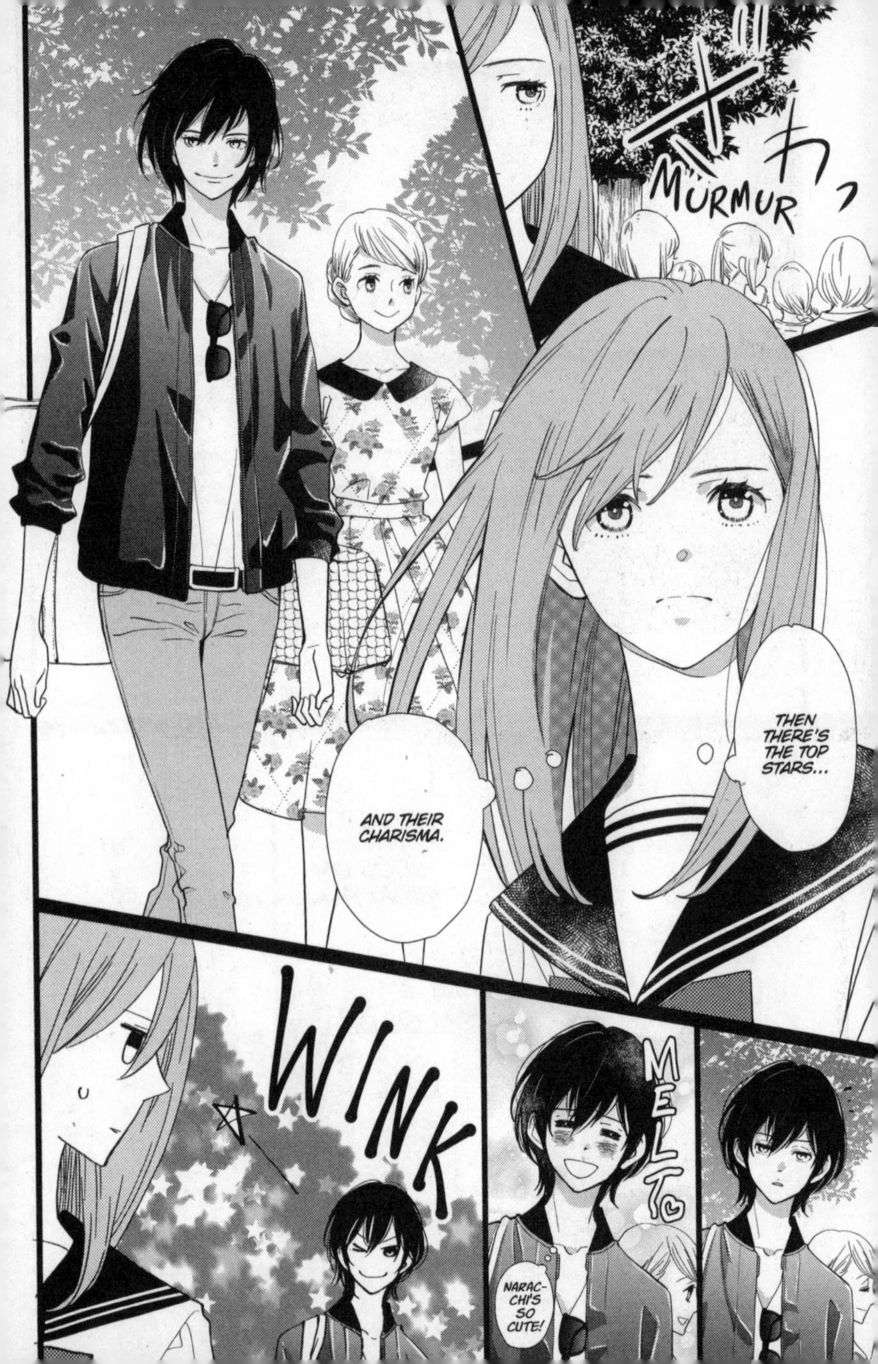
MURMUR
わっ
THEN THERE'S THE TOP STARS...
AND THEIR CHARISMA.
MELT
NARACHI'S SO CUTE!
WINK

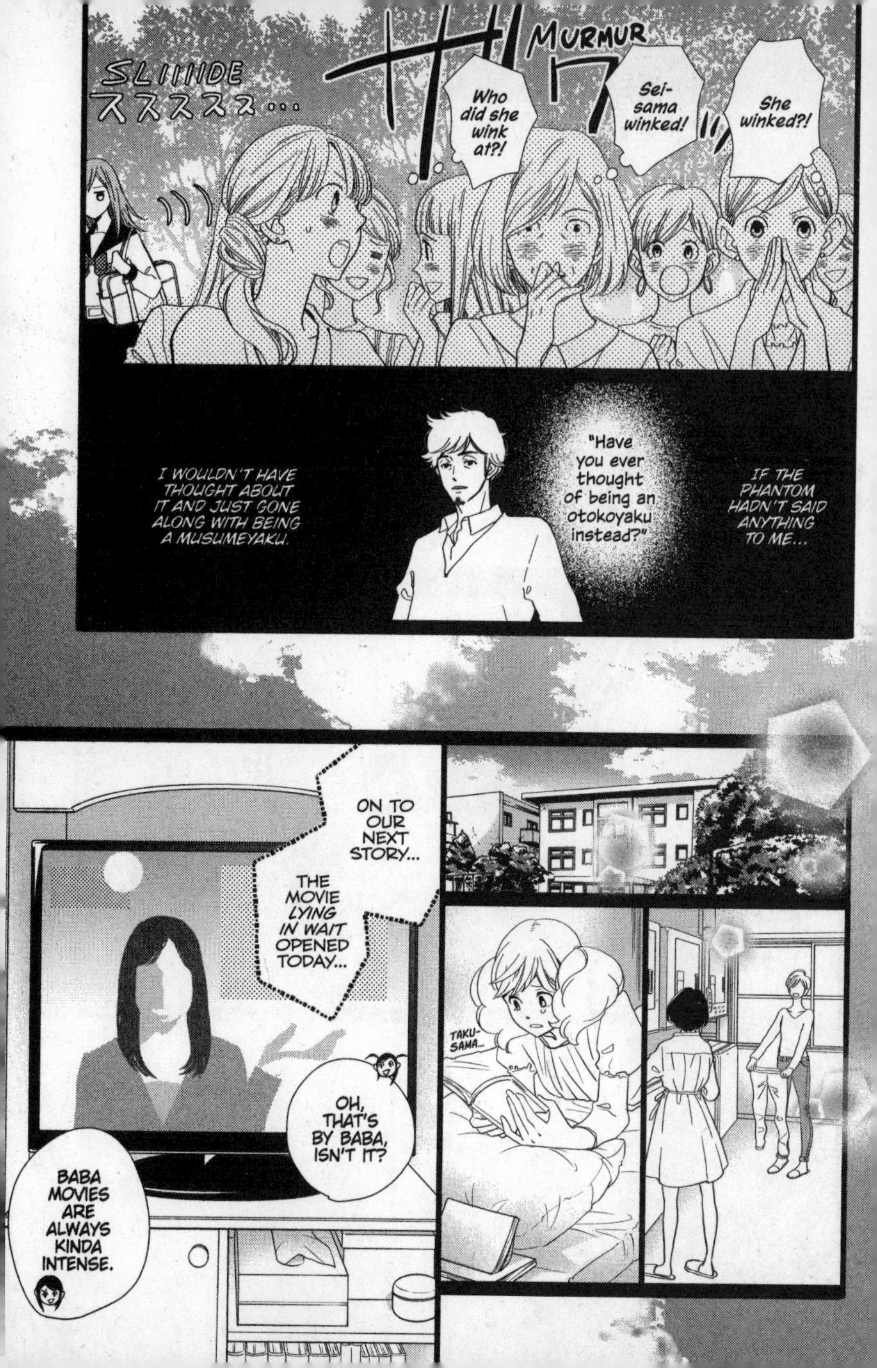
MURMUR
She winked?!
Sei-sama winked!
Who did she wink at?!
SLIIIIDE ススススス...
IF THE PHANTOM HADN'T SAID ANYTHING TO ME...
"Have you ever thought of being an otokoyaku instead?"
I WOULDN'T HAVE THOUGHT ABOUT IT AND JUST GONE ALONG WITH BEING A MUSUMEYAKU.
TAKU-SAMA...
ON TO OUR NEXT STORY...
THE MOVIE LYING IN WAIT OPENED TODAY...
OH, THAT'S BY BABA, ISN'T IT?
BABA MOVIES ARE ALWAYS KINDA INTENSE.

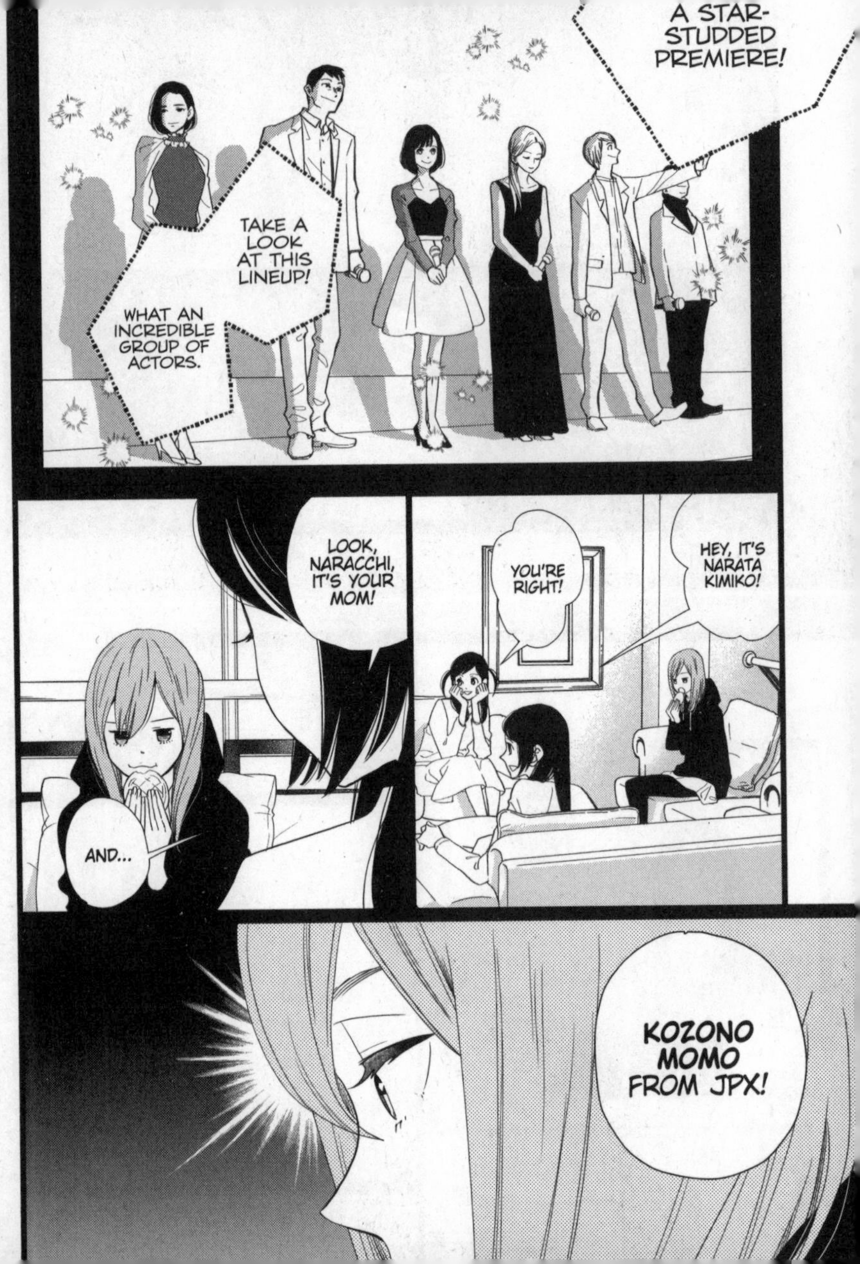
A STAR-STUDDED PREMIERE!
TAKE A LOOK AT THIS LINEUP!
WHAT AN INCREDIBLE GROUP OF ACTORS.
HEY, IT'S NARATA KIMIKO!
YOU'RE RIGHT!
LOOK, NARACCHI, IT'S YOUR MOM!
AND...
KOZONO MOMO FROM JPX!

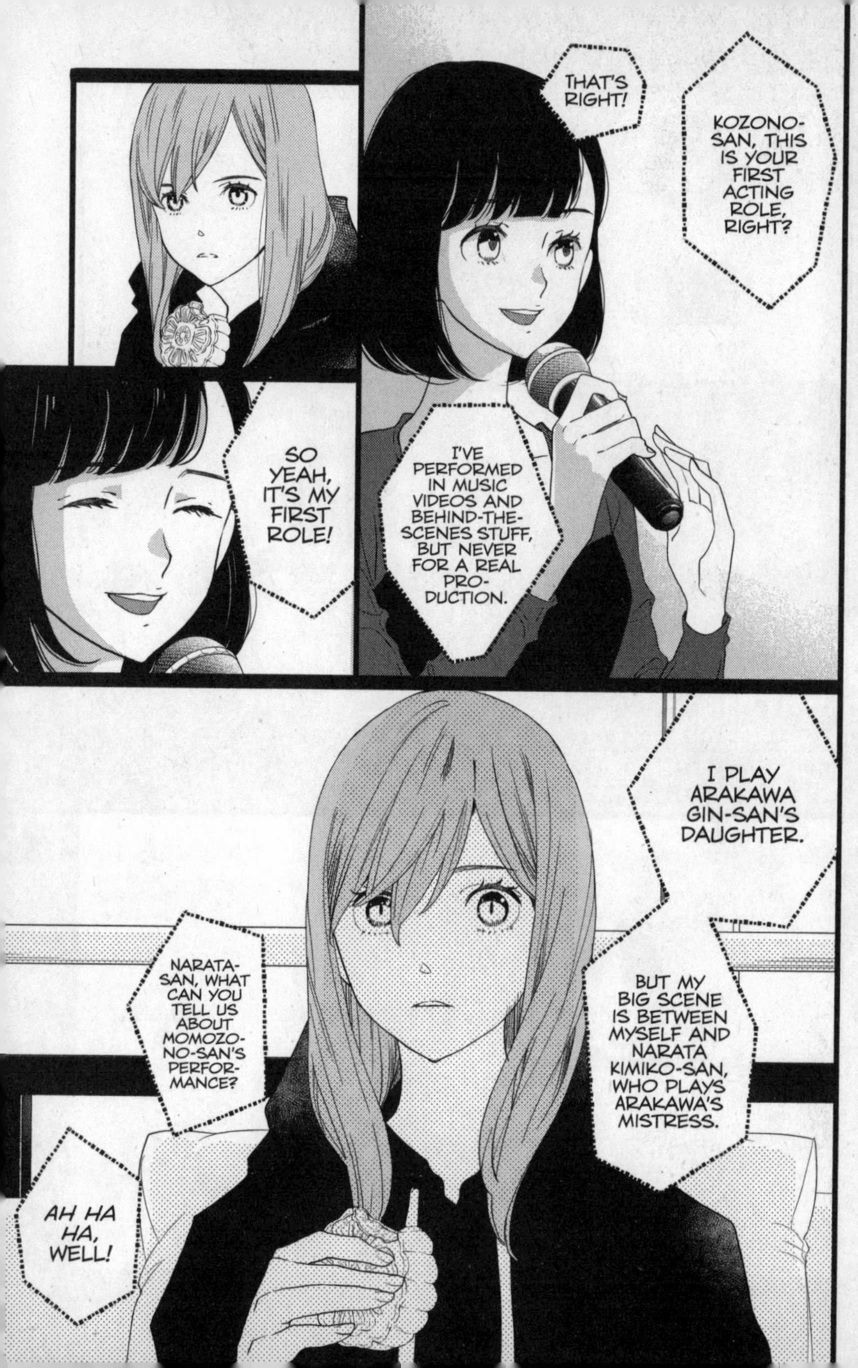
KOZONO-SAN, THIS IS YOUR FIRST ACTING ROLE, RIGHT?
THAT'S RIGHT!
I'VE PERFORMED IN MUSIC VIDEOS AND BEHIND-THE-SCENES STUFF, BUT NEVER FOR A REAL PRO-DUCTION.
SO YEAH, IT'S MY FIRST ROLE!
I PLAY ARAKAWA GIN-SAN'S DAUGHTER.
BUT MY BIG SCENE IS BETWEEN MYSELF AND NARATA KIMIKO-SAN, WHO PLAYS ARAKAWA'S MISTRESS.
NARATA-SAN, WHAT CAN YOU TELL US ABOUT MOMOZONO-NO-SAN'S PERFOR-MANCE?
AH HA HA, WELL!

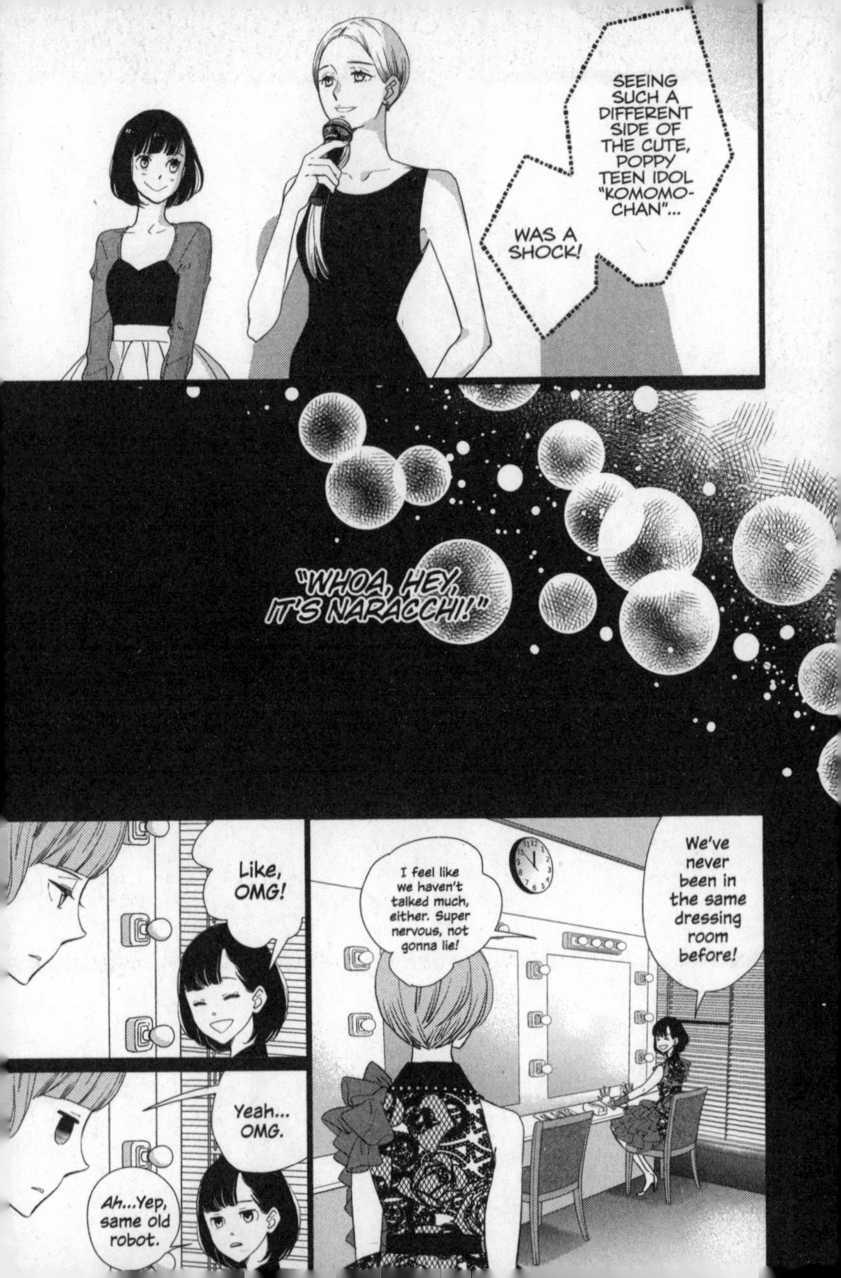
SEEING SUCH A DIFFERENT SIDE OF THE CUTE, POPPY TEEN IDOL "KOMOMO-CHAN"...
WAS A SHOCK!
"WHOA, HEY, IT'S NARACCHI!"
We've never been in the same dressing room before!
I feel like we haven't talked much, either. Super nervous, not gonna lie!
Like, OMG!
Yeah... OMG.
Ah...Yep, same old robot.

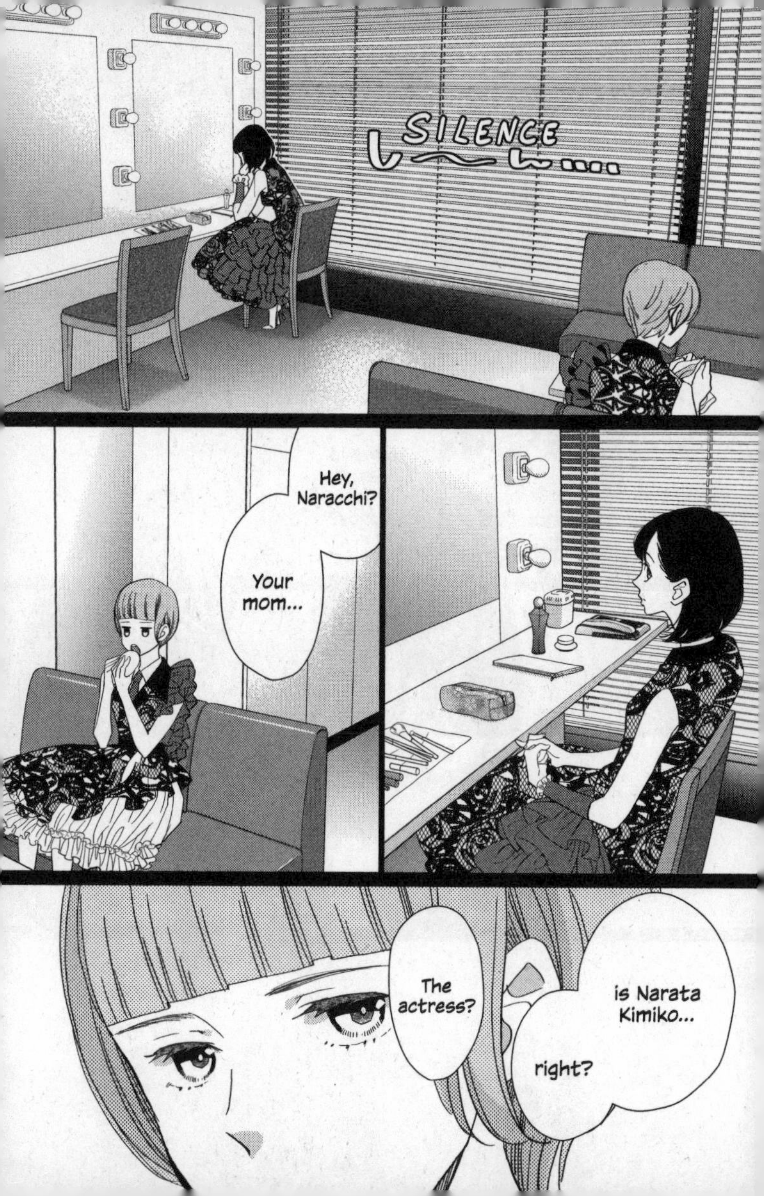
SILENCE
し〜ん....
Hey, Naracchi?
Your mom...
is Narata Kimiko...
right?
The actress?

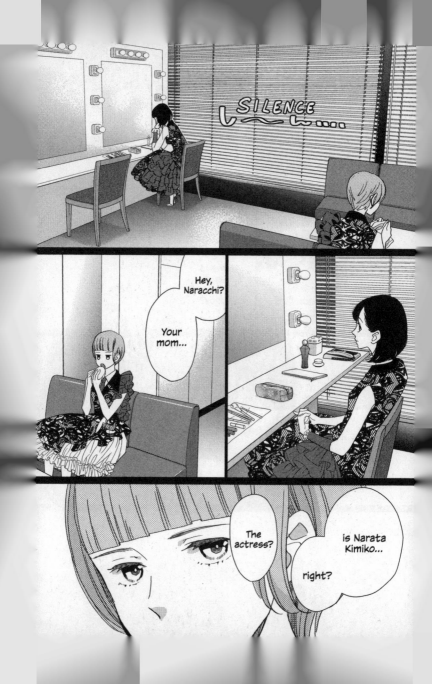

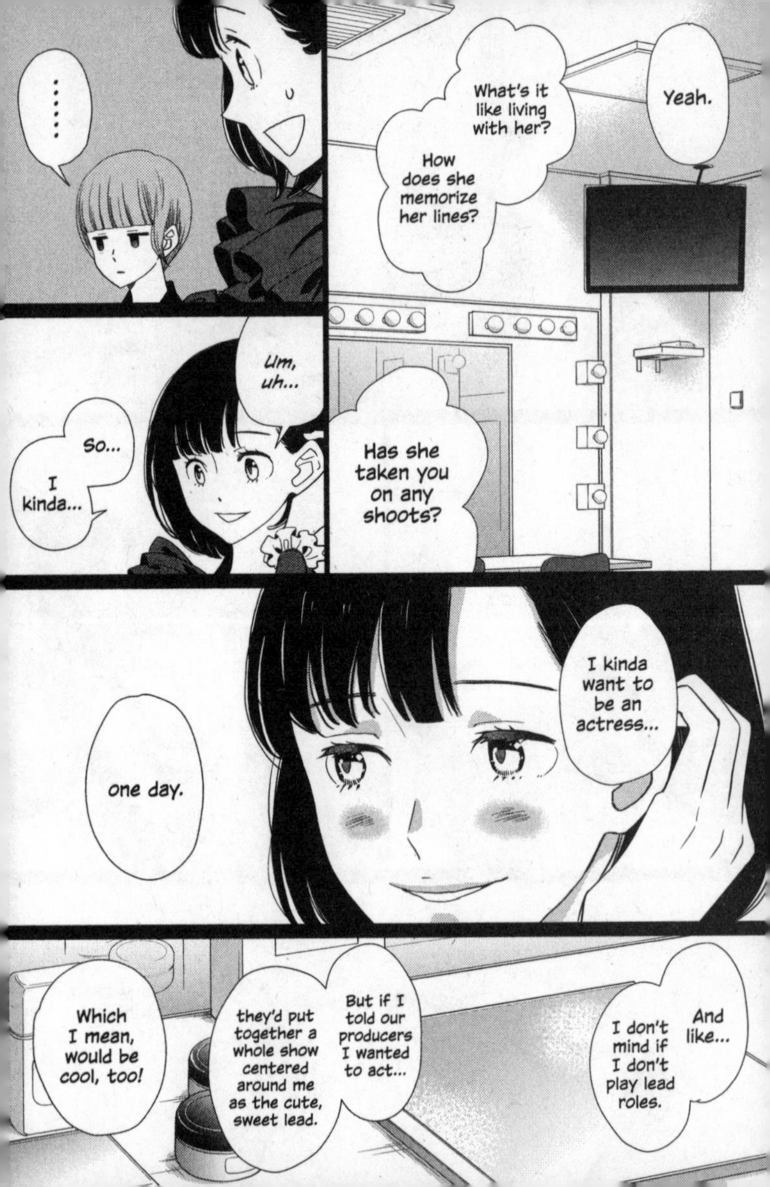
Yeah.
What's it like living with her?
How does she memorize her lines?
......
Has she taken you on any shoots?
Um, uh...
So...
I kinda...
I kinda want to be an actress...
one day.
And like...
I don't mind if I don't play lead roles.
But if I told our producers I wanted to act...
they'd put together a whole show centered around me as the cute, sweet lead.
Which I mean, would be cool, too!

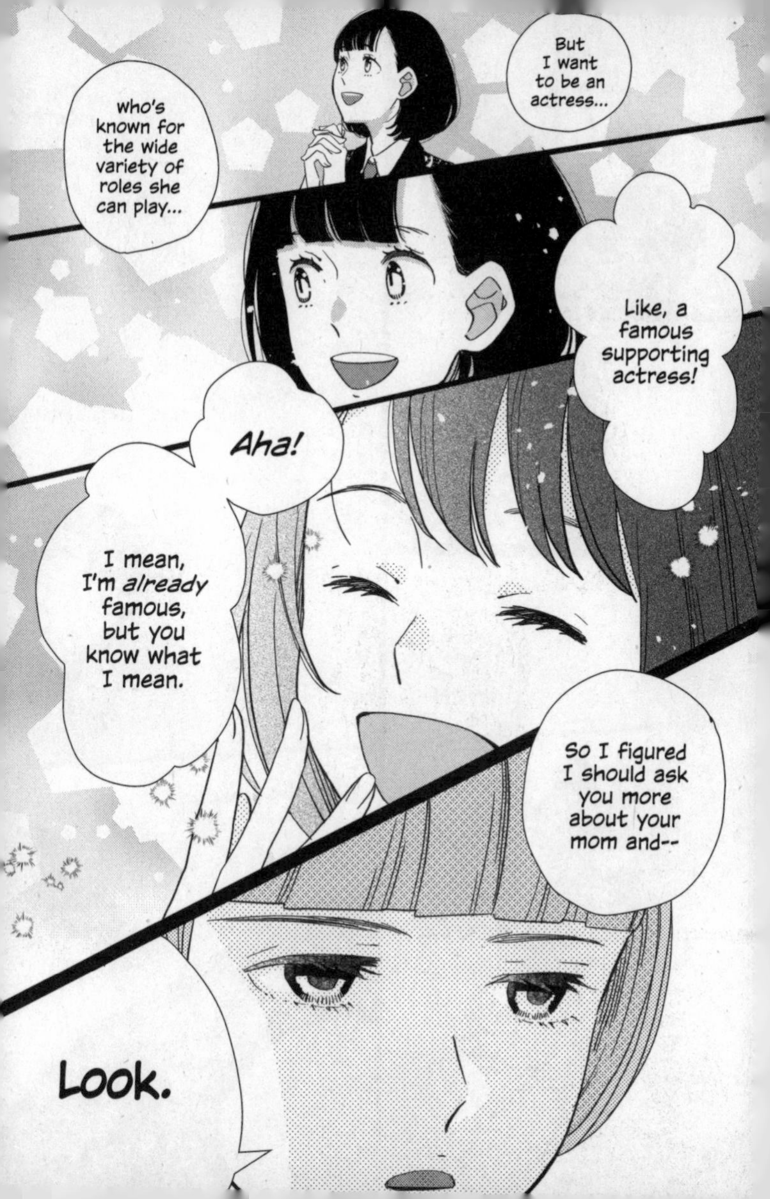
But I want to be an actress...
who's known for the wide variety of roles she can play...
Like, a famous supporting actress!
Aha!
I mean, I'm *already* famous, but you know what I mean.
So I figured I should ask you more about your mom and--
Look.

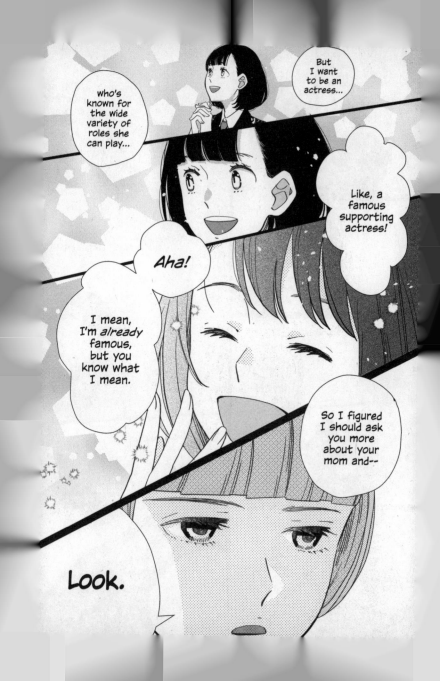

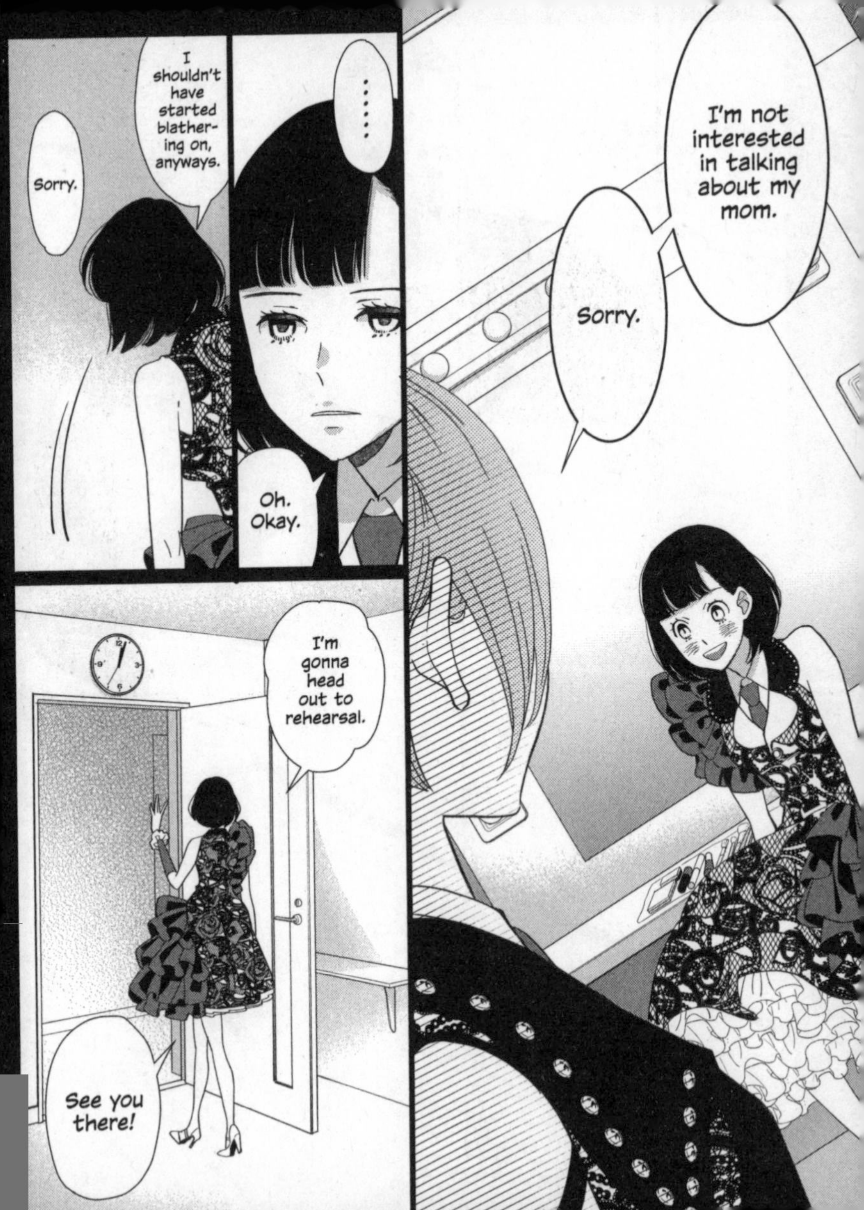
I'm not interested in talking about my mom.
Sorry.
……
Oh. Okay.
I shouldn't have started blather-ing on, anyways.
Sorry.
I'm gonna head out to rehearsal.
See you there!

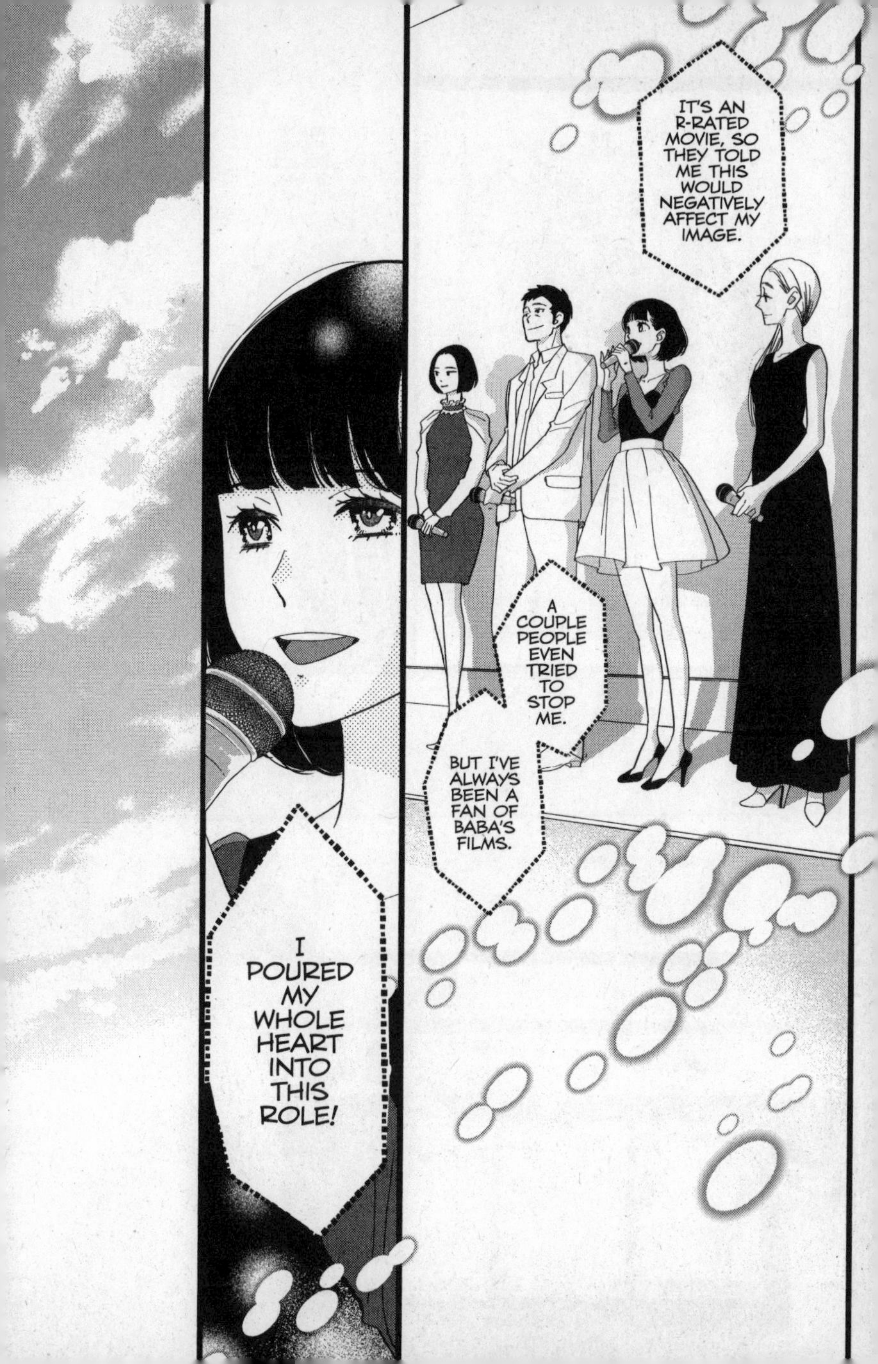
IT'S AN R-RATED MOVIE, SO THEY TOLD ME THIS WOULD NEGATIVELY AFFECT MY IMAGE.
A COUPLE PEOPLE EVEN TRIED TO STOP ME.
BUT I'VE ALWAYS BEEN A FAN OF BABA'S FILMS.
I POURED MY WHOLE HEART INTO THIS ROLE!

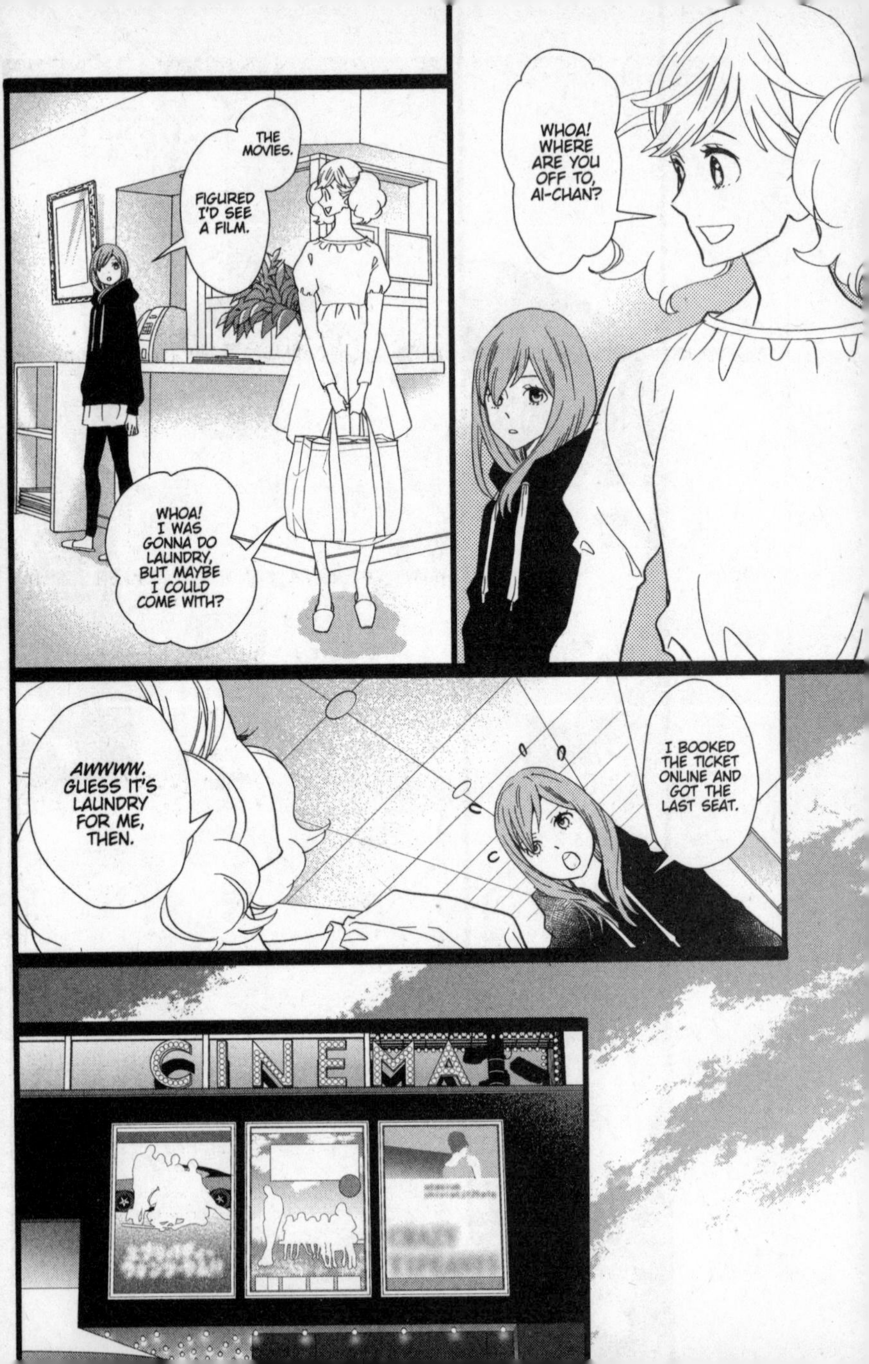
WHOA! WHERE ARE YOU OFF TO, AI-CHAN?
THE MOVIES.
FIGURED I'D SEE A FILM.
WHOA! I WAS GONNA DO LAUNDRY, BUT MAYBE I COULD COME WITH?
I BOOKED THE TICKET ONLINE AND GOT THE LAST SEAT.
AWWWW. GUESS IT'S LAUNDRY FOR ME, THEN.
CINEMA

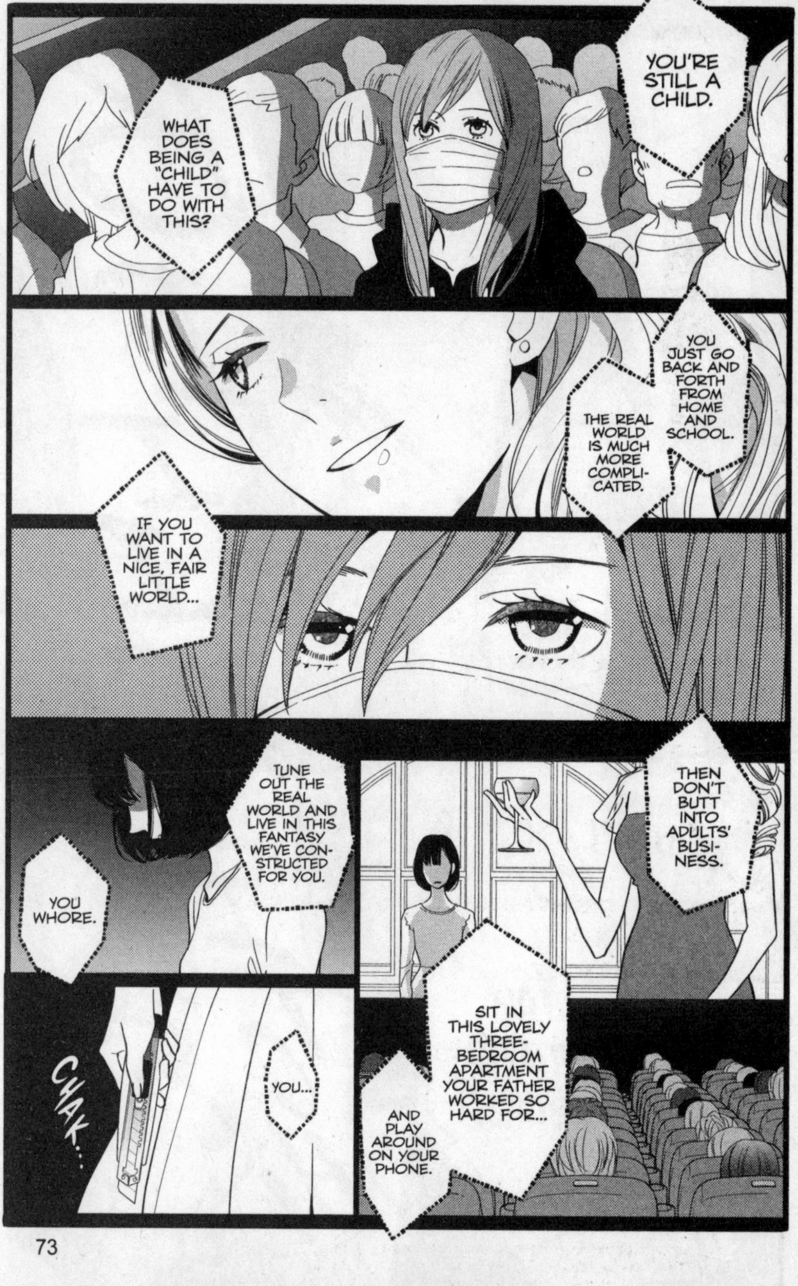
YOU'RE STILL A CHILD.
WHAT DOES BEING A "CHILD" HAVE TO DO WITH THIS?
YOU JUST GO BACK AND FORTH FROM HOME AND SCHOOL.
THE REAL WORLD IS MUCH MORE COMPLICATED.
IF YOU WANT TO LIVE IN A NICE, FAIR LITTLE WORLD...
THEN DON'T BUTT INTO ADULTS' BUSINESS.
TUNE OUT THE REAL WORLD AND LIVE IN THIS FANTASY WE'VE CONSTRUCTED FOR YOU.
YOU WHORE.
SIT IN THIS LOVELY THREE-BEDROOM APARTMENT YOUR FATHER WORKED SO HARD FOR...
AND PLAY AROUND ON YOUR PHONE.
YOU...
CHAK...

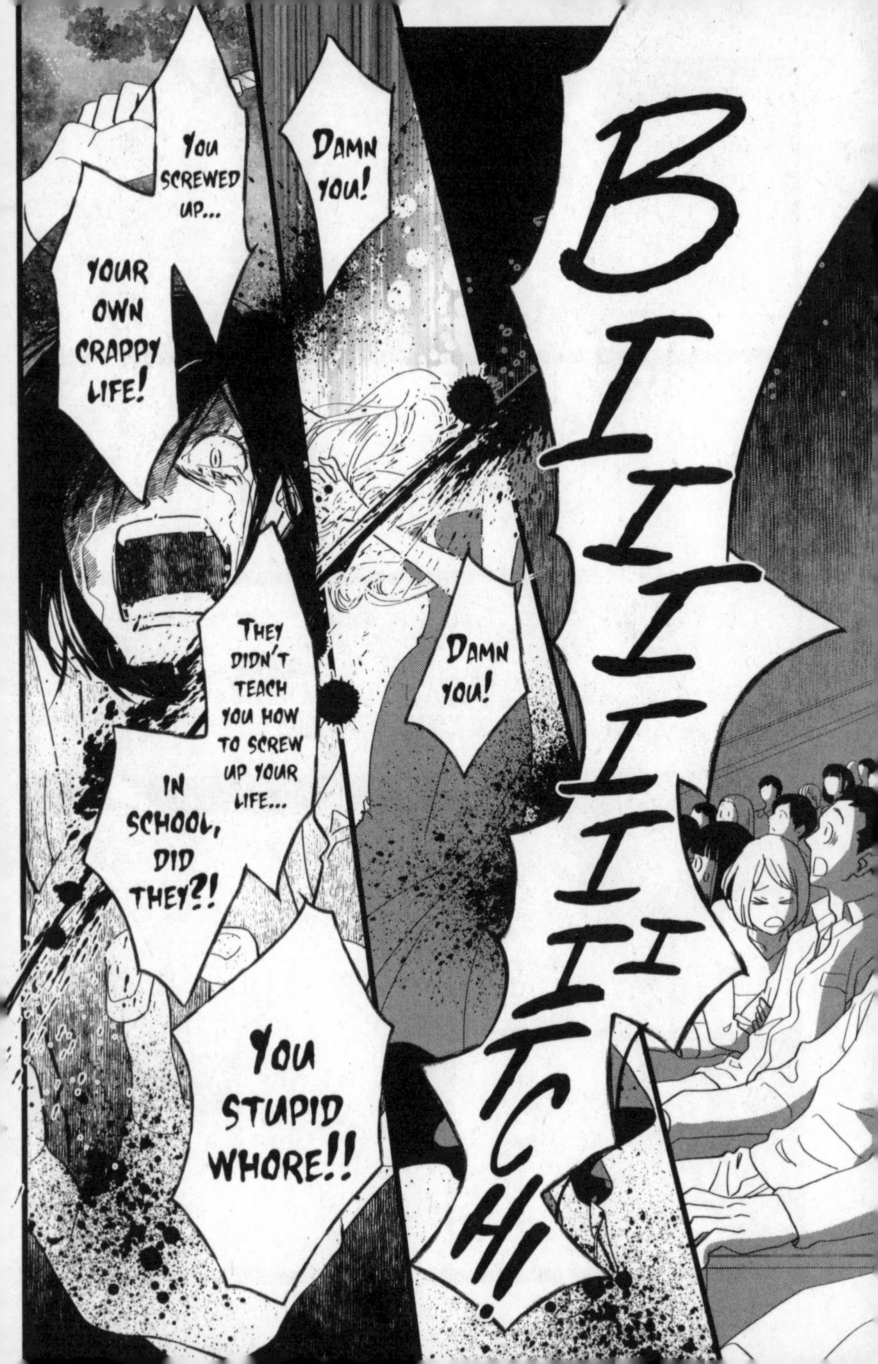
Damn you!
You screwed up... your own crappy life!
Damn you!
They didn't teach you how to screw up your life...
in school, did they?!
You stupid whore!!
BIIIIIITCH!

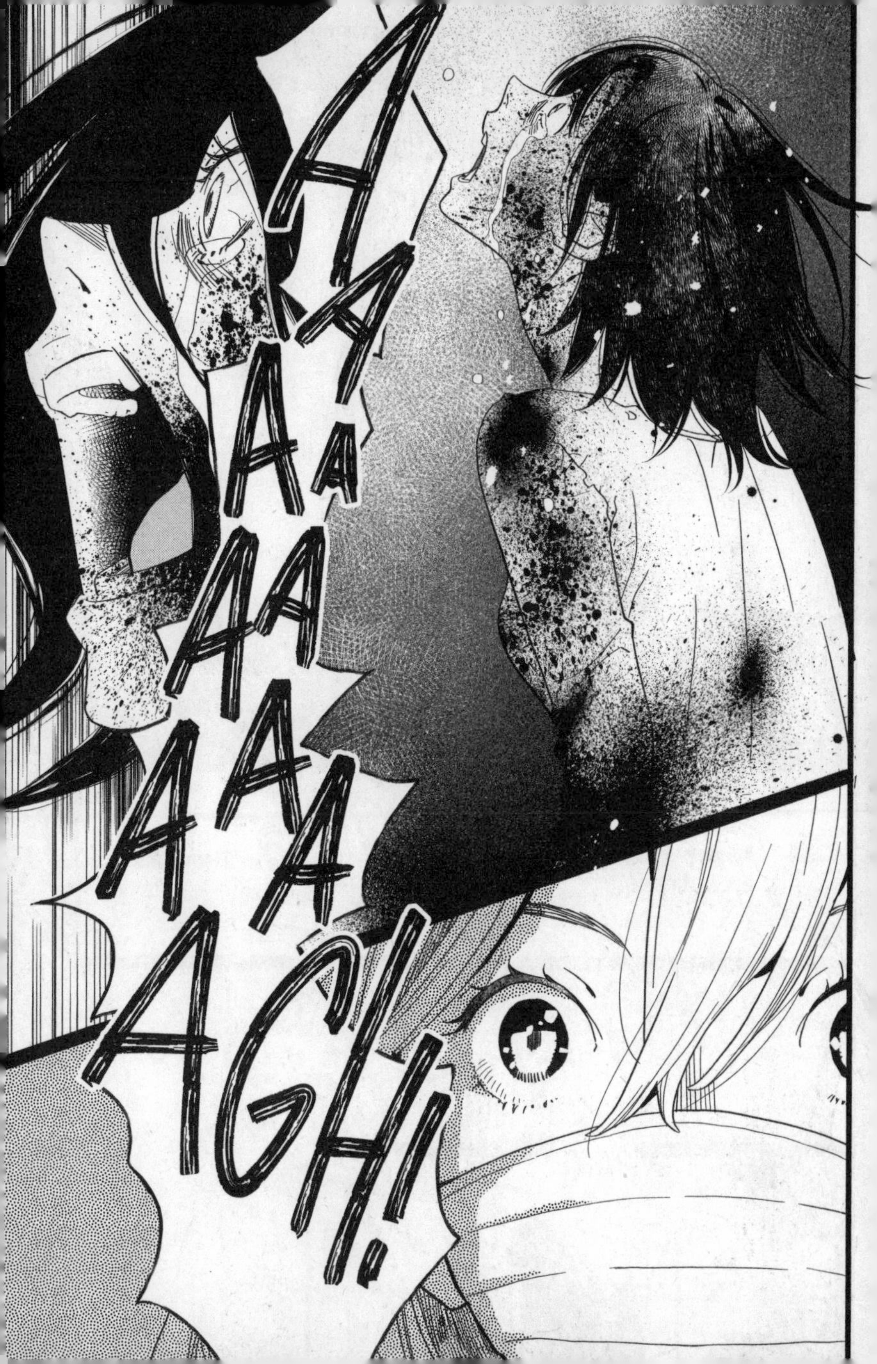
AAAAAAAAAAAGH!

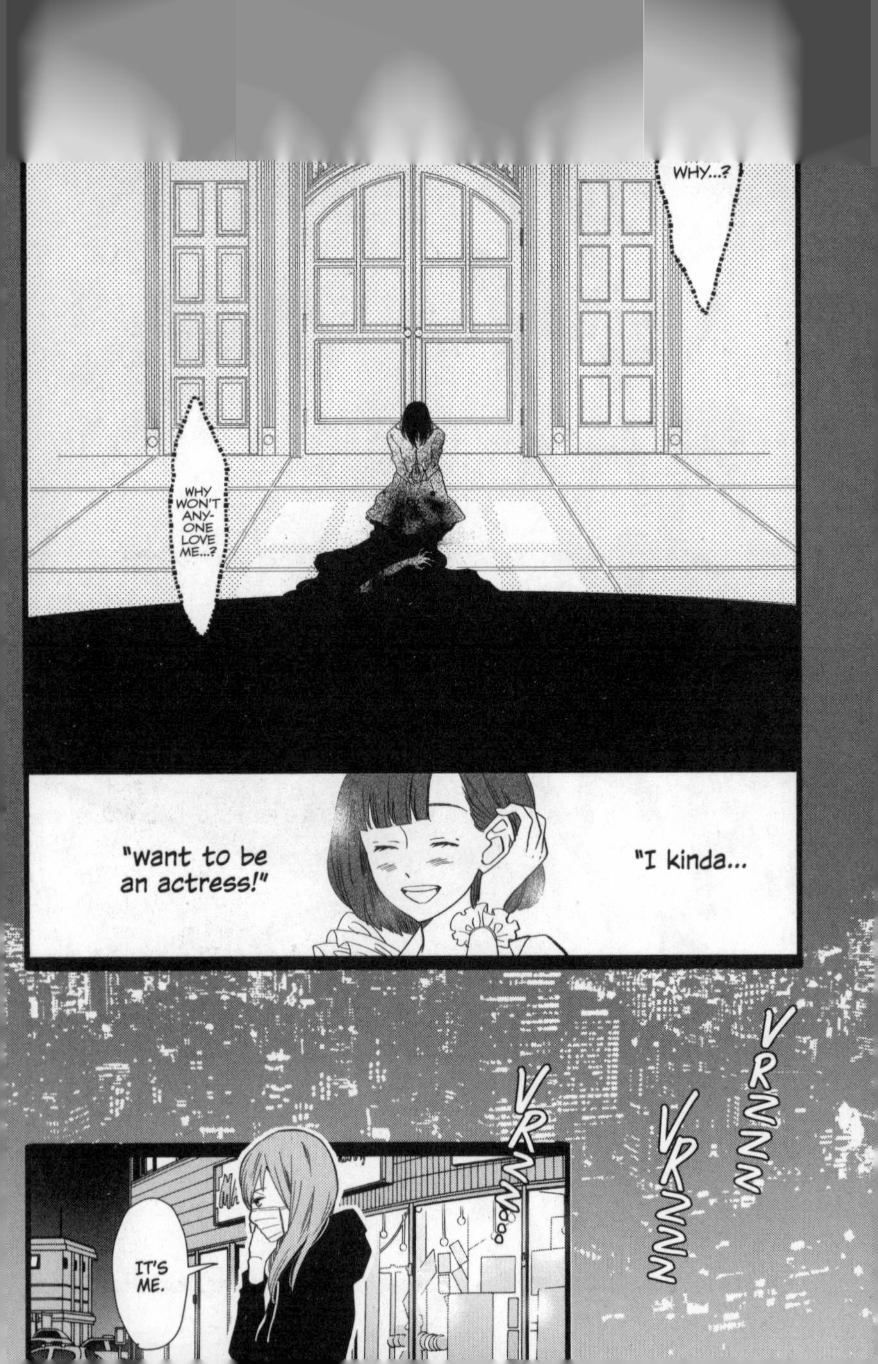
WHY...?
WHY WON'T ANYONE LOVE ME...?
"I kinda...
"want to be an actress!"
VRZZZ
VRZZZZ
VRZZooo
IT'S ME.

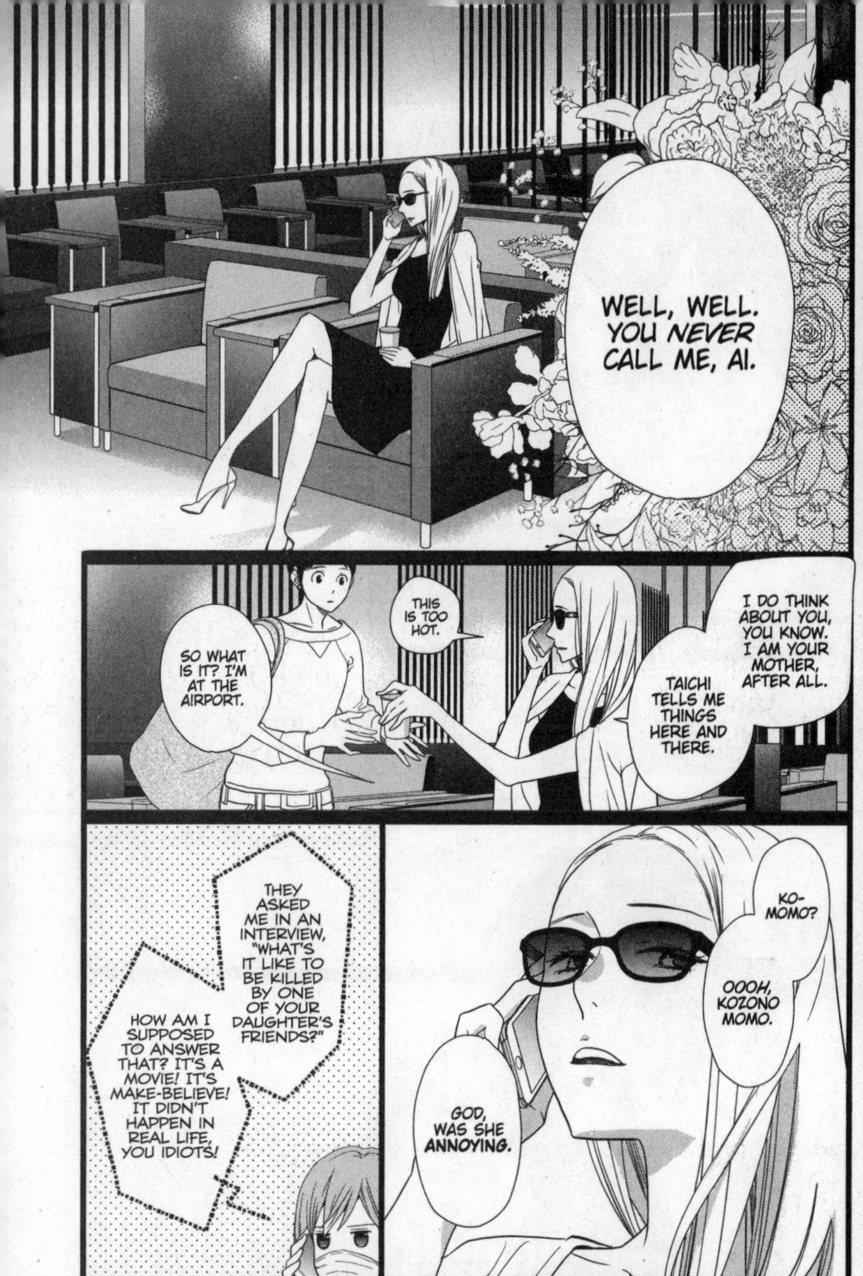
WELL, WELL. YOU *NEVER* CALL ME, AI.
I DO THINK ABOUT YOU, YOU KNOW. I AM YOUR MOTHER, AFTER ALL.
TAICHI TELLS ME THINGS HERE AND THERE.
THIS IS TOO HOT.
SO WHAT IS IT? I'M AT THE AIRPORT.
KO-MOMO?
OOOH, KOZONO MOMO.
GOD, WAS SHE **ANNOYING**.
THEY ASKED ME IN AN INTERVIEW, "WHAT'S IT LIKE TO BE KILLED BY ONE OF YOUR DAUGHTER'S FRIENDS?"
HOW AM I SUPPOSED TO ANSWER THAT? IT'S A MOVIE! IT'S MAKE-BELIEVE! IT DIDN'T HAPPEN IN REAL LIFE, YOU IDIOTS!

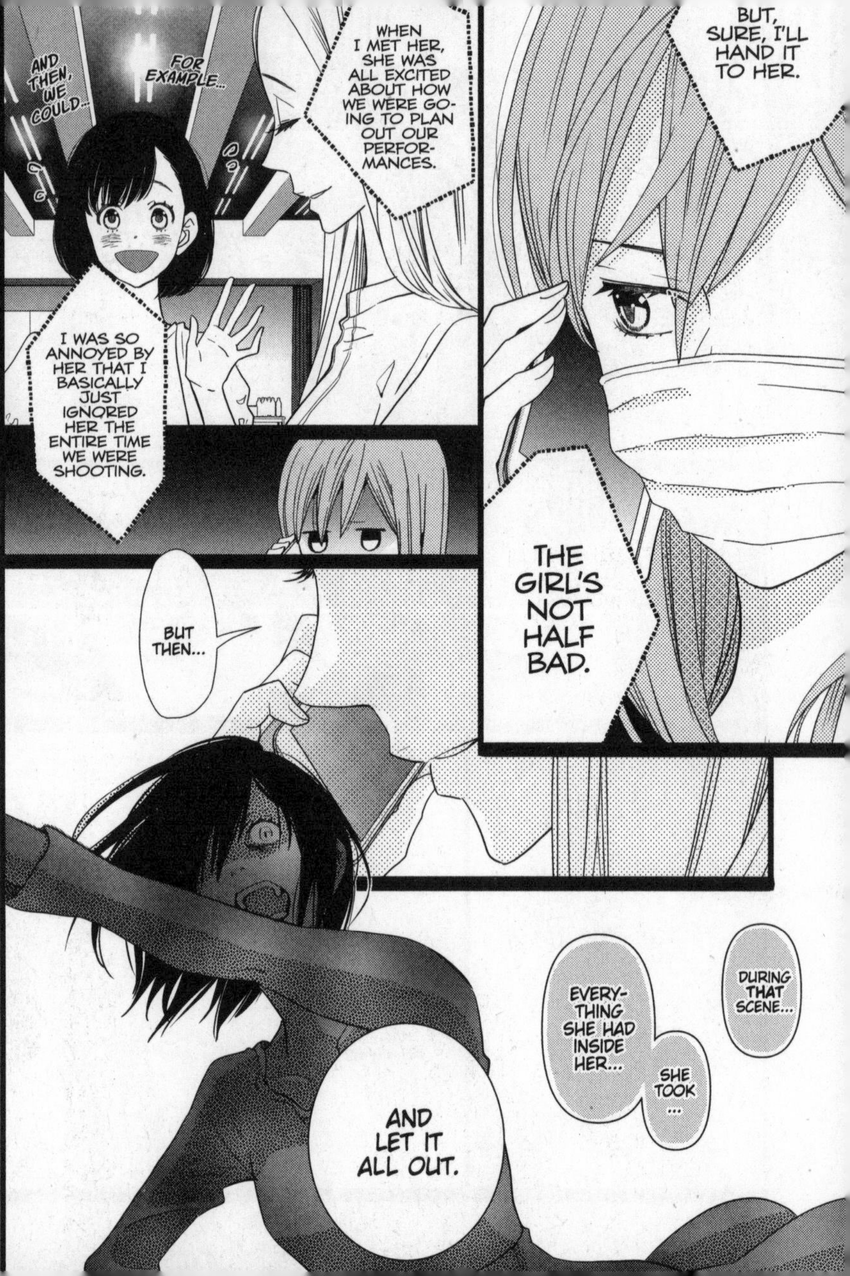
BUT, SURE, I'LL HAND IT TO HER.
THE GIRL'S NOT HALF BAD.
WHEN I MET HER, SHE WAS ALL EXCITED ABOUT HOW WE WERE GOING TO PLAN OUT OUR PERFORMANCES.
FOR EXAMPLE...
AND THEN, WE COULD...
I WAS SO ANNOYED BY HER THAT I BASICALLY JUST IGNORED HER THE ENTIRE TIME WE WERE SHOOTING.
BUT THEN...
DURING THAT SCENE...
EVERYTHING SHE HAD INSIDE HER...
SHE TOOK...
AND LET IT ALL OUT.

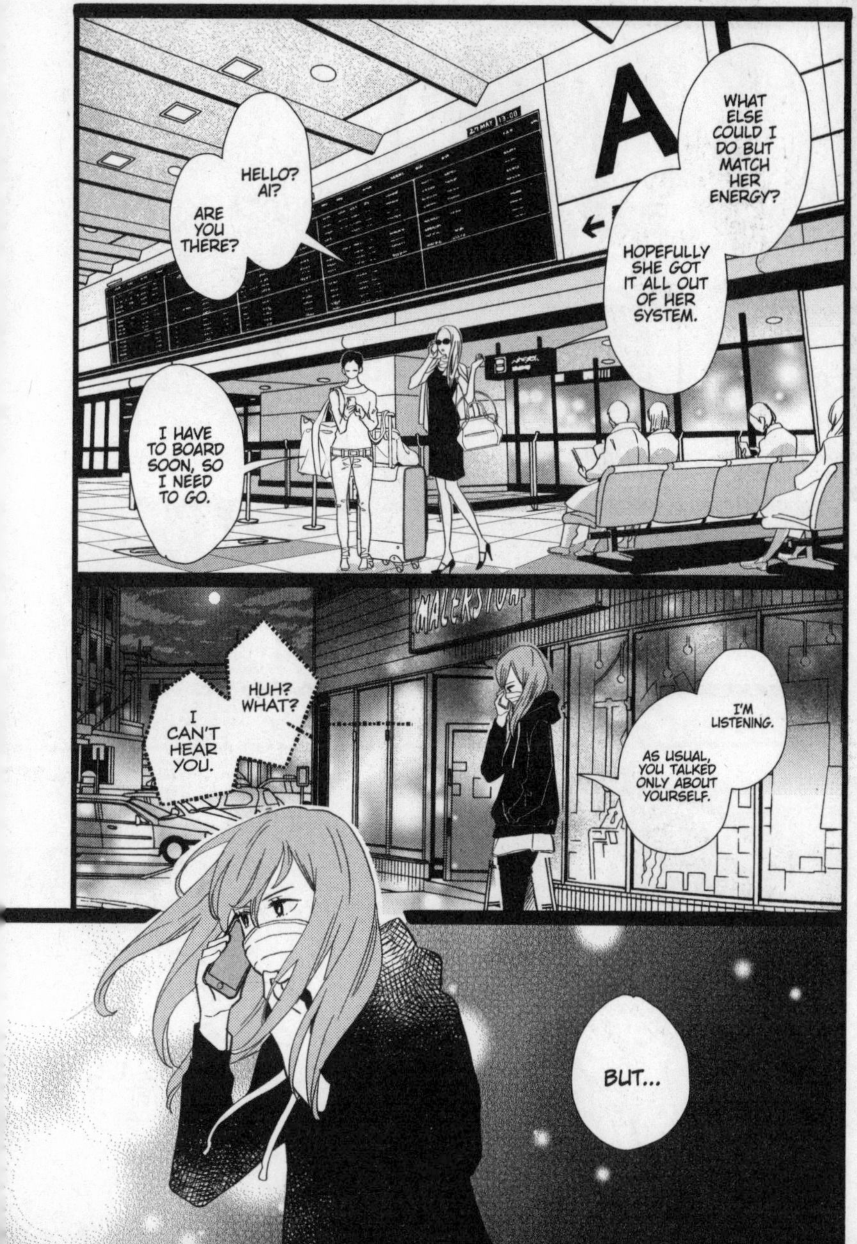
WHAT ELSE COULD I DO BUT MATCH HER ENERGY?
HOPEFULLY SHE GOT IT ALL OUT OF HER SYSTEM.
HELLO? AI?
ARE YOU THERE?
I HAVE TO BOARD SOON, SO I NEED TO GO.
I'M LISTENING.
AS USUAL, YOU TALKED ONLY ABOUT YOURSELF.
HUH? WHAT?
I CAN'T HEAR YOU.
BUT...

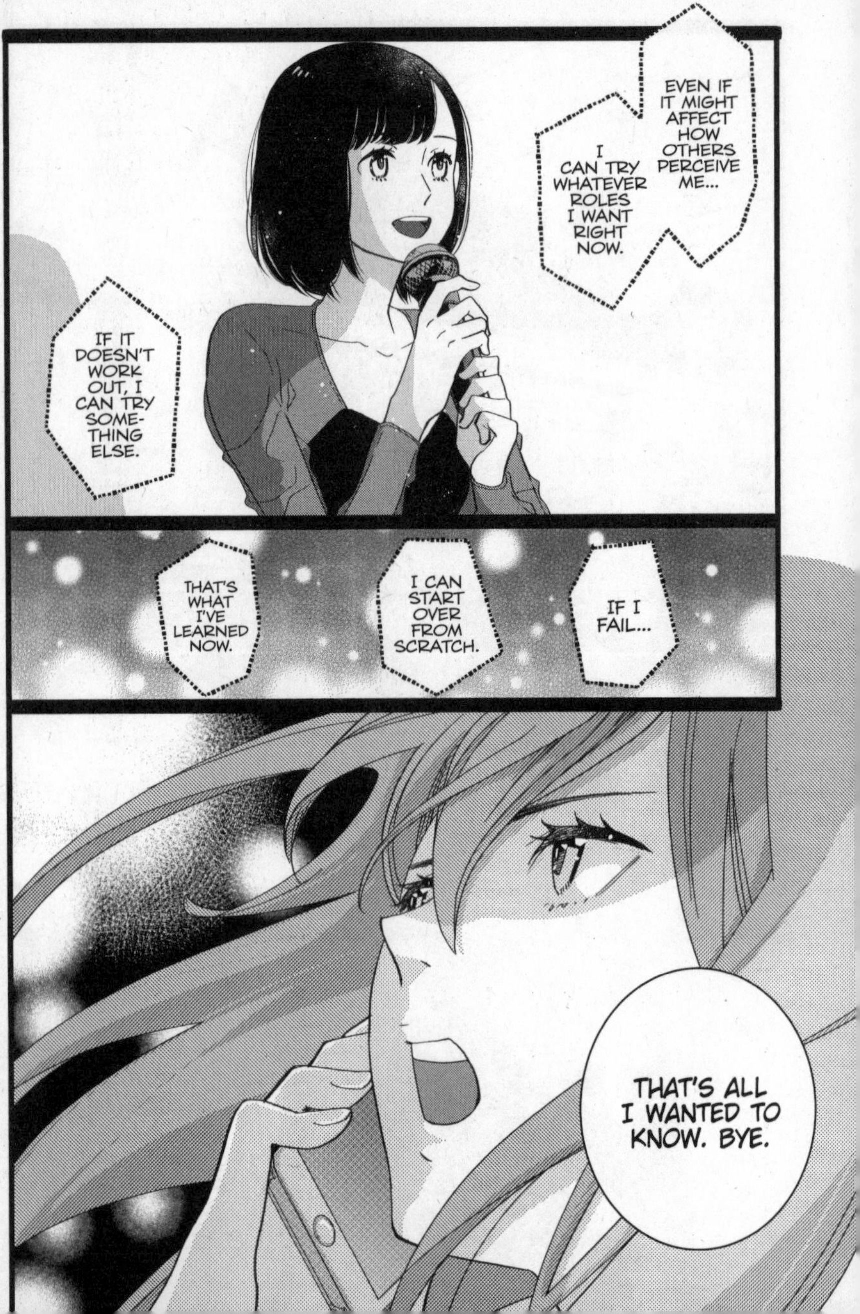
EVEN IF IT MIGHT AFFECT HOW OTHERS PERCEIVE ME...
I CAN TRY WHATEVER ROLES I WANT RIGHT NOW.
IF IT DOESN'T WORK OUT, I CAN TRY SOME-THING ELSE.
IF I FAIL...
I CAN START OVER FROM SCRATCH.
THAT'S WHAT I'VE LEARNED NOW.
THAT'S ALL I WANTED TO KNOW. BYE.

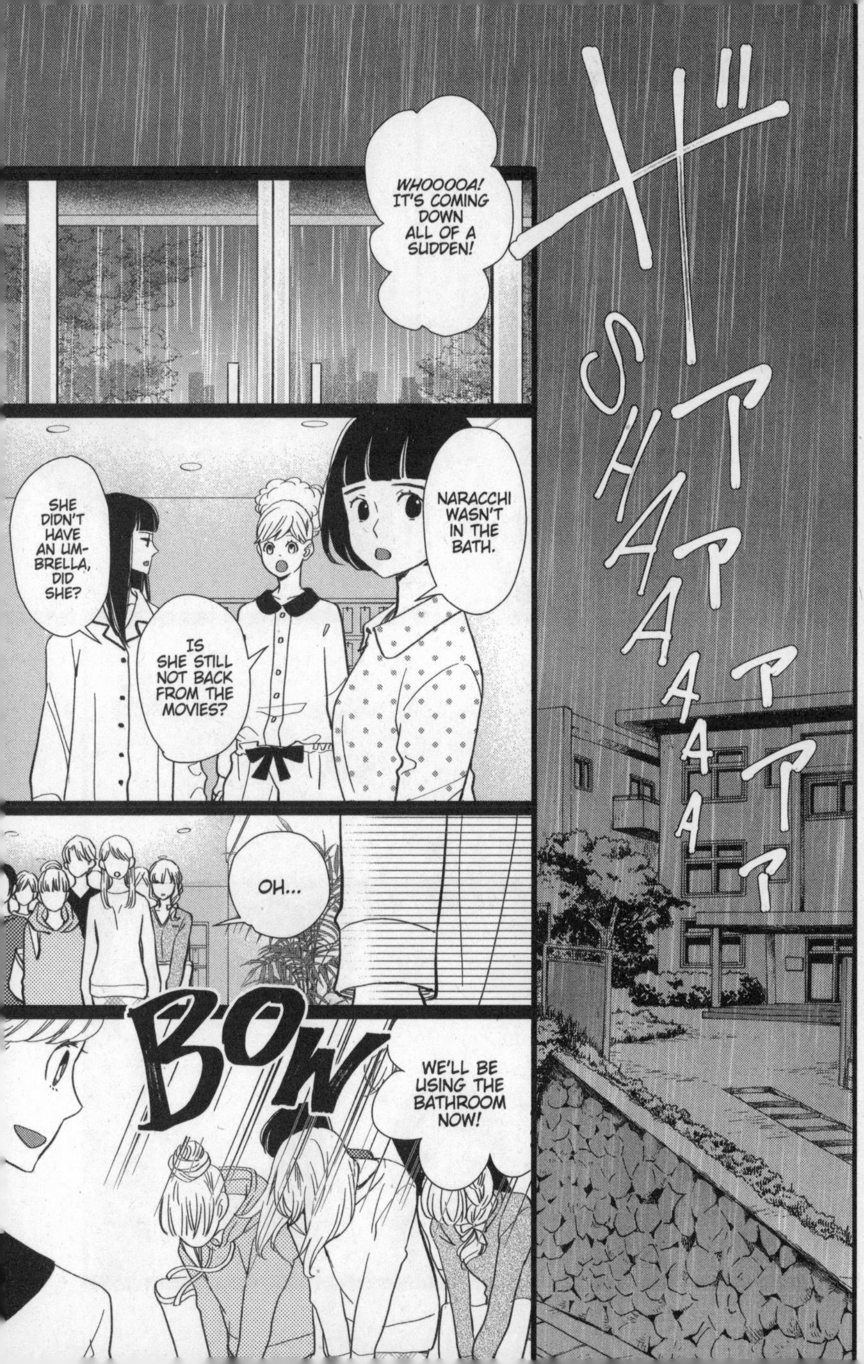
SHAAAA
WHOOOOA! IT'S COMING DOWN ALL OF A SUDDEN!
NARACCHI WASN'T IN THE BATH.
IS SHE STILL NOT BACK FROM THE MOVIES?
SHE DIDN'T HAVE AN UM-BRELLA, DID SHE?
OH...
WE'LL BE USING THE BATHROOM NOW!
BOW

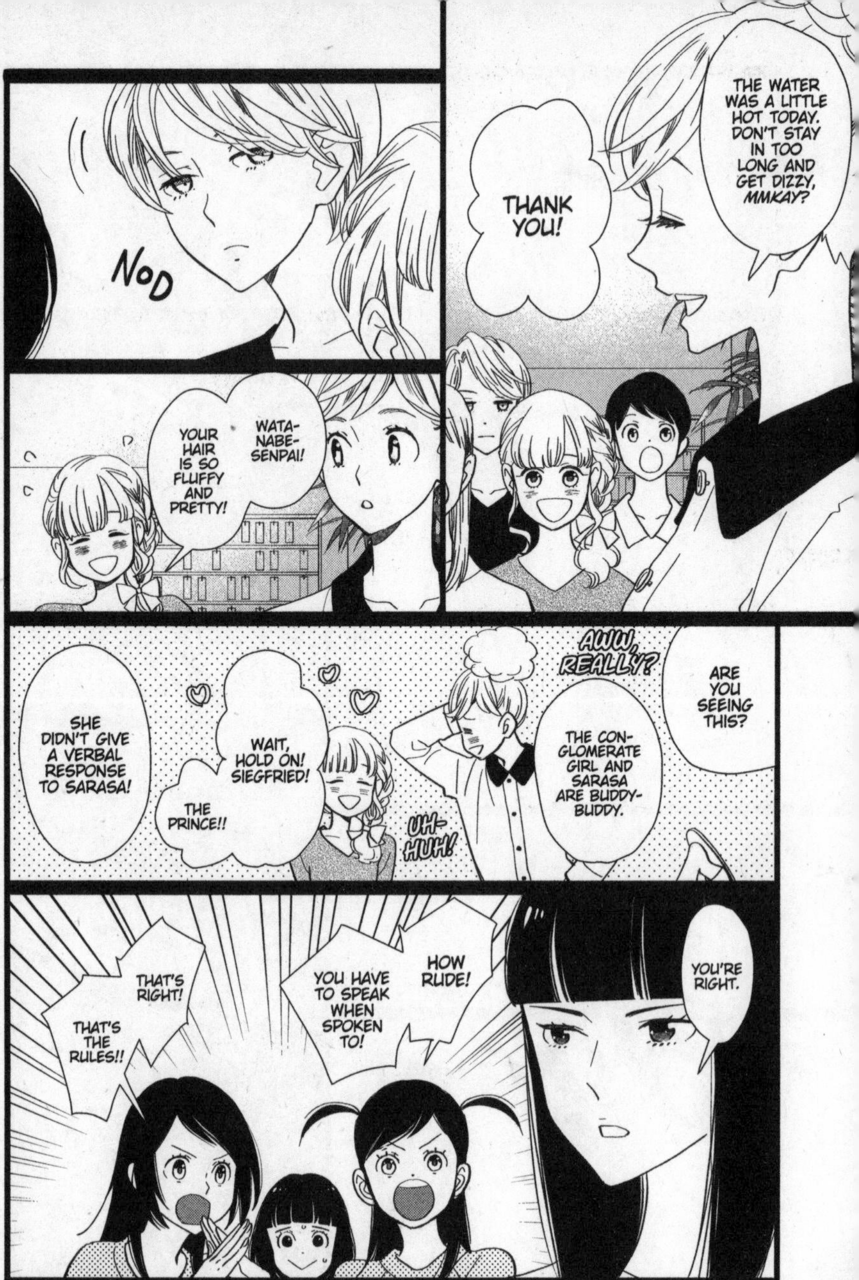
THE WATER WAS A LITTLE HOT TODAY. DON'T STAY IN TOO LONG AND GET DIZZY, MMKAY?
THANK YOU!
NOD
WATA-NABE-SENPAI!
YOUR HAIR IS SO FLUFFY AND PRETTY!
ARE YOU SEEING THIS?
AWW, REALLY?
THE CON-GLOMERATE GIRL AND SARASA ARE BUDDY-BUDDY.
UH-HUH!
WAIT, HOLD ON! SIEGFRIED!
THE PRINCE!!
SHE DIDN'T GIVE A VERBAL RESPONSE TO SARASA!
YOU'RE RIGHT.
HOW RUDE!
YOU HAVE TO SPEAK WHEN SPOKEN TO!
THAT'S RIGHT!
THAT'S THE RULES!!

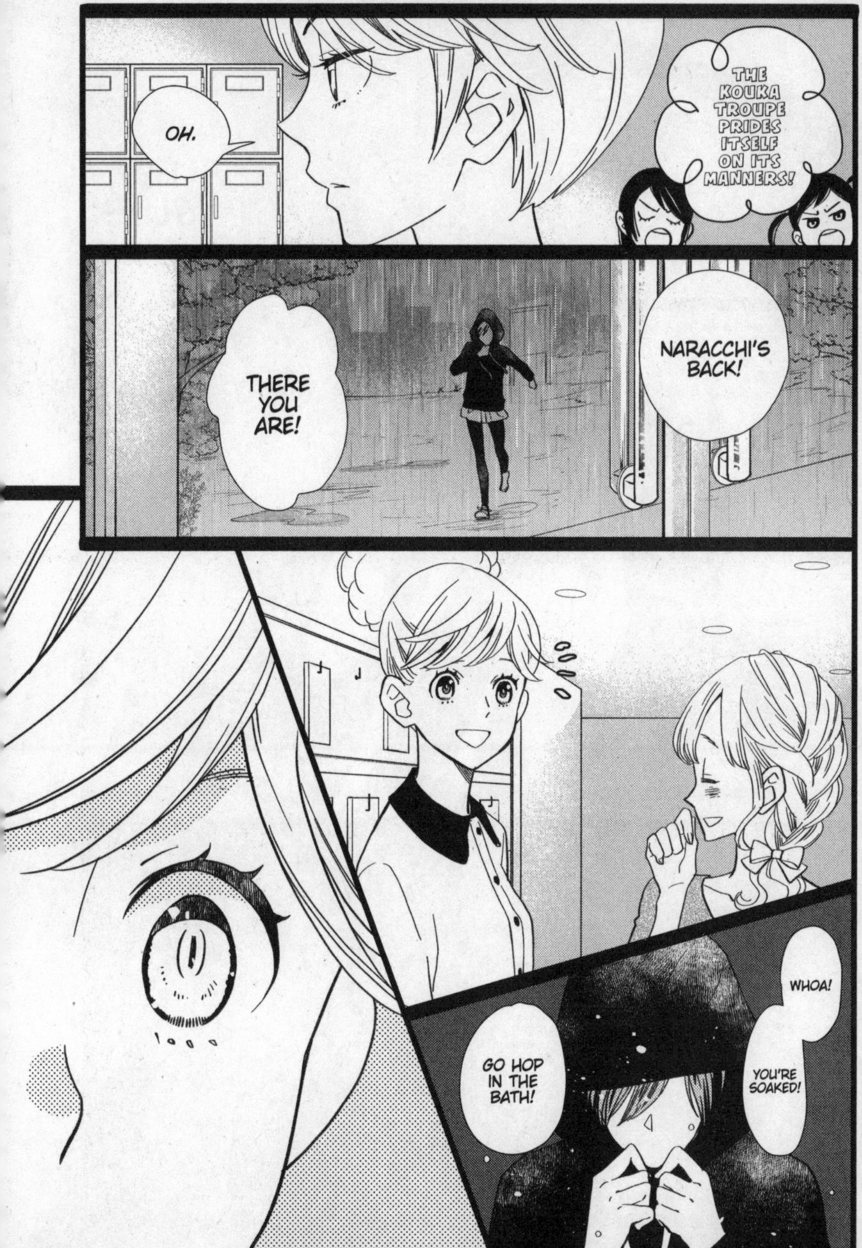
THE KOUKA TROUPE PRIDES ITSELF ON ITS MANNERS!
OH.
NARACCHI'S BACK!
THERE YOU ARE!
WHOA!
YOU'RE SOAKED!
GO HOP IN THE BATH!

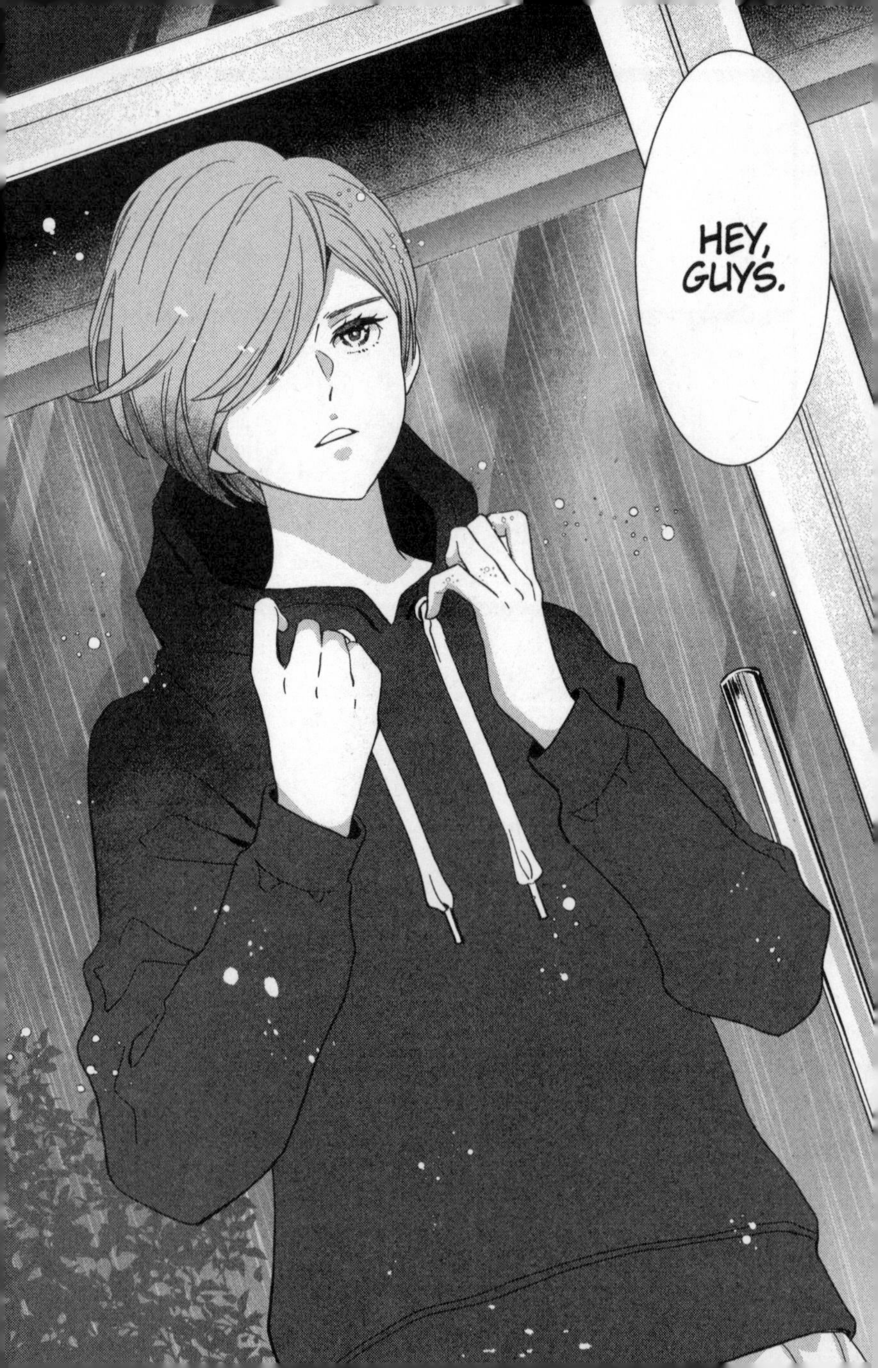
HEY, GUYS.

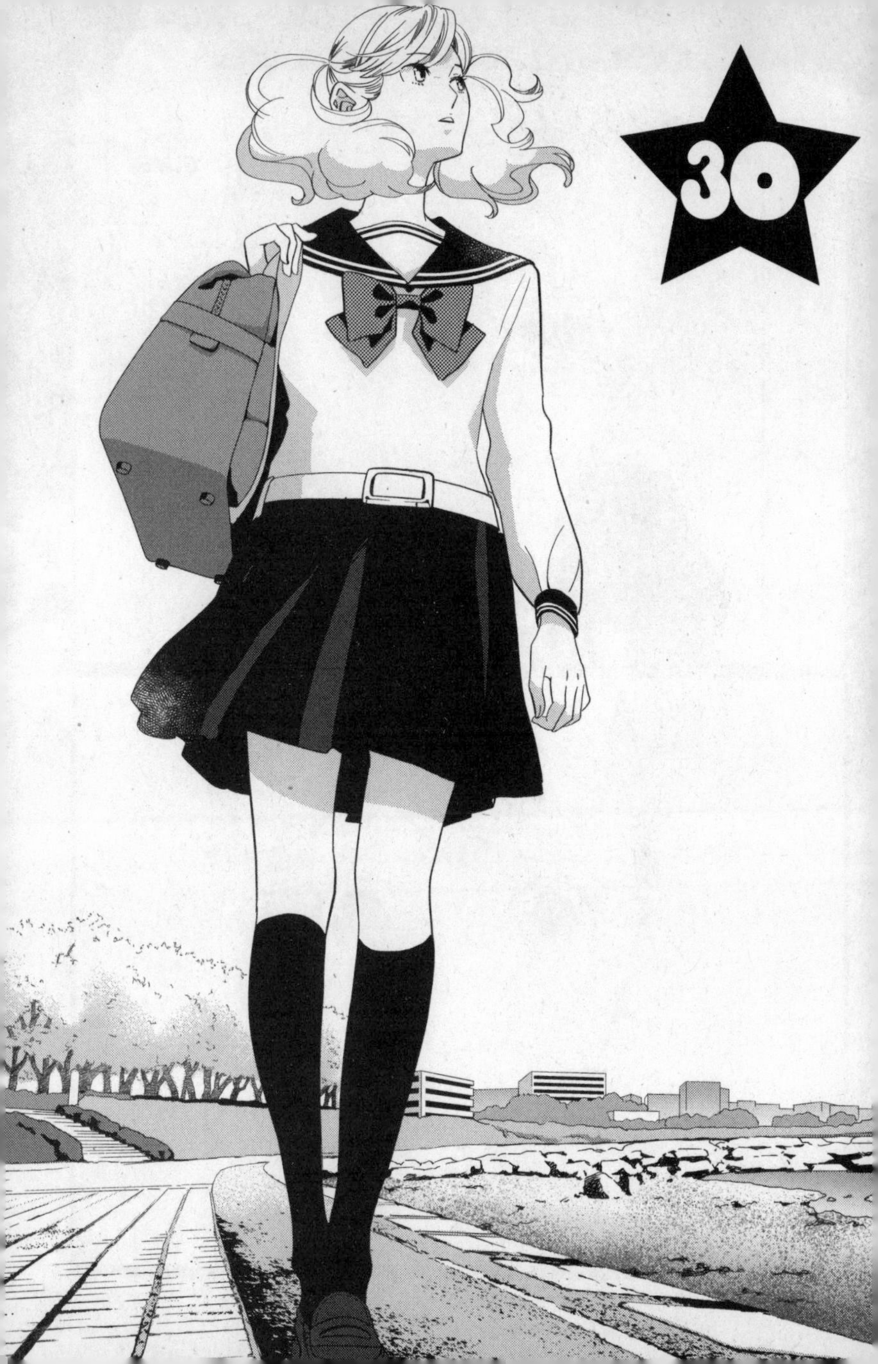
30

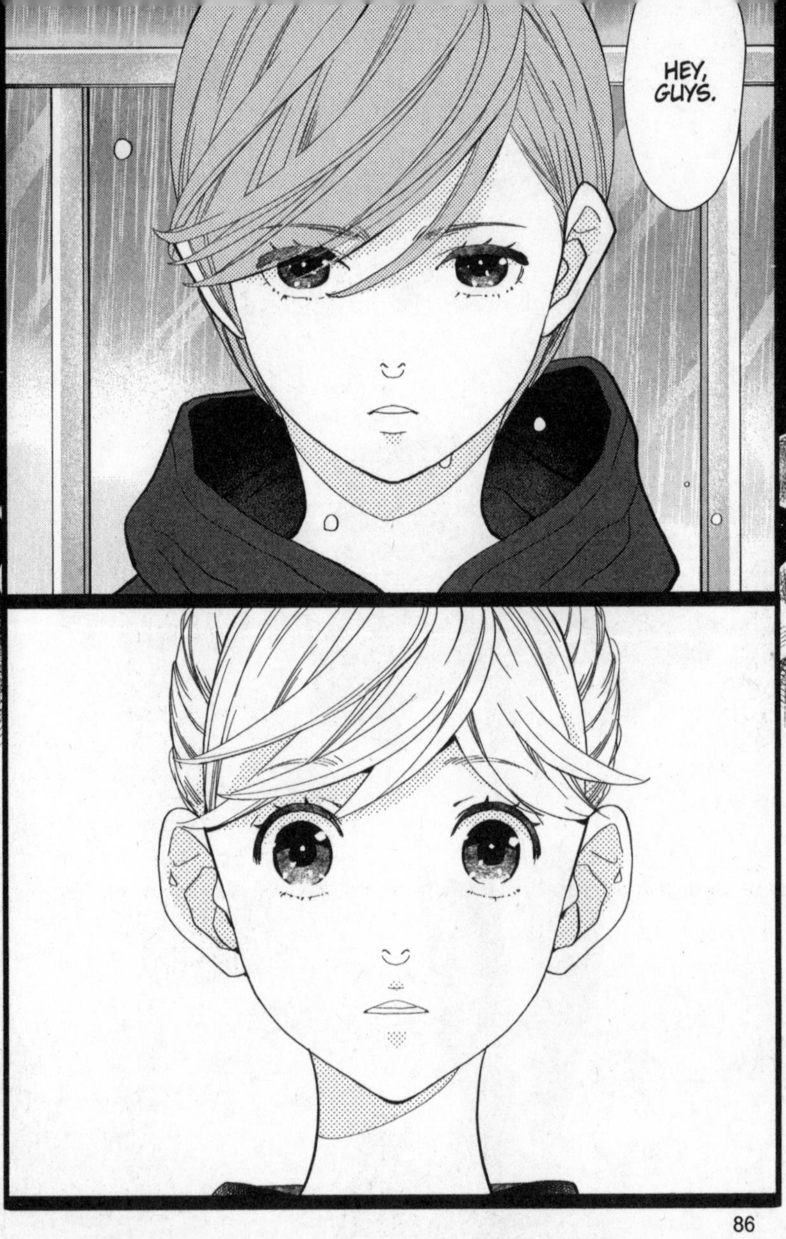
HEY, GUYS.

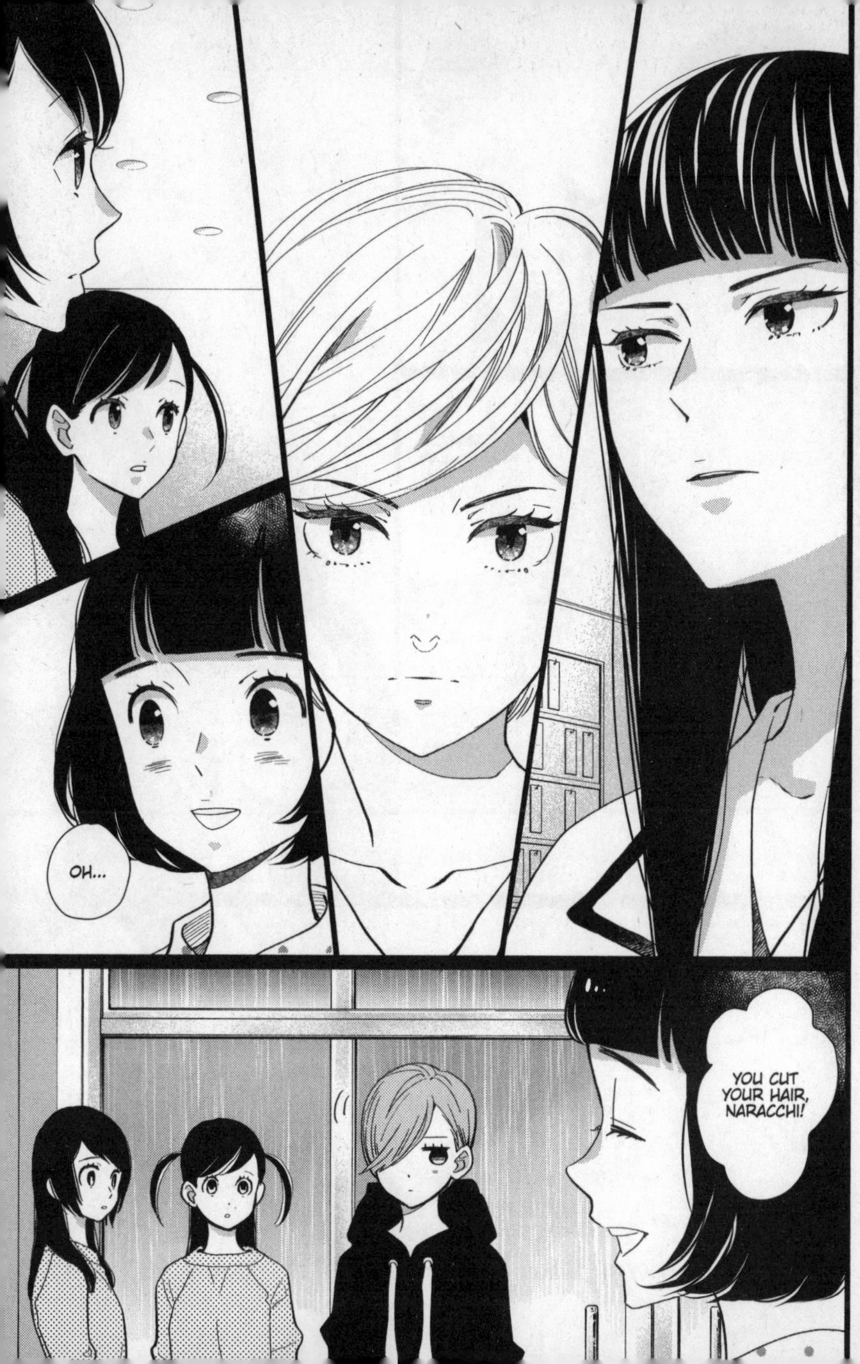
OH...
YOU CUT YOUR HAIR, NARACCHI!

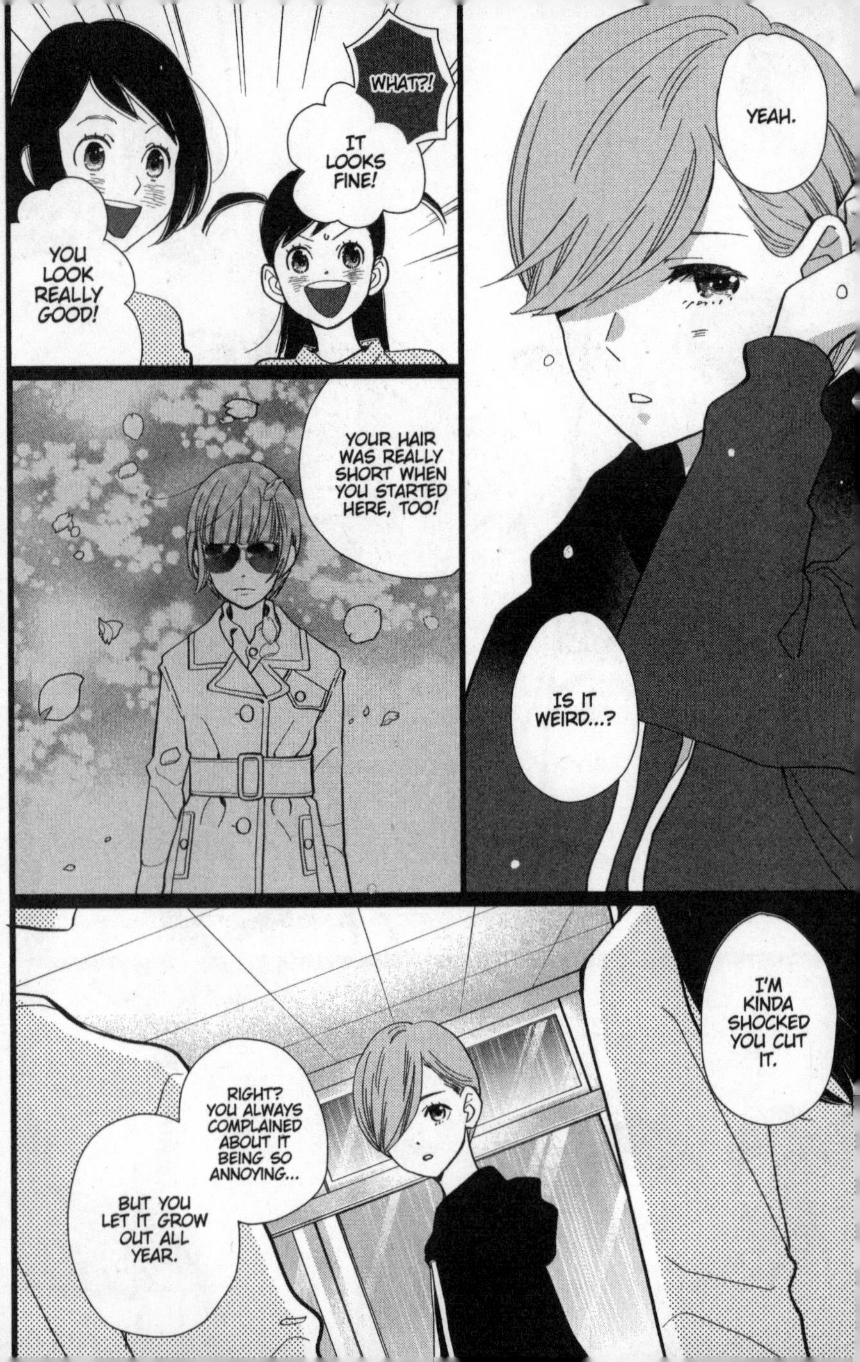
YEAH.
IS IT WEIRD...?
WHAT?!
IT LOOKS FINE!
YOU LOOK REALLY GOOD!
YOUR HAIR WAS REALLY SHORT WHEN YOU STARTED HERE, TOO!
I'M KINDA SHOCKED YOU CUT IT.
RIGHT? YOU ALWAYS COMPLAINED ABOUT IT BEING SO ANNOYING...
BUT YOU LET IT GROW OUT ALL YEAR.

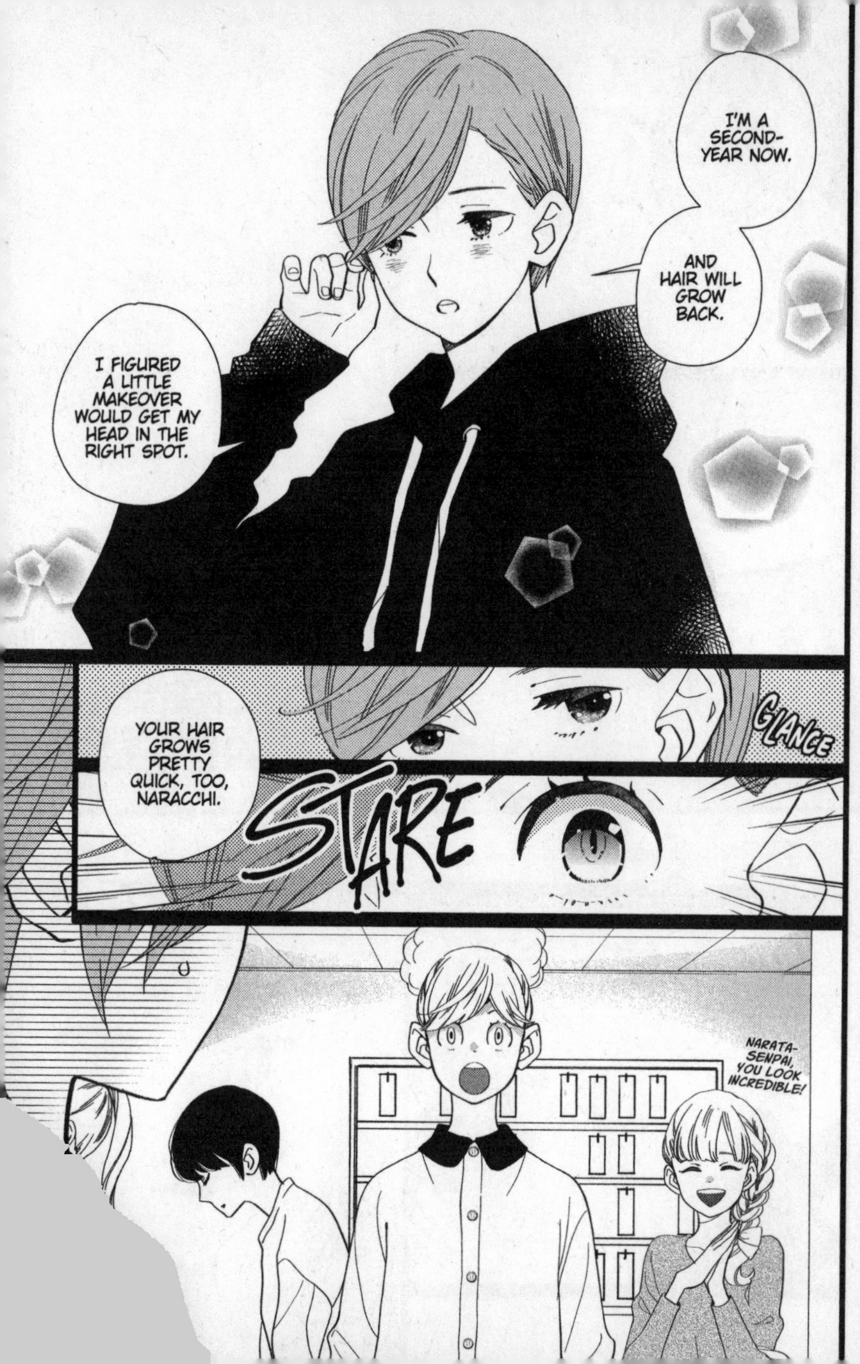
I'M A SECOND-YEAR NOW.
AND HAIR WILL GROW BACK.
I FIGURED A LITTLE MAKEOVER WOULD GET MY HEAD IN THE RIGHT SPOT.
GLANCE
STARE
YOUR HAIR GROWS PRETTY QUICK, TOO, NARACCHI.
NARATA-SENPAI, YOU LOOK INCREDIBLE!

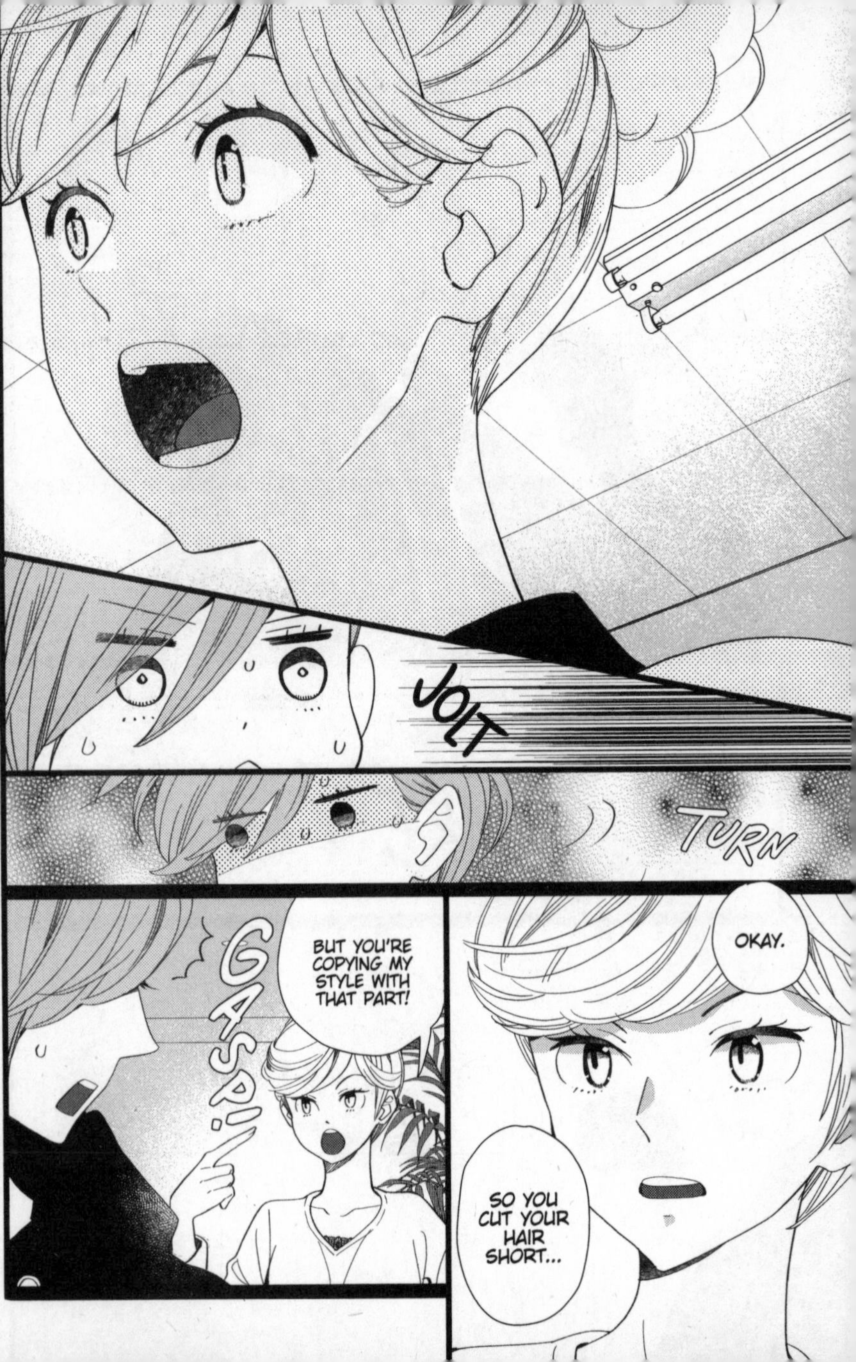
JOLT
TURN
OKAY.
SO YOU CUT YOUR HAIR SHORT...
BUT YOU'RE COPYING MY STYLE WITH THAT PART!
GASP!

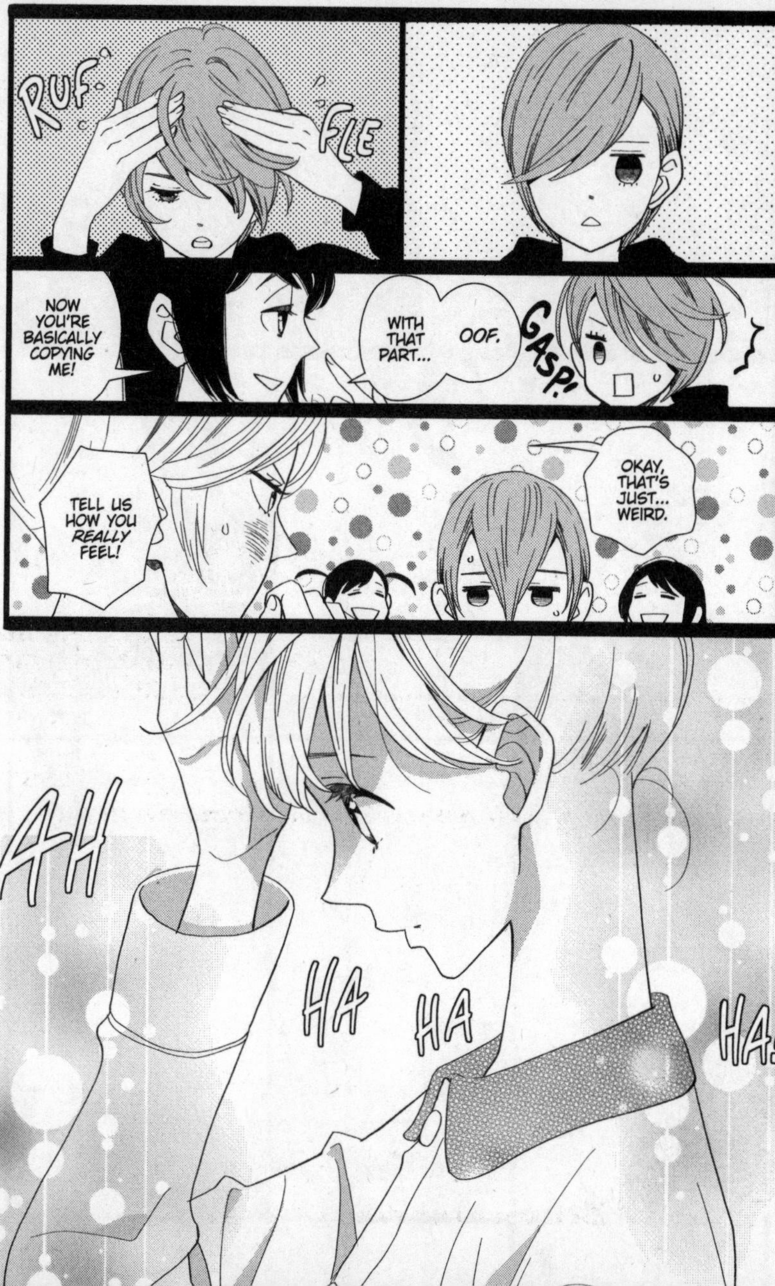
RUF FLE
GASP!
WITH THAT PART... OOF.
NOW YOU'RE BASICALLY COPYING ME!
OKAY, THAT'S JUST... WEIRD.
TELL US HOW YOU *REALLY* FEEL!
AH HA HA HA!

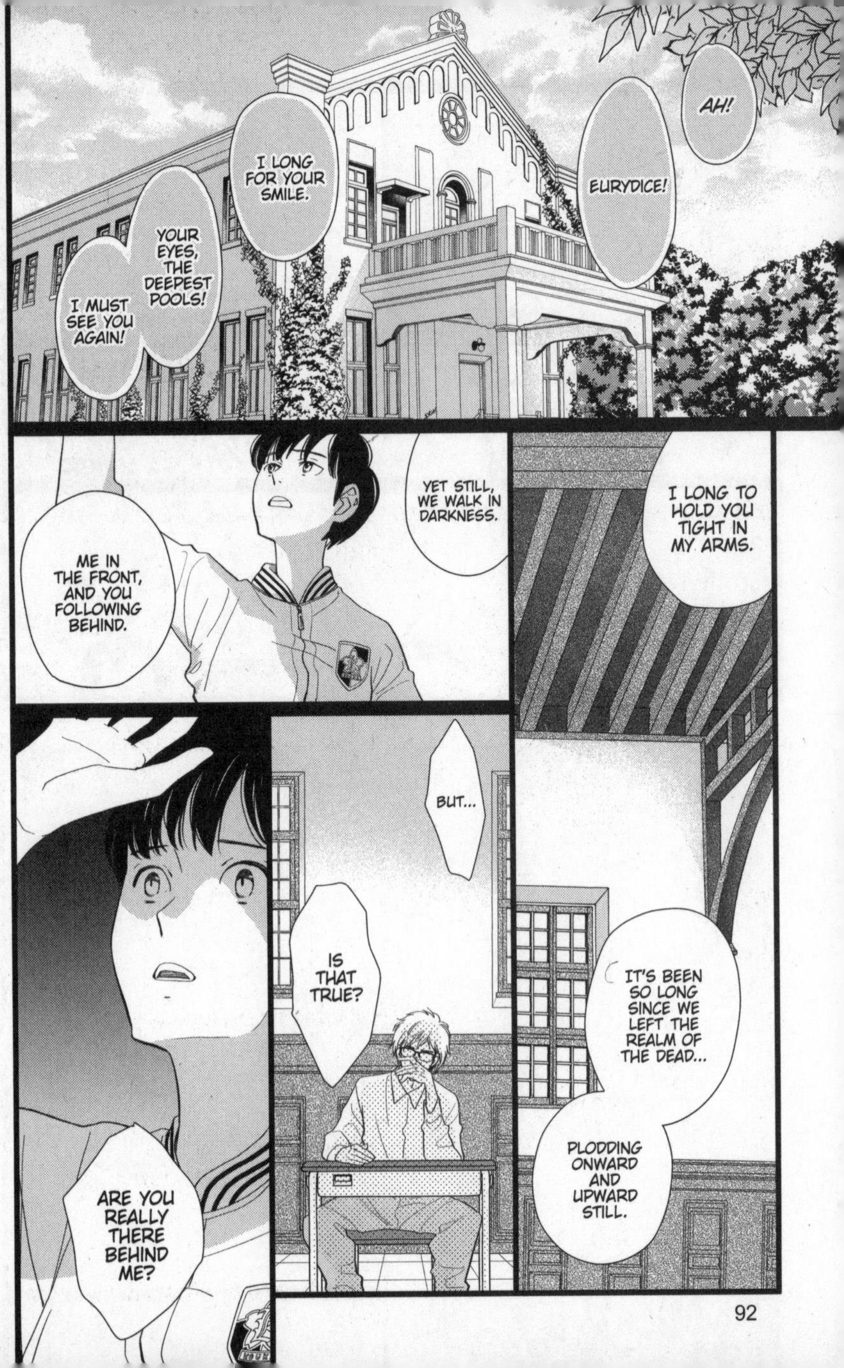
AH!
EURYDICE!
I LONG FOR YOUR SMILE.
YOUR EYES, THE DEEPEST POOLS!
I MUST SEE YOU AGAIN!
I LONG TO HOLD YOU TIGHT IN MY ARMS.
YET STILL, WE WALK IN DARKNESS.
ME IN THE FRONT, AND YOU FOLLOWING BEHIND.
IT'S BEEN SO LONG SINCE WE LEFT THE REALM OF THE DEAD...
PLODDING ONWARD AND UPWARD STILL.
BUT...
IS THAT TRUE?
ARE YOU REALLY THERE BEHIND ME?

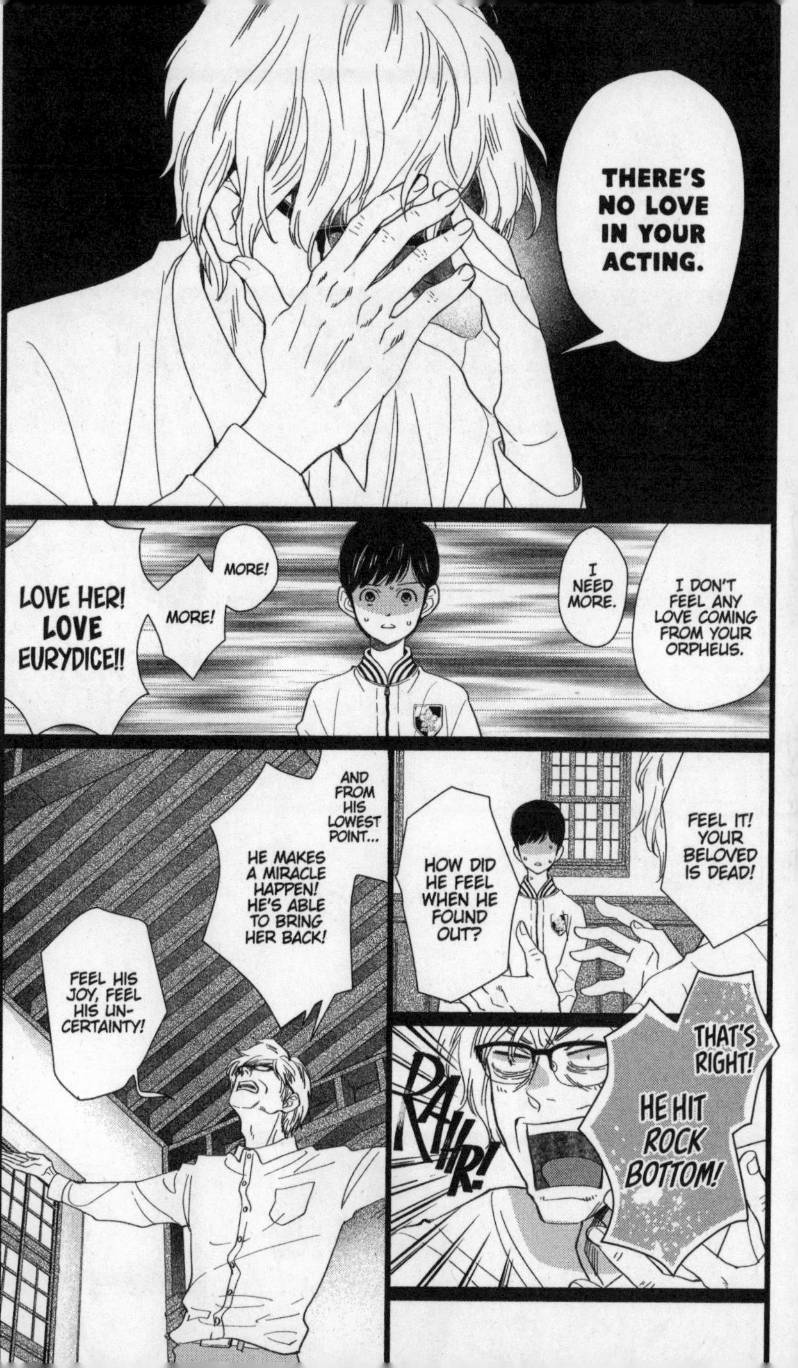
THERE'S NO LOVE IN YOUR ACTING.
I DON'T FEEL ANY LOVE COMING FROM YOUR ORPHEUS.
I NEED MORE.
MORE!
MORE!
LOVE HER! LOVE EURYDICE!!
FEEL IT! YOUR BELOVED IS DEAD!
HOW DID HE FEEL WHEN HE FOUND OUT?
THAT'S RIGHT!
HE HIT ROCK BOTTOM!
RAHR!
AND FROM HIS LOWEST POINT...
HE MAKES A MIRACLE HAPPEN! HE'S ABLE TO BRING HER BACK!
FEEL HIS JOY, FEEL HIS UN-CERTAINTY!

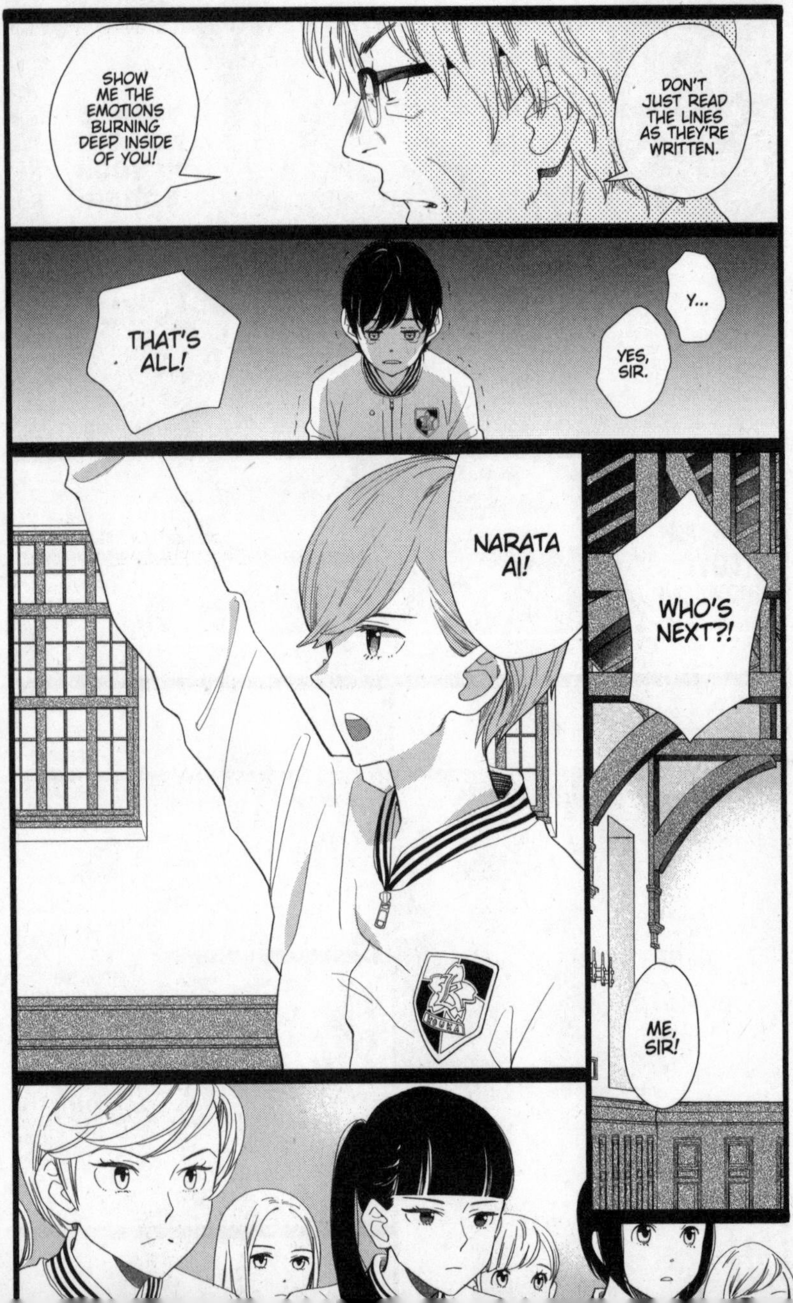
DON'T JUST READ THE LINES AS THEY'RE WRITTEN.
SHOW ME THE EMOTIONS BURNING DEEP INSIDE OF YOU!
THAT'S ALL!
Y...
YES, SIR.
WHO'S NEXT?!
ME, SIR!
NARATA AI!

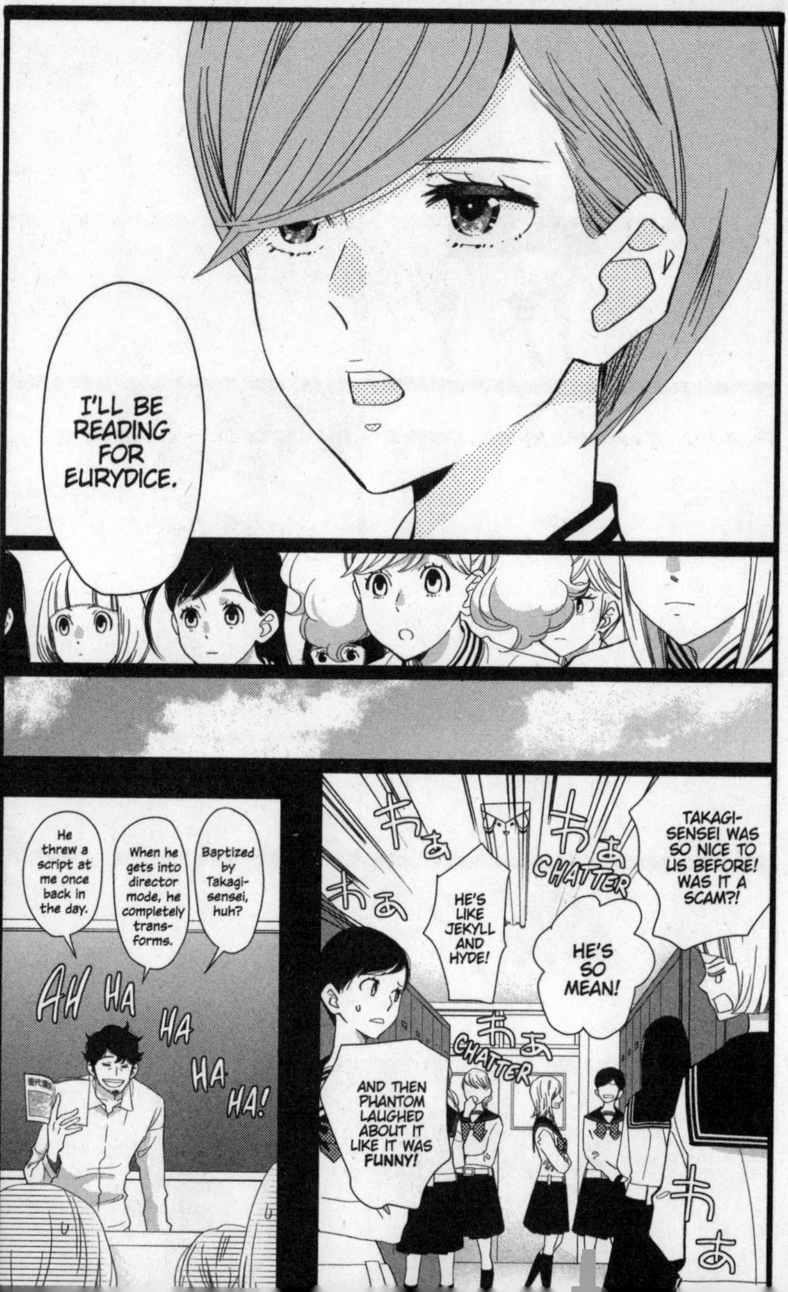
I'LL BE READING FOR EURYDICE.
TAKAGI-SENSEI WAS SO NICE TO US BEFORE! WAS IT A SCAM?!
CHATTER
HE'S SO MEAN!
HE'S LIKE JEKYLL AND HYDE!
CHATTER
AND THEN PHANTOM LAUGHED ABOUT IT LIKE IT WAS FUNNY!
Baptized by Takagi-sensei, huh?
When he gets into director mode, he completely trans-forms.
He threw a script at me once back in the day.
AH HA HA HA HA!

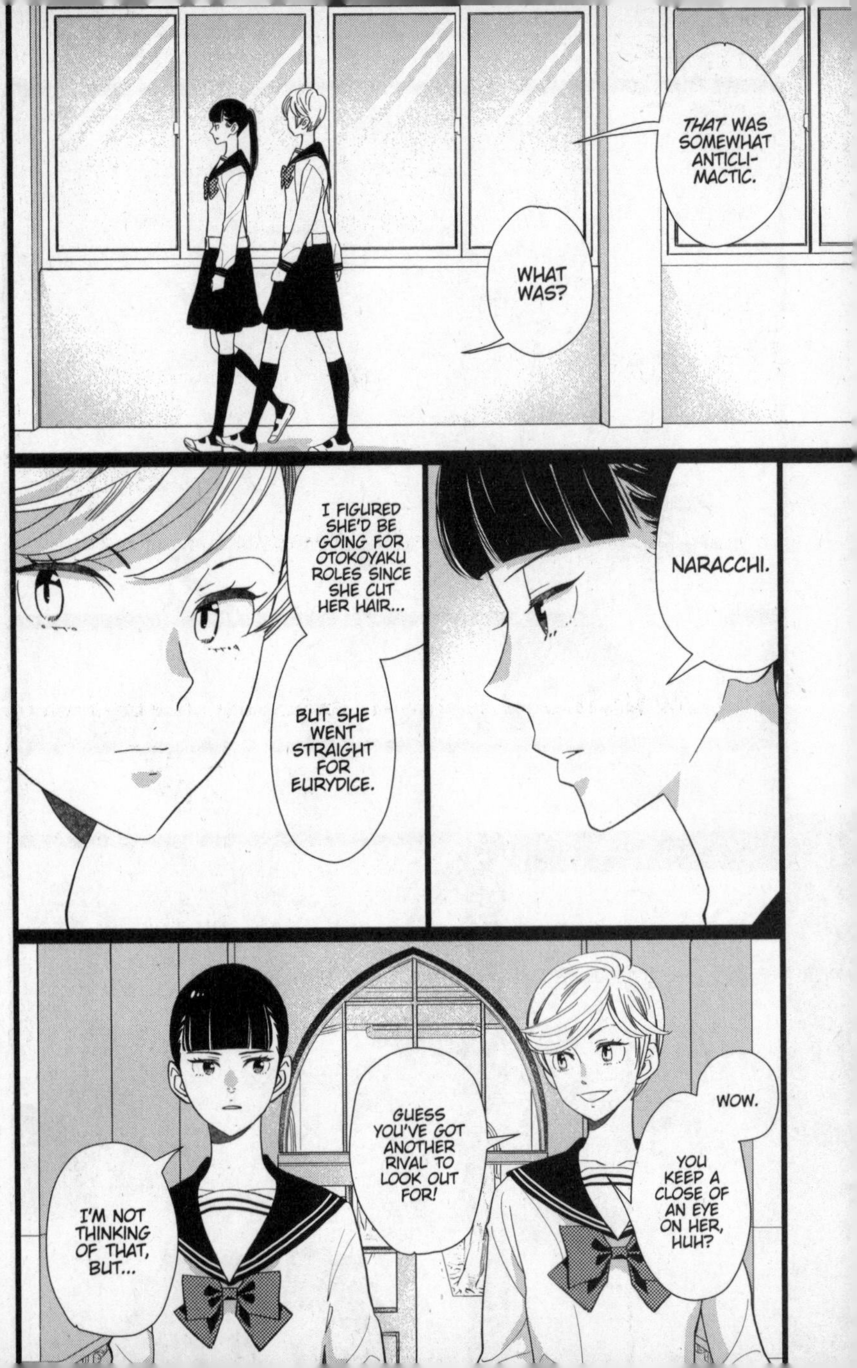
THAT WAS SOMEWHAT ANTICLIMACTIC.
WHAT WAS?
NARACCHI.
I FIGURED SHE'D BE GOING FOR OTOKOYAKU ROLES SINCE SHE CUT HER HAIR...
BUT SHE WENT STRAIGHT FOR EURYDICE.
WOW.
YOU KEEP A CLOSE OF AN EYE ON HER, HUH?
GUESS YOU'VE GOT ANOTHER RIVAL TO LOOK OUT FOR!
I'M NOT THINKING OF THAT, BUT...

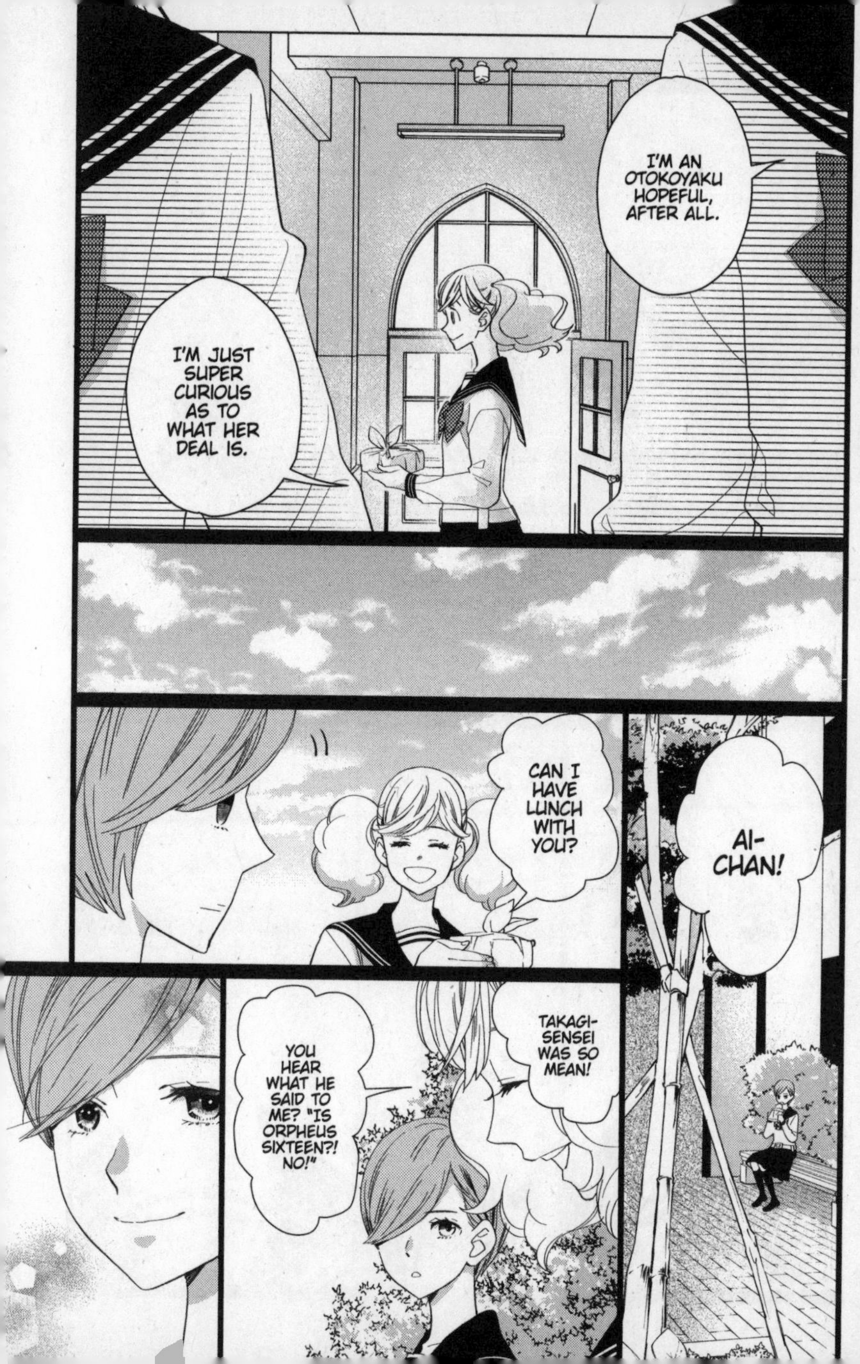
I'M AN OTOKOYAKU HOPEFUL, AFTER ALL.
I'M JUST SUPER CURIOUS AS TO WHAT HER DEAL IS.
AI-CHAN!
CAN I HAVE LUNCH WITH YOU?
TAKAGI-SENSEI WAS SO MEAN!
YOU HEAR WHAT HE SAID TO ME? "IS ORPHEUS SIXTEEN?! NO!"

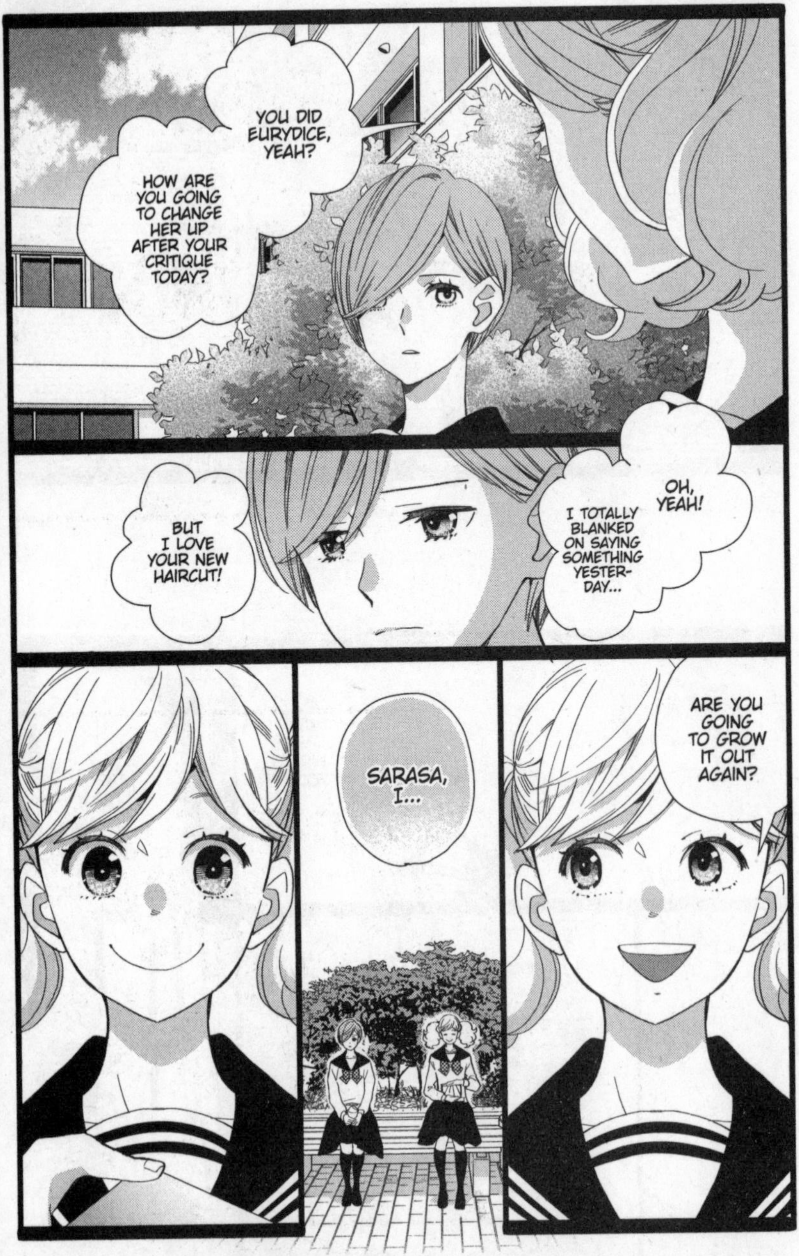
YOU DID EURYDICE, YEAH?
HOW ARE YOU GOING TO CHANGE HER UP AFTER YOUR CRITIQUE TODAY?
OH, YEAH!
I TOTALLY BLANKED ON SAYING SOMETHING YESTER-DAY...
BUT I LOVE YOUR NEW HAIRCUT!
ARE YOU GOING TO GROW IT OUT AGAIN?
SARASA, I...

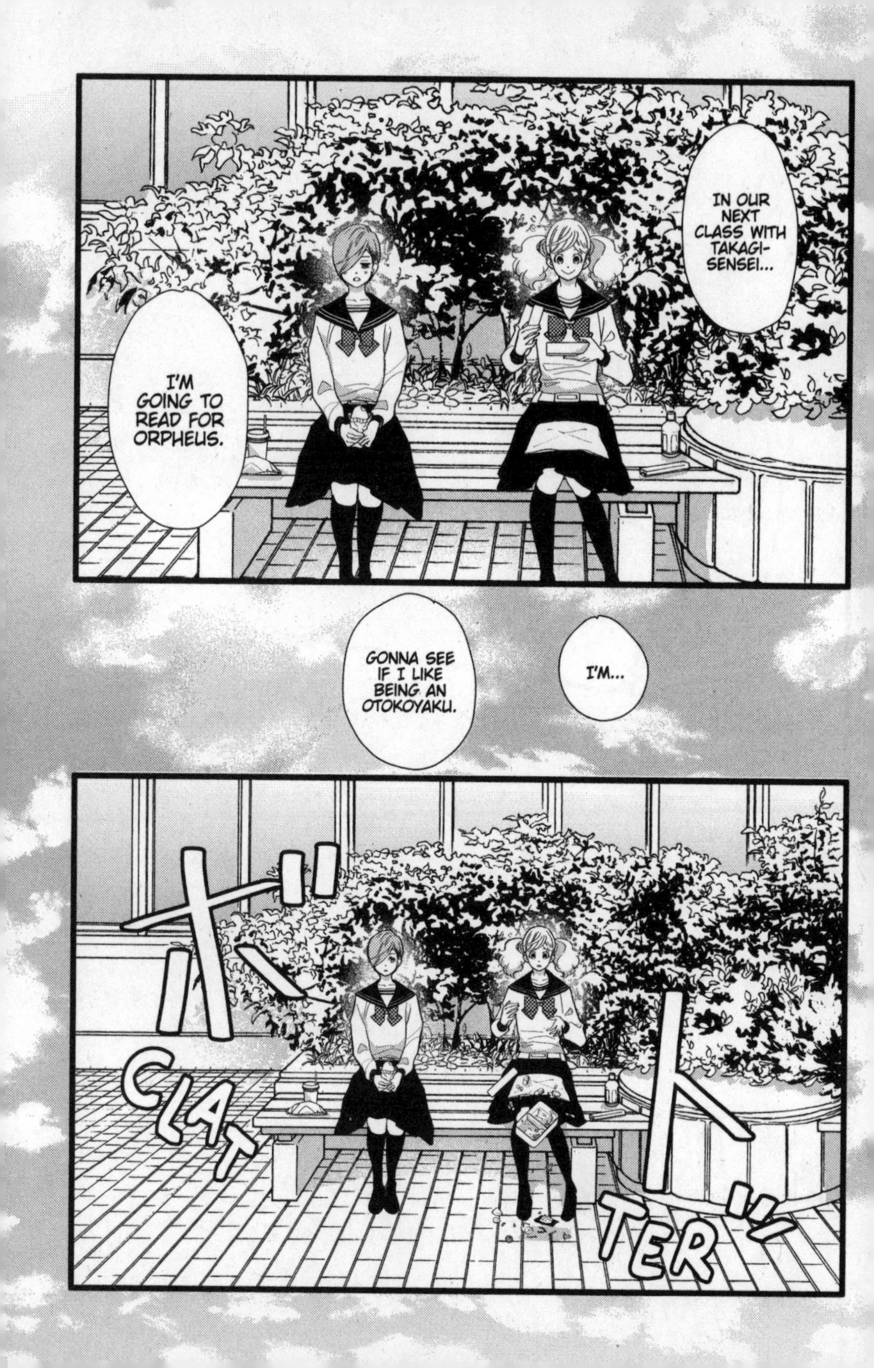
IN OUR NEXT CLASS WITH TAKAGI-SENSEI...
I'M GOING TO READ FOR ORPHEUS.
I'M...
GONNA SEE IF I LIKE BEING AN OTOKOYAKU.
CLATTER

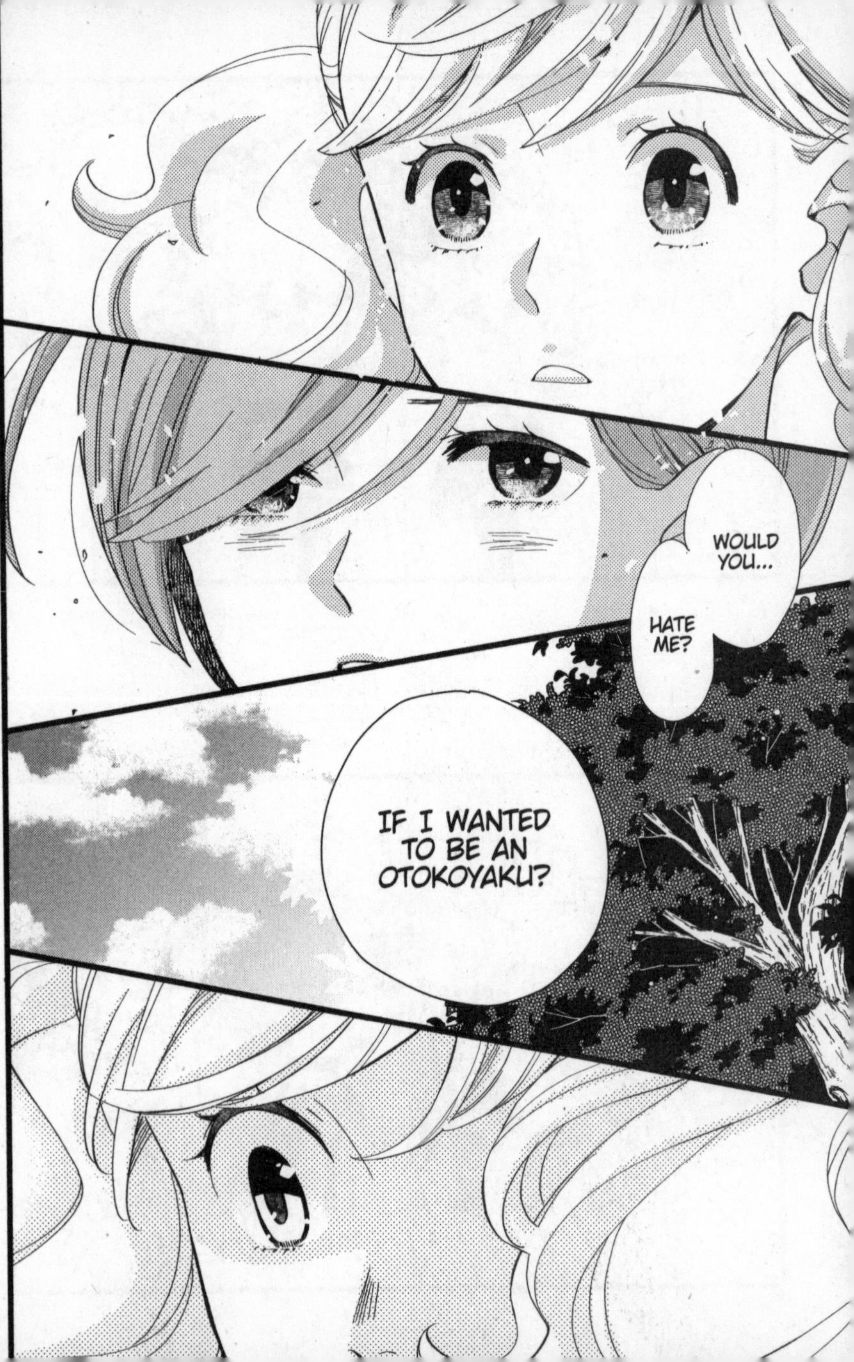
WOULD YOU...
HATE ME?
IF I WANTED TO BE AN OTOKOYAKU?

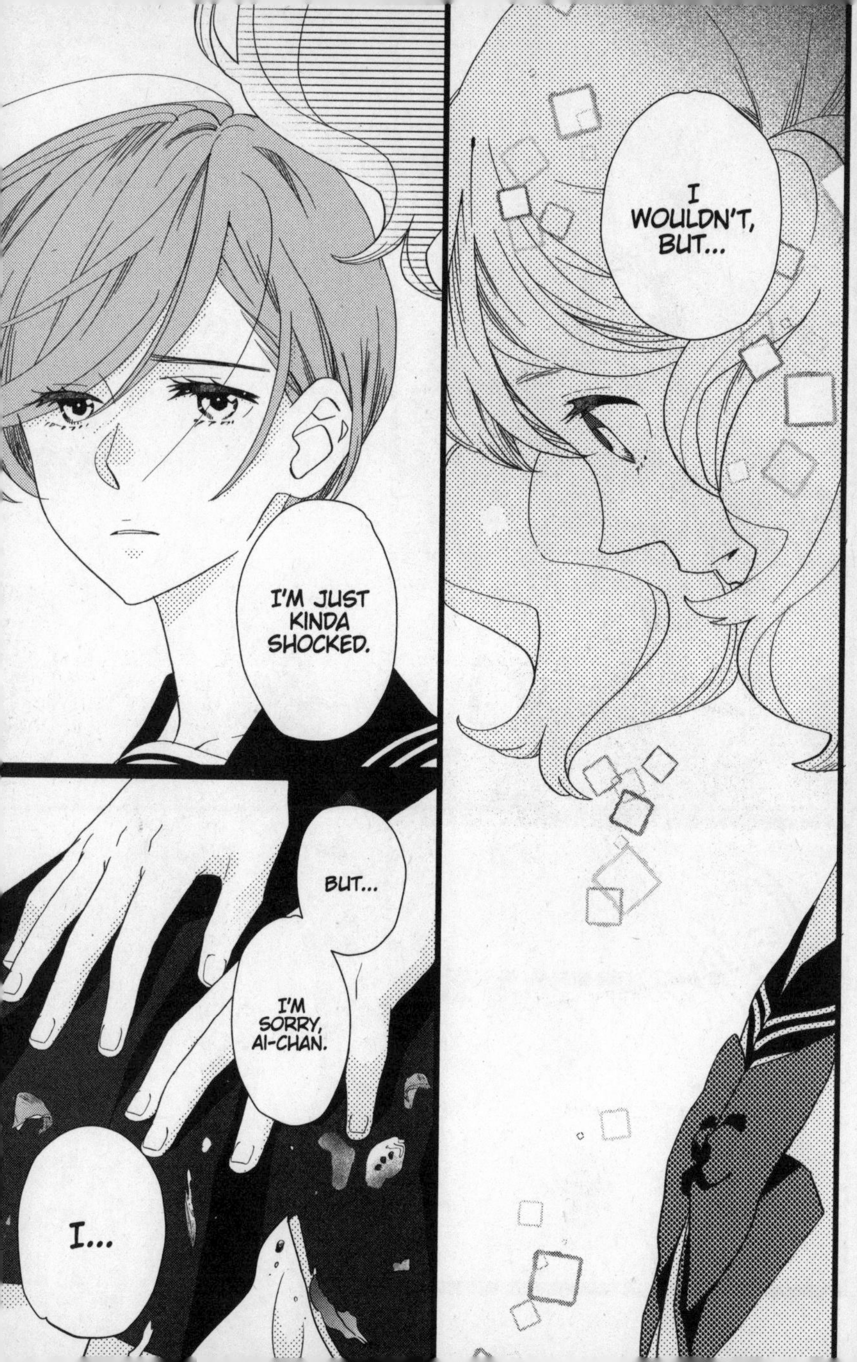
I WOULDN'T, BUT...
I'M JUST KINDA SHOCKED.
BUT...
I'M SORRY, AI-CHAN.
I...

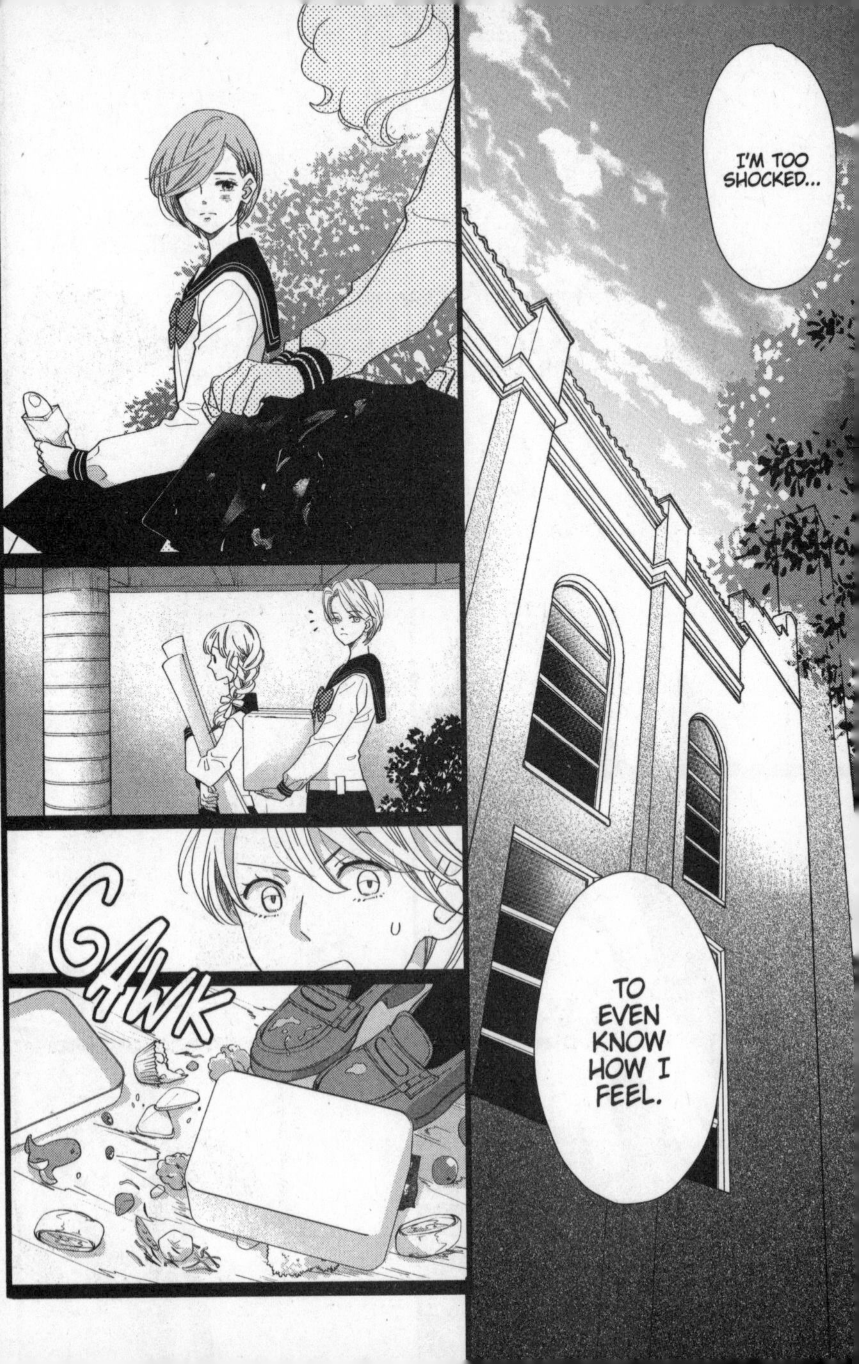
I'M TOO SHOCKED...
TO EVEN KNOW HOW I FEEL.
GAWK

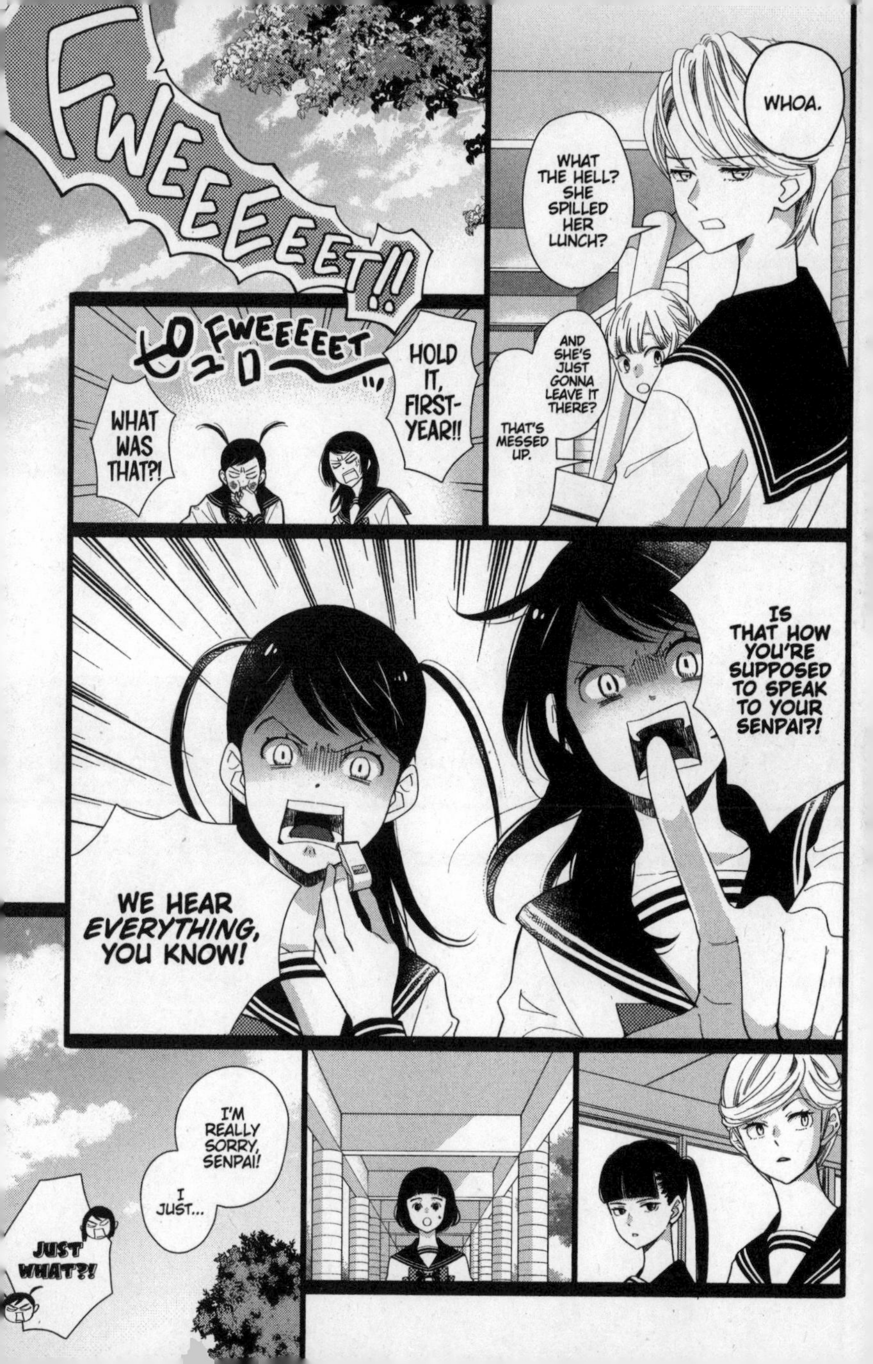
WHOA.
WHAT THE HELL? SHE SPILLED HER LUNCH?
AND SHE'S JUST GONNA LEAVE IT THERE?
THAT'S MESSED UP.
FWEEEEEET!!
FWEEEEEET
HOLD IT, FIRST-YEAR!!
WHAT WAS THAT?!
IS THAT HOW YOU'RE SUPPOSED TO SPEAK TO YOUR SENPAI?!
WE HEAR *EVERYTHING*, YOU KNOW!
I'M REALLY SORRY, SENPAI!
I JUST...
JUST WHAT?!

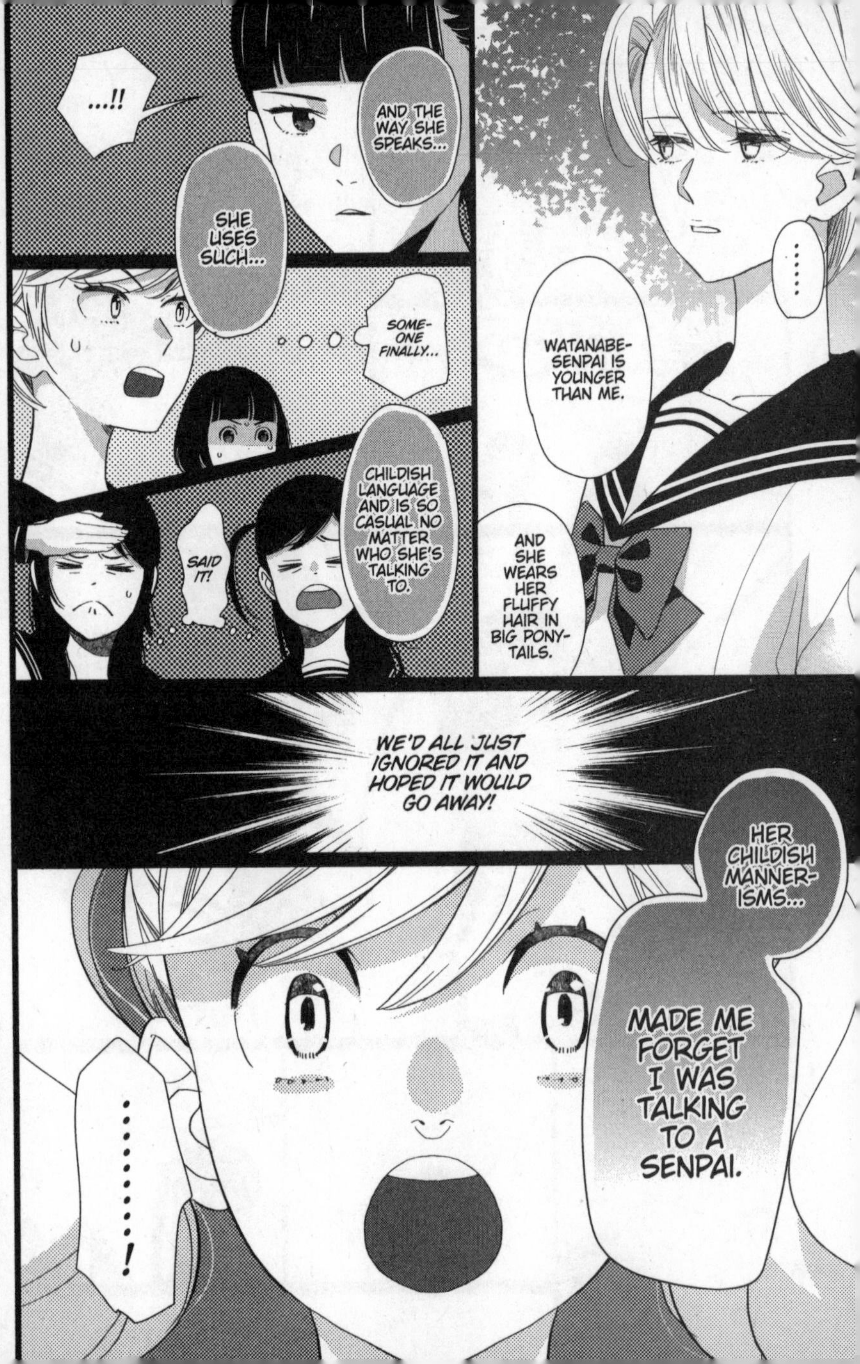
......
WATANABE-SENPAI IS YOUNGER THAN ME.
AND SHE WEARS HER FLUFFY HAIR IN BIG PONY-TAILS.
AND THE WAY SHE SPEAKS...
...!!
SHE USES SUCH...
SOME-ONE FINALLY...
CHILDISH LANGUAGE AND IS SO CASUAL NO MATTER WHO SHE'S TALKING TO.
SAID IT!
WE'D ALL JUST IGNORED IT AND HOPED IT WOULD GO AWAY!
HER CHILDISH MANNER-ISMS...
MADE ME FORGET I WAS TALKING TO A SENPAI.
........!

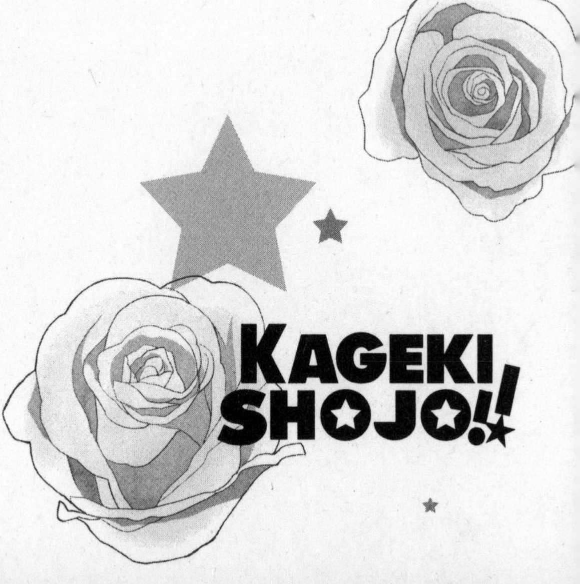
KAGEKI SHOJO!!

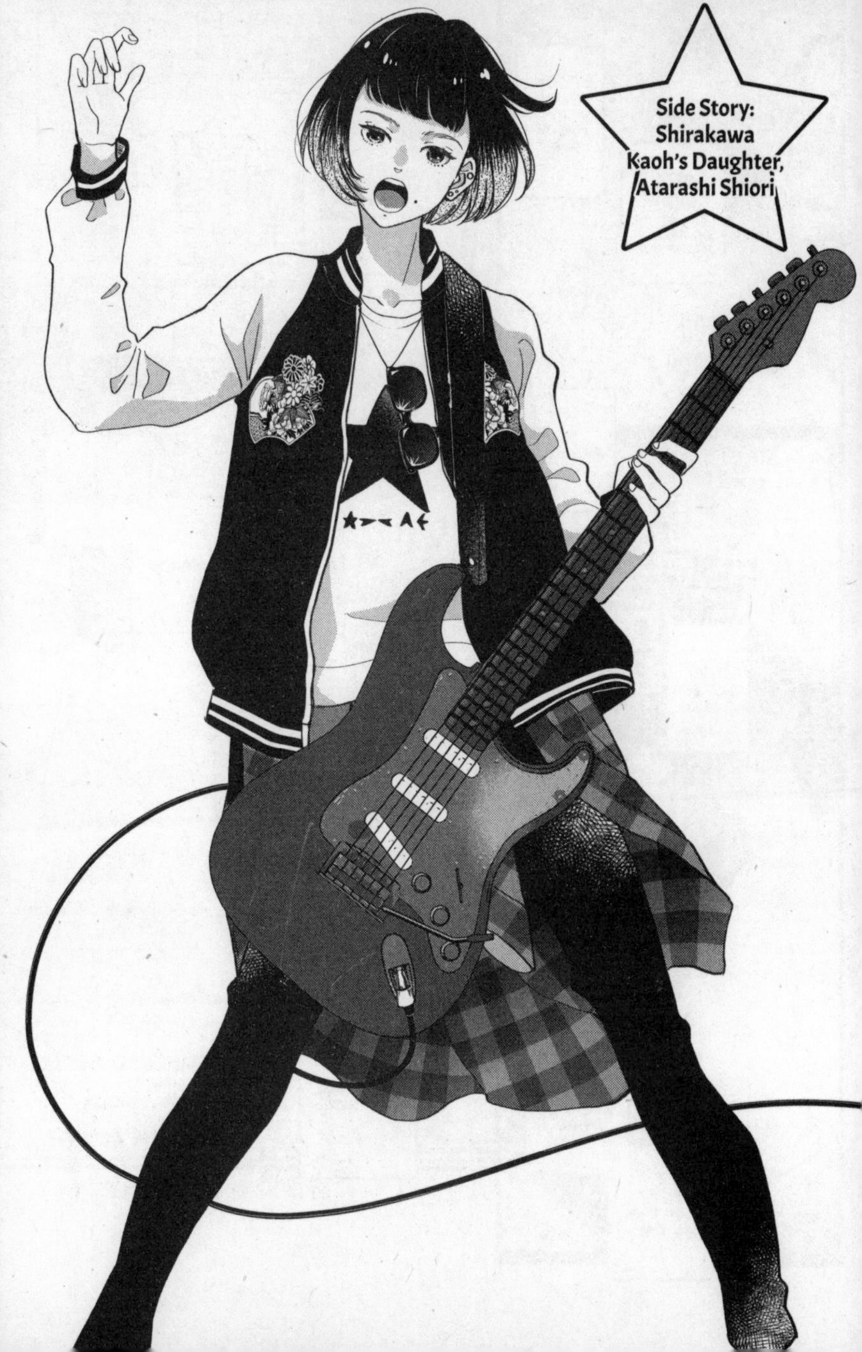
Side Story: Shirakawa Kaoh's Daughter, Atarashi Shiori

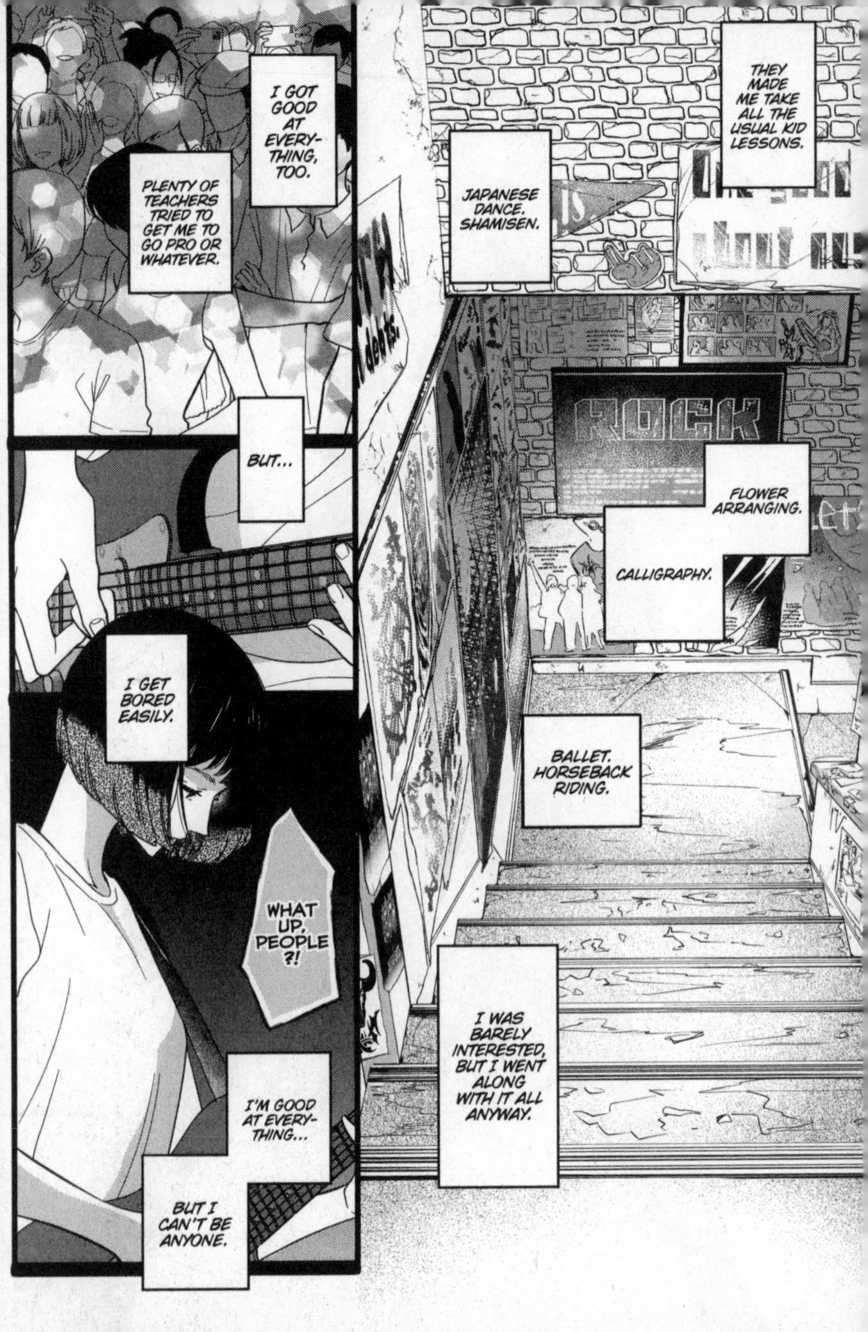

THEY MADE ME TAKE ALL THE USUAL KID LESSONS.
JAPANESE DANCE. SHAMISEN.
ROCK
FLOWER ARRANGING.
CALLIGRAPHY.
BALLET. HORSEBACK RIDING.
I WAS BARELY INTERESTED, BUT I WENT ALONG WITH IT ALL ANYWAY.
I GOT GOOD AT EVERYTHING, TOO.
PLENTY OF TEACHERS TRIED TO GET ME TO GO PRO OR WHATEVER.
BUT...
I GET BORED EASILY.
WHAT UP, PEOPLE?!
I'M GOOD AT EVERYTHING...
BUT I CAN'T BE ANYONE.

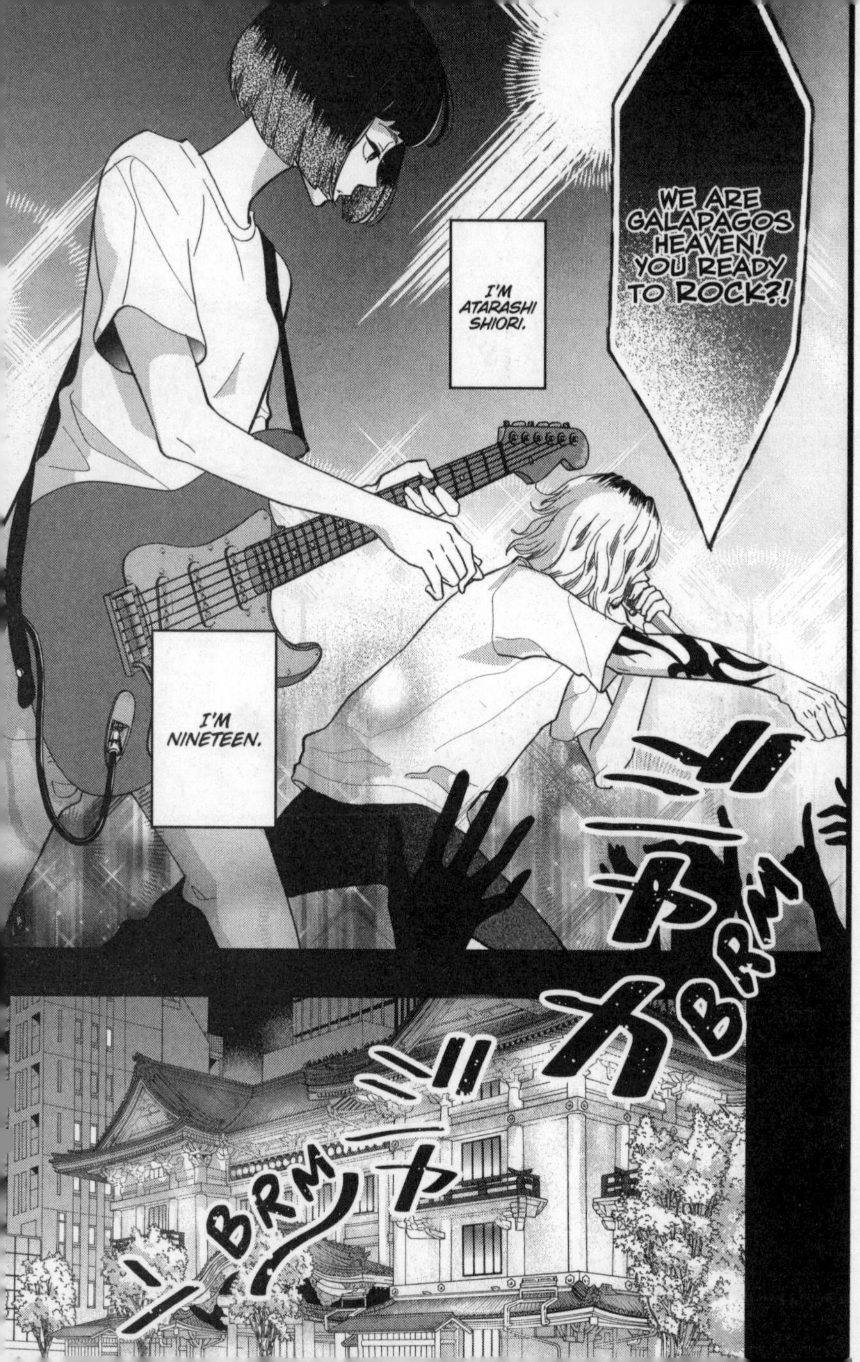
WE ARE GALAPAGOS HEAVEN! YOU READY TO ROCK?!
I'M ATARASHI SHIORI.
I'M NINETEEN.
BRRM
BRM

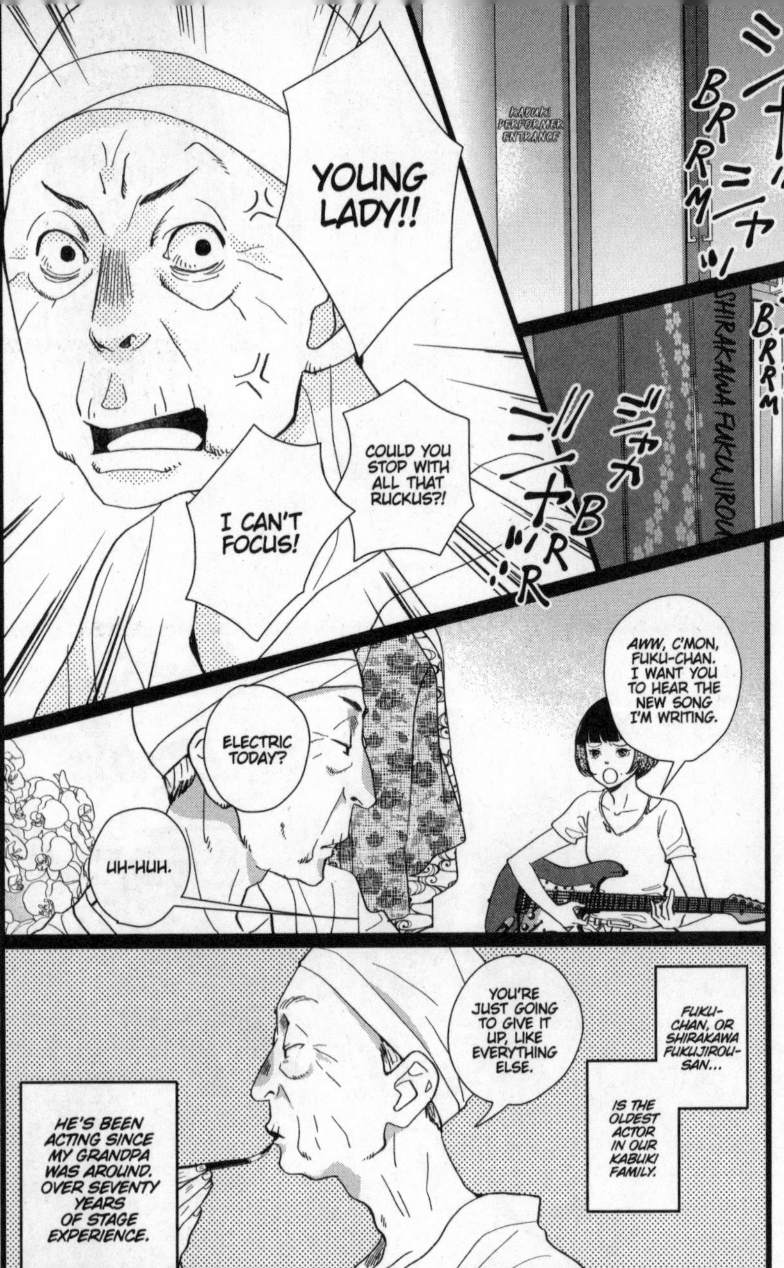

BRRRM
KABUKI PERFORMER ENTRANCE
BRRRM
SHIRAKAWA FUKUJIROU
BRRR
YOUNG LADY!!
COULD YOU STOP WITH ALL THAT RUCKUS?!
I CAN'T FOCUS!
AWW, C'MON, FUKU-CHAN. I WANT YOU TO HEAR THE NEW SONG I'M WRITING.
ELECTRIC TODAY?
UH-HUH.
FUKU-CHAN, OR SHIRAKAWA FUKUJIROU-SAN...
IS THE OLDEST ACTOR IN OUR KABUKI FAMILY.
YOU'RE JUST GOING TO GIVE IT UP, LIKE EVERYTHING ELSE.
HE'S BEEN ACTING SINCE MY GRANDPA WAS AROUND. OVER SEVENTY YEARS OF STAGE EXPERIENCE.

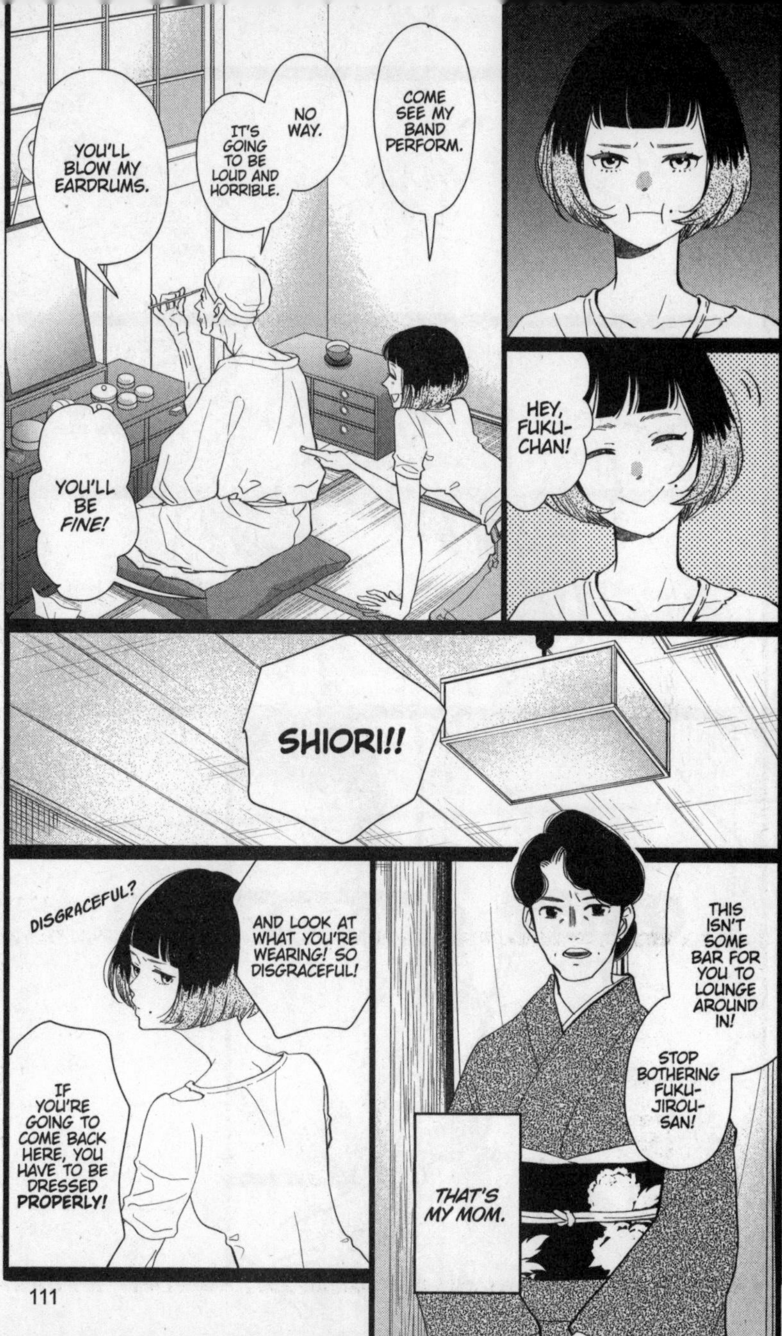
HEY, FUKU-CHAN!
COME SEE MY BAND PERFORM.
NO WAY.
IT'S GOING TO BE LOUD AND HORRIBLE.
YOU'LL BLOW MY EARDRUMS.
YOU'LL BE FINE!
SHIORI!!
THIS ISN'T SOME BAR FOR YOU TO LOUNGE AROUND IN!
STOP BOTHERING FUKU-JIROU-SAN!
THAT'S MY MOM.
AND LOOK AT WHAT YOU'RE WEARING! SO DISGRACEFUL!
DISGRACEFUL?
IF YOU'RE GOING TO COME BACK HERE, YOU HAVE TO BE DRESSED PROPERLY!

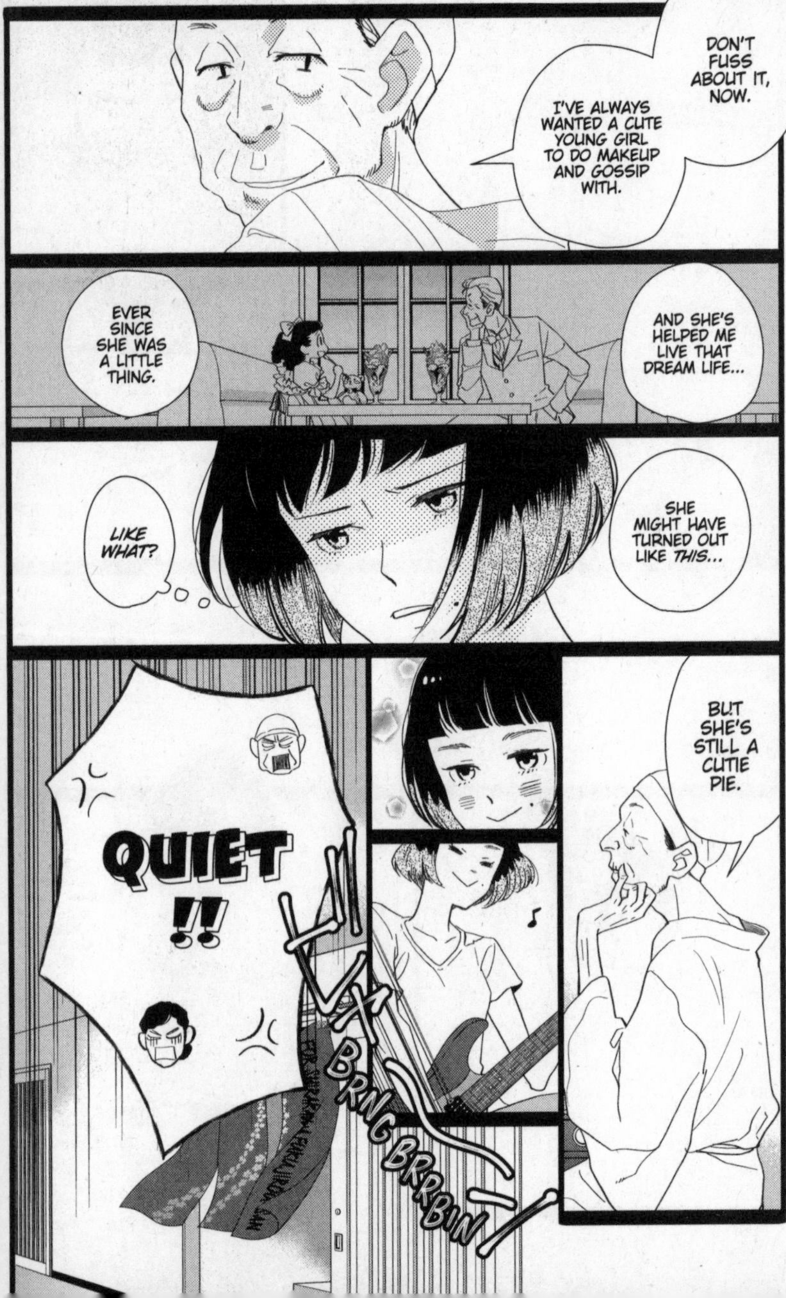
DON'T FUSS ABOUT IT, NOW.
I'VE ALWAYS WANTED A CUTE YOUNG GIRL TO DO MAKEUP AND GOSSIP WITH.
AND SHE'S HELPED ME LIVE THAT DREAM LIFE...
EVER SINCE SHE WAS A LITTLE THING.
SHE MIGHT HAVE TURNED OUT LIKE *THIS*...
LIKE WHAT?
BUT SHE'S STILL A CUTIE PIE.
BRNG BRRBIN
QUIET!!

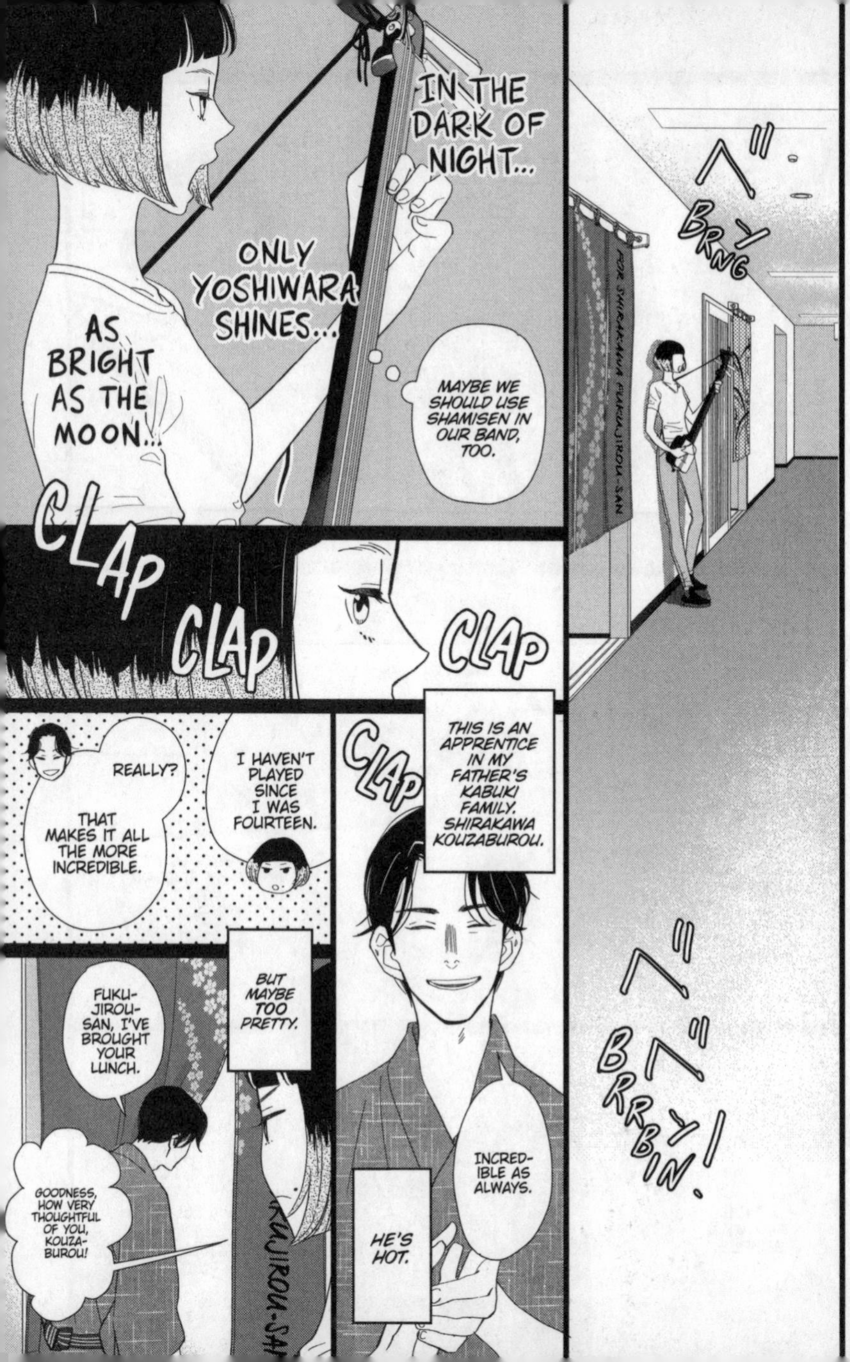
BRNG
FOR SHIRAKAWA FUKUJIROU-SAN
BRRBIN!
IN THE DARK OF NIGHT...
ONLY YOSHIWARA SHINES...
AS BRIGHT AS THE MOON...
MAYBE WE SHOULD USE SHAMISEN IN OUR BAND, TOO.
CLAP
CLAP
CLAP
CLAP
THIS IS AN APPRENTICE IN MY FATHER'S KABUKI FAMILY. SHIRAKAWA KOUZABUROU.
INCREDIBLE AS ALWAYS.
HE'S HOT.
I HAVEN'T PLAYED SINCE I WAS FOURTEEN.
REALLY?
THAT MAKES IT ALL THE MORE INCREDIBLE.
BUT MAYBE TOO PRETTY.
FUKUJIROU-SAN, I'VE BROUGHT YOUR LUNCH.
GOODNESS, HOW VERY THOUGHTFUL OF YOU, KOUZABUROU!
KUJIROU-SAN

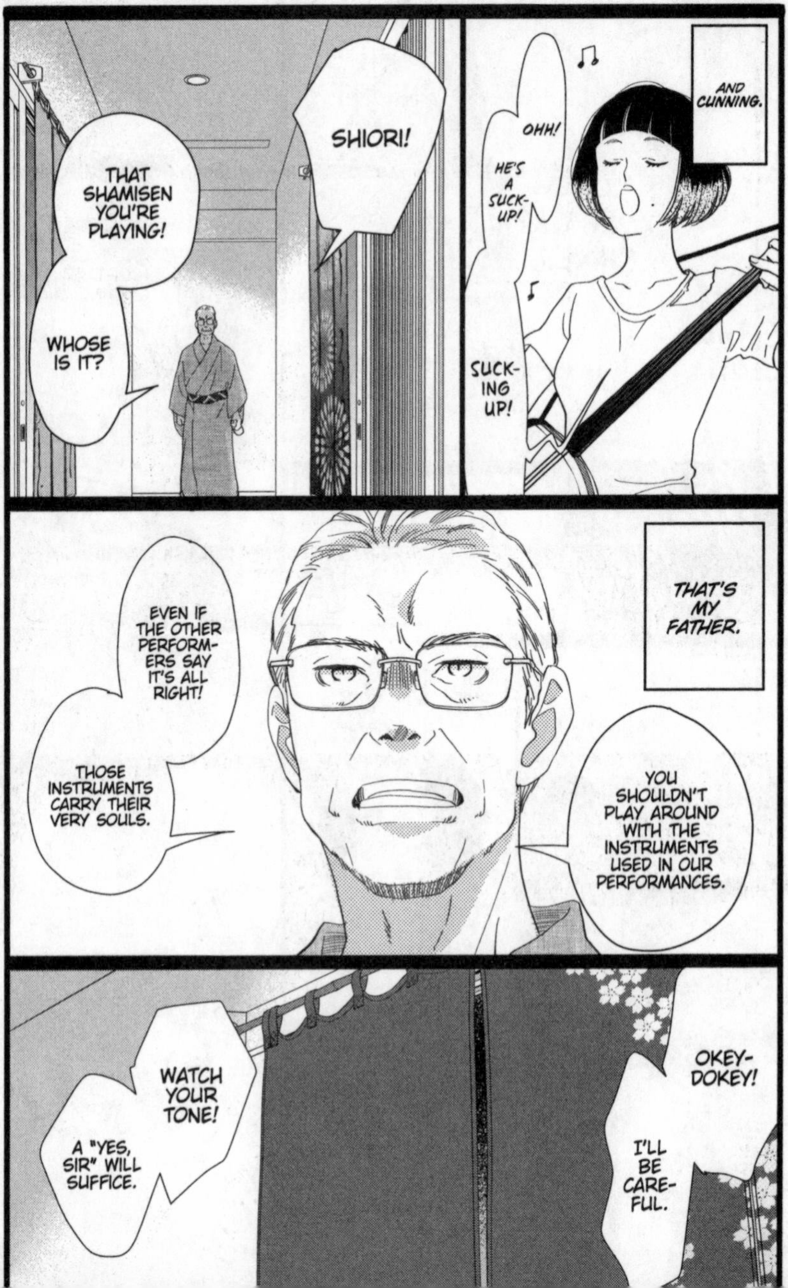
AND CUNNING.
OHH!
HE'S A SUCK-UP!
SUCK-ING UP!
SHIORI!
THAT SHAMISEN YOU'RE PLAYING!
WHOSE IS IT?
THAT'S MY FATHER.
YOU SHOULDN'T PLAY AROUND WITH THE INSTRUMENTS USED IN OUR PERFORMANCES.
EVEN IF THE OTHER PERFORM-ERS SAY IT'S ALL RIGHT!
THOSE INSTRUMENTS CARRY THEIR VERY SOULS.
OKEY-DOKEY!
I'LL BE CARE-FUL.
WATCH YOUR TONE!
A "YES, SIR" WILL SUFFICE.

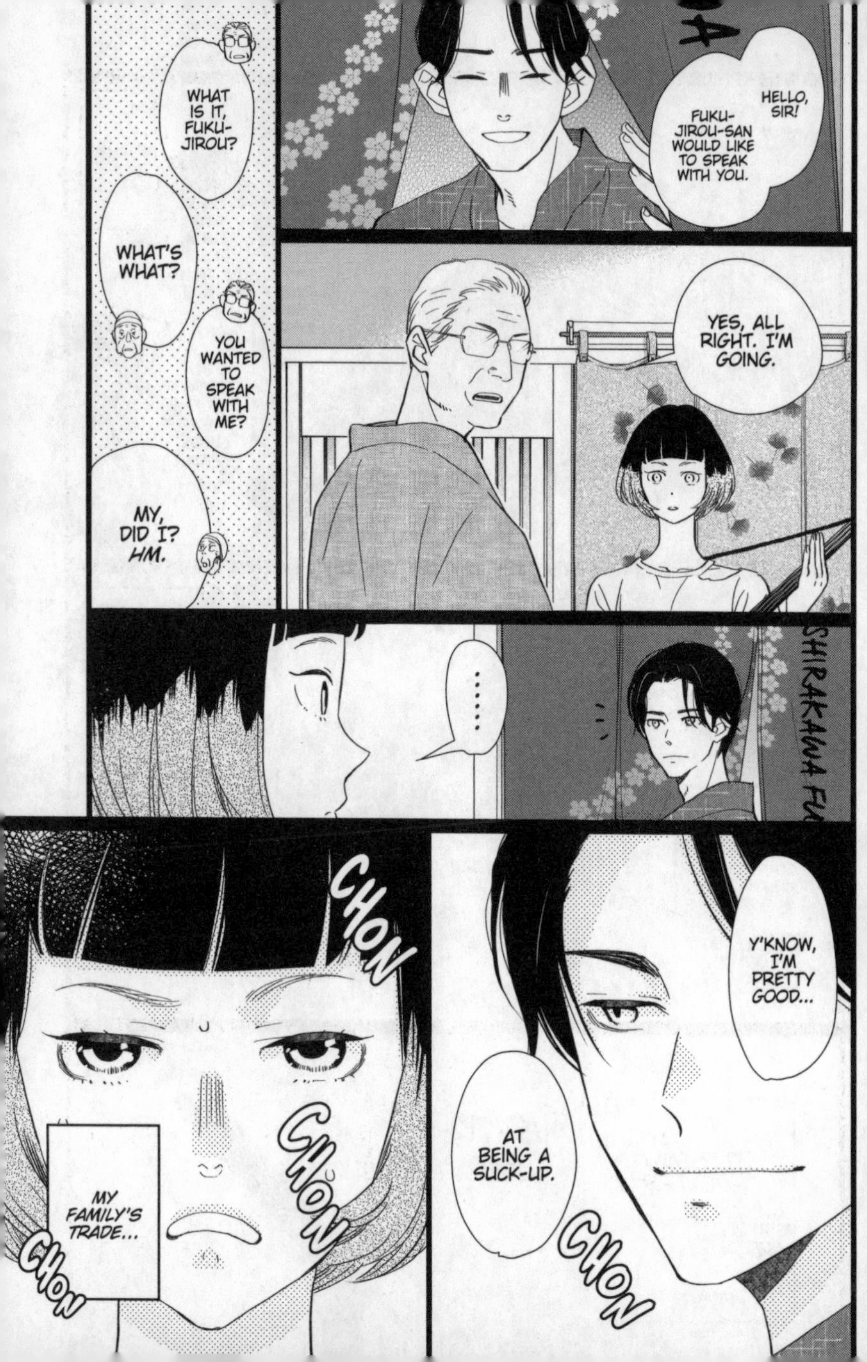
HELLO, SIR!
FUKU-JIROU-SAN WOULD LIKE TO SPEAK WITH YOU.
YES, ALL RIGHT. I'M GOING.
WHAT IS IT, FUKU-JIROU?
WHAT'S WHAT?
YOU WANTED TO SPEAK WITH ME?
MY, DID I? *HM.*
SHIRAKAWA FU
......
Y'KNOW, I'M PRETTY GOOD...
AT BEING A SUCK-UP.
CHON
CHON
CHON
MY FAMILY'S TRADE...
CHON

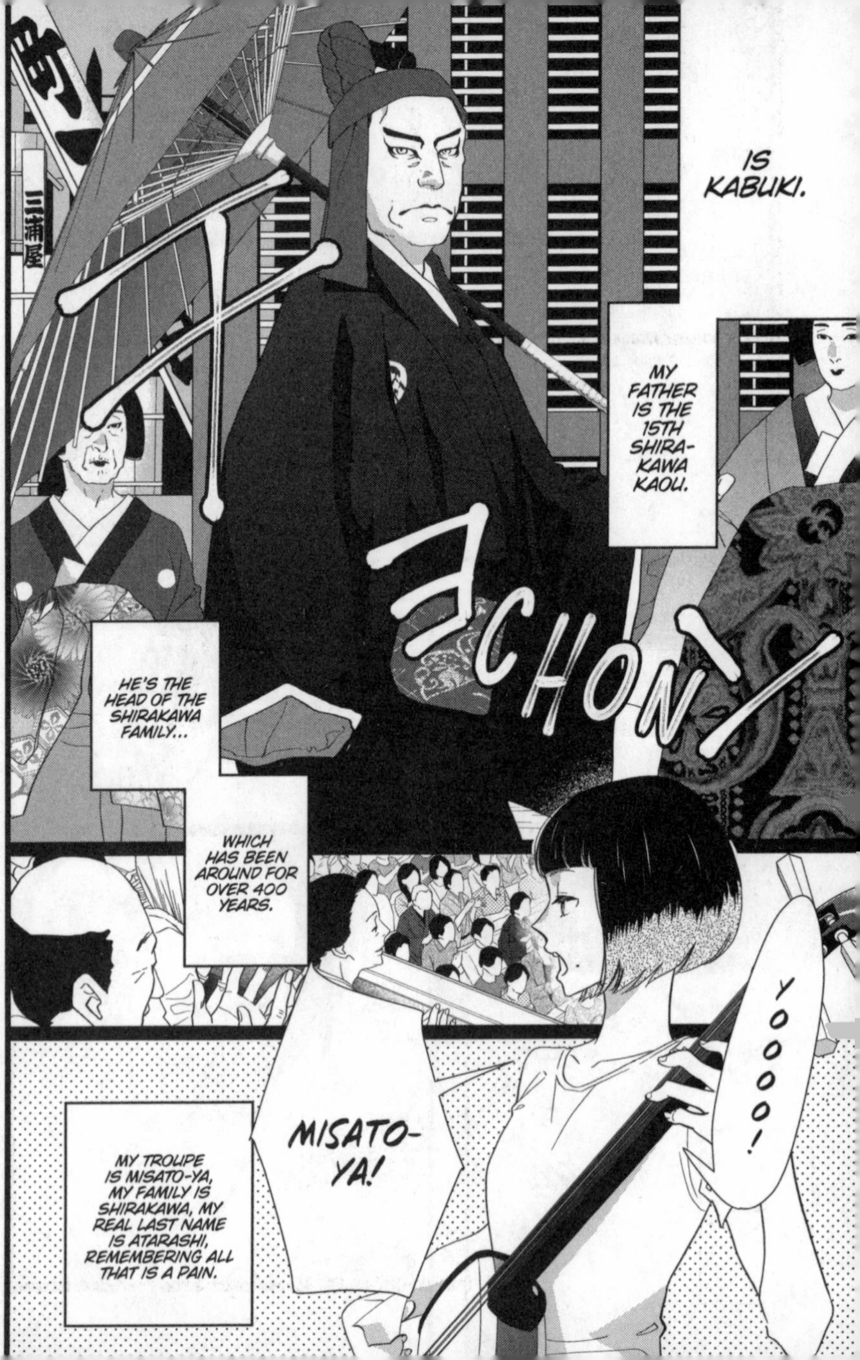
IS KABUKI.
MY FATHER IS THE 15TH SHIRA-KAWA KAOU.
三浦屋
CHON
HE'S THE HEAD OF THE SHIRAKAWA FAMILY...
WHICH HAS BEEN AROUND FOR OVER 400 YEARS.
YOOOOO!
MISATO-YA!
MY TROUPE IS MISATO-YA, MY FAMILY IS SHIRAKAWA, MY REAL LAST NAME IS ATARASHI, REMEMBERING ALL THAT IS A PAIN.

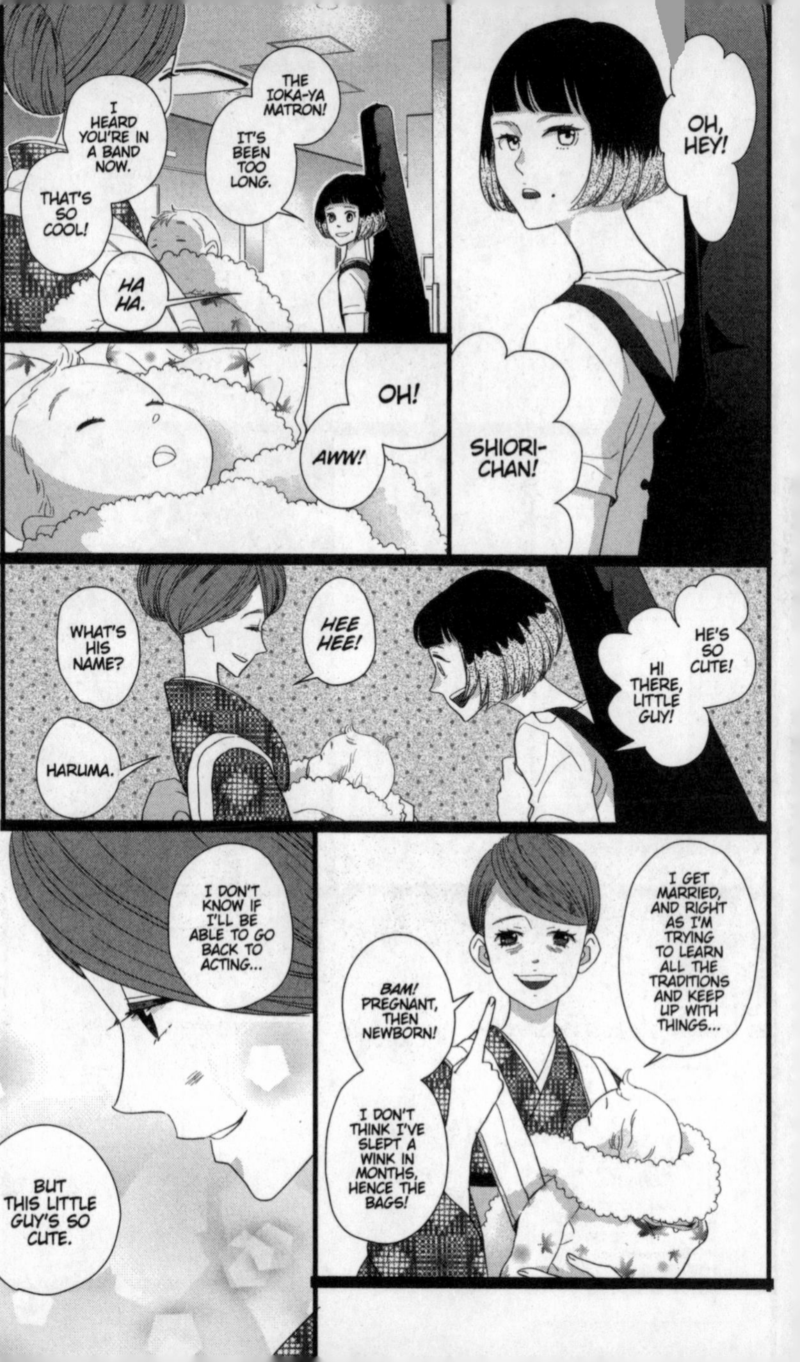
OH, HEY!
SHIORI-CHAN!
THE IOKA-YA MATRON!
IT'S BEEN TOO LONG.
I HEARD YOU'RE IN A BAND NOW.
THAT'S SO COOL!
HA HA.
OH!
AWW!
HE'S SO CUTE!
HI THERE, LITTLE GUY!
HEE HEE!
WHAT'S HIS NAME?
HARUMA.
I GET MARRIED, AND RIGHT AS I'M TRYING TO LEARN ALL THE TRADITIONS AND KEEP UP WITH THINGS...
BAM! PREGNANT, THEN NEWBORN!
I DON'T THINK I'VE SLEPT A WINK IN MONTHS, HENCE THE BAGS!
I DON'T KNOW IF I'LL BE ABLE TO GO BACK TO ACTING...
BUT THIS LITTLE GUY'S SO CUTE.

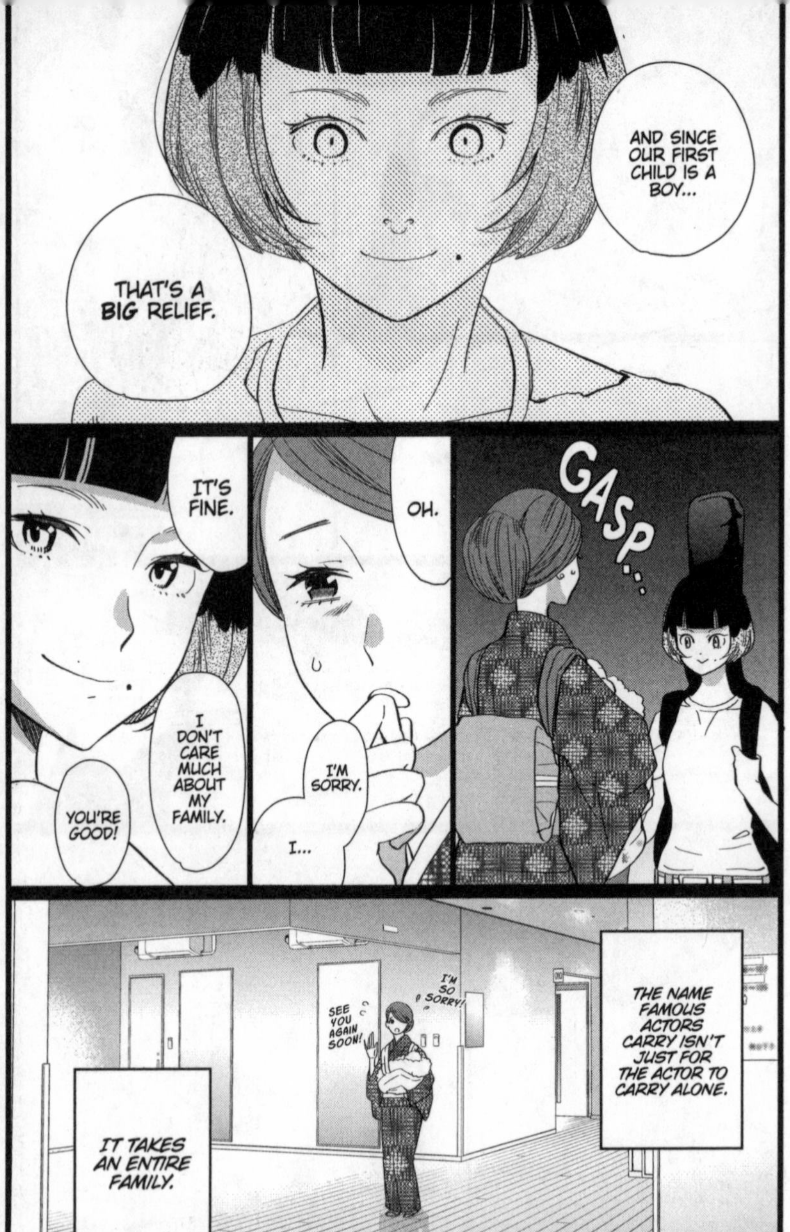
AND SINCE OUR FIRST CHILD IS A BOY...
THAT'S A BIG RELIEF.
GASP...
OH.
I'M SORRY.
I...
IT'S FINE.
I DON'T CARE MUCH ABOUT MY FAMILY.
YOU'RE GOOD!
THE NAME FAMOUS ACTORS CARRY ISN'T JUST FOR THE ACTOR TO CARRY ALONE.
I'M SO SORRY!
SEE YOU AGAIN SOON!
IT TAKES AN ENTIRE FAMILY.

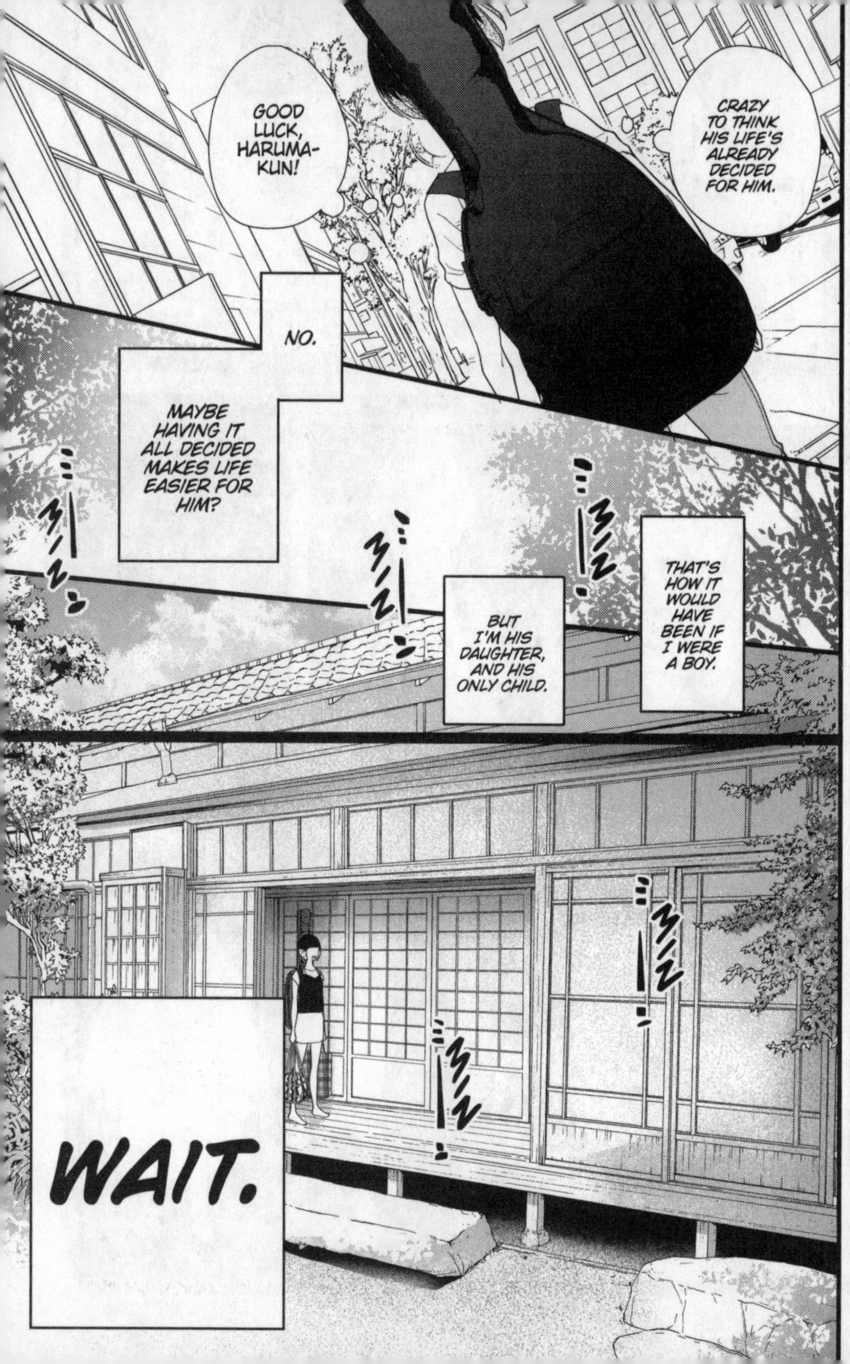
CRAZY TO THINK HIS LIFE'S ALREADY DECIDED FOR HIM.
GOOD LUCK, HARUMA-KUN!
NO.
MAYBE HAVING IT ALL DECIDED MAKES LIFE EASIER FOR HIM?
MIN
MIN
MIN
THAT'S HOW IT WOULD HAVE BEEN IF I WERE A BOY.
BUT I'M HIS DAUGHTER, AND HIS ONLY CHILD.
MIN
MIN
WAIT.

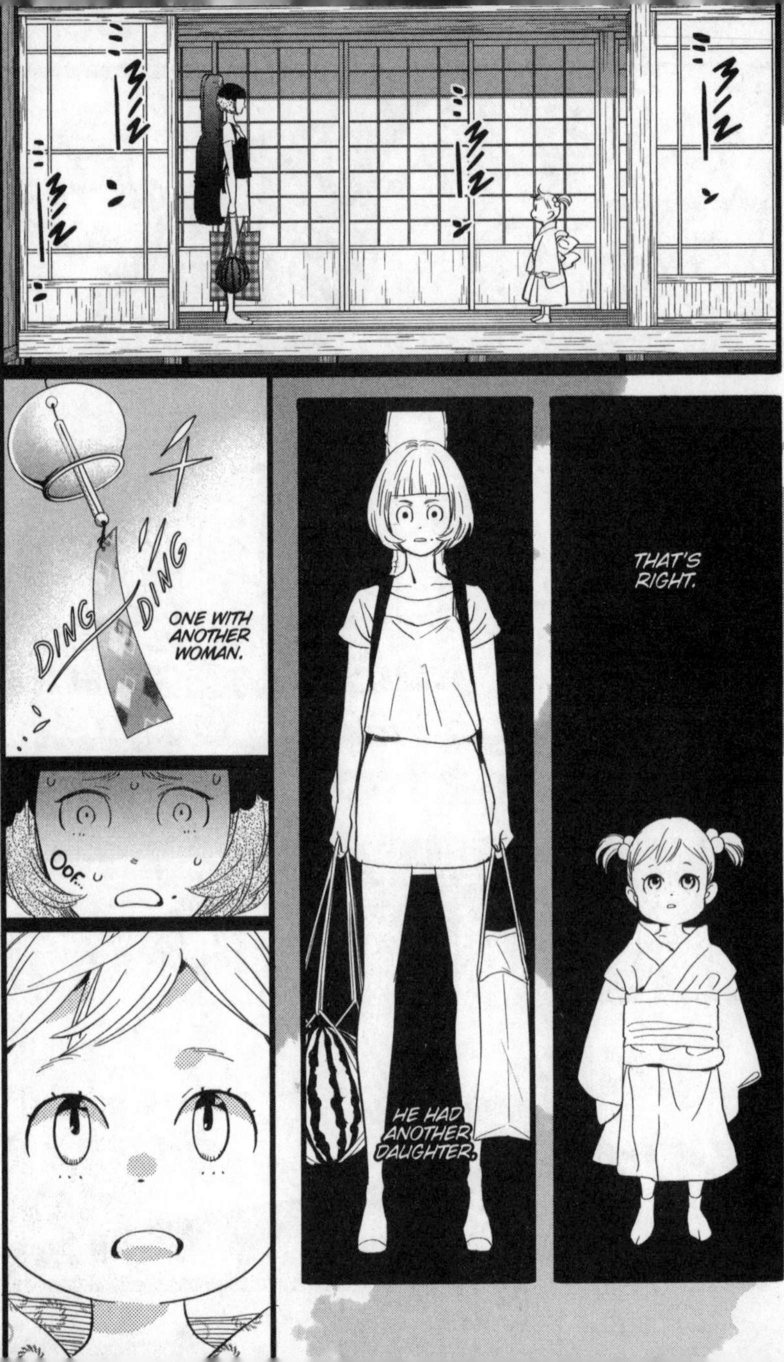

ミーン
ミーン
ミーン
ミーン
THAT'S RIGHT.
HE HAD ANOTHER DAUGHTER.
DING DING
ONE WITH ANOTHER WOMAN.
Oof...

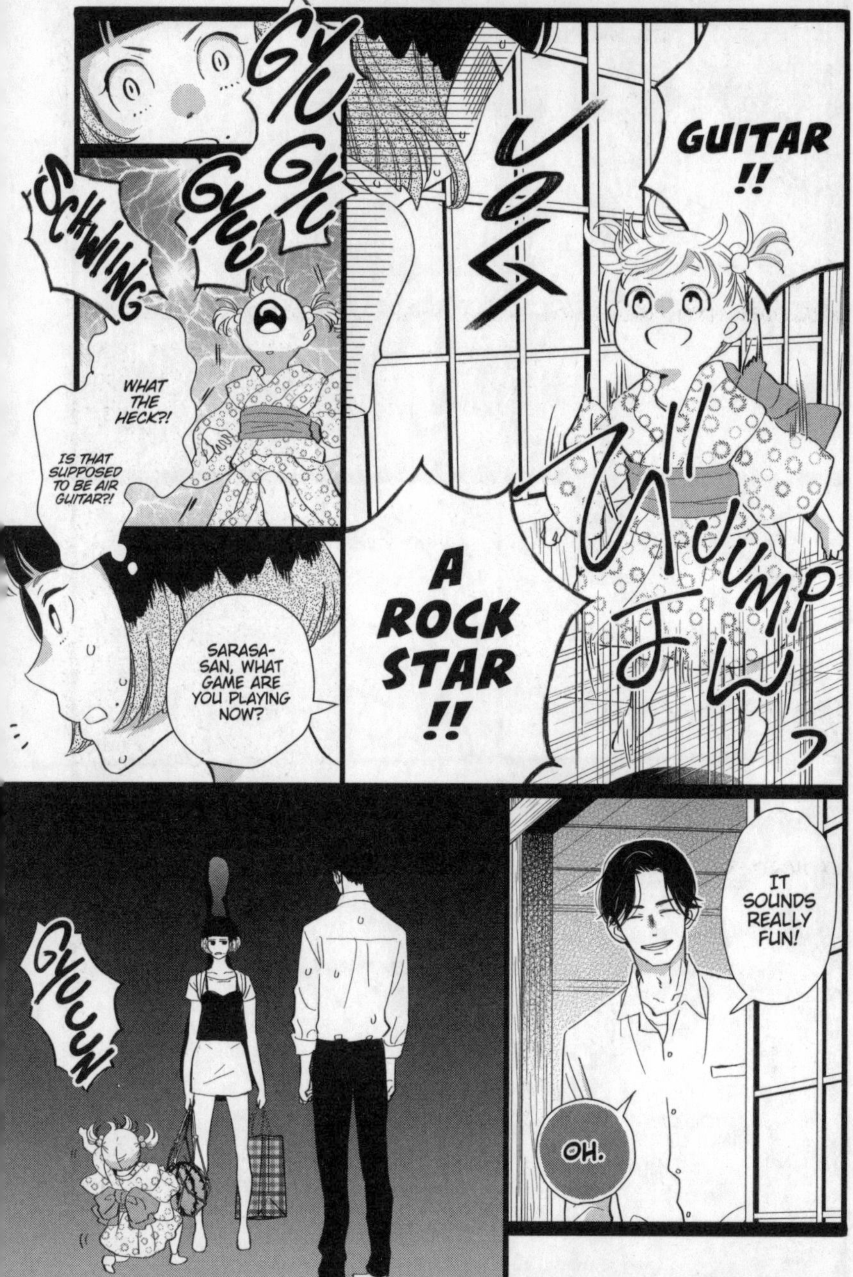
GUITAR !!
VOLT
A ROCK STAR !!
JUMP
GYU GYU GYUU
SCHWIING
WHAT THE HECK?!
IS THAT SUPPOSED TO BE AIR GUITAR?!
SARASA-SAN, WHAT GAME ARE YOU PLAYING NOW?
IT SOUNDS REALLY FUN!
OH.
GYUUUN

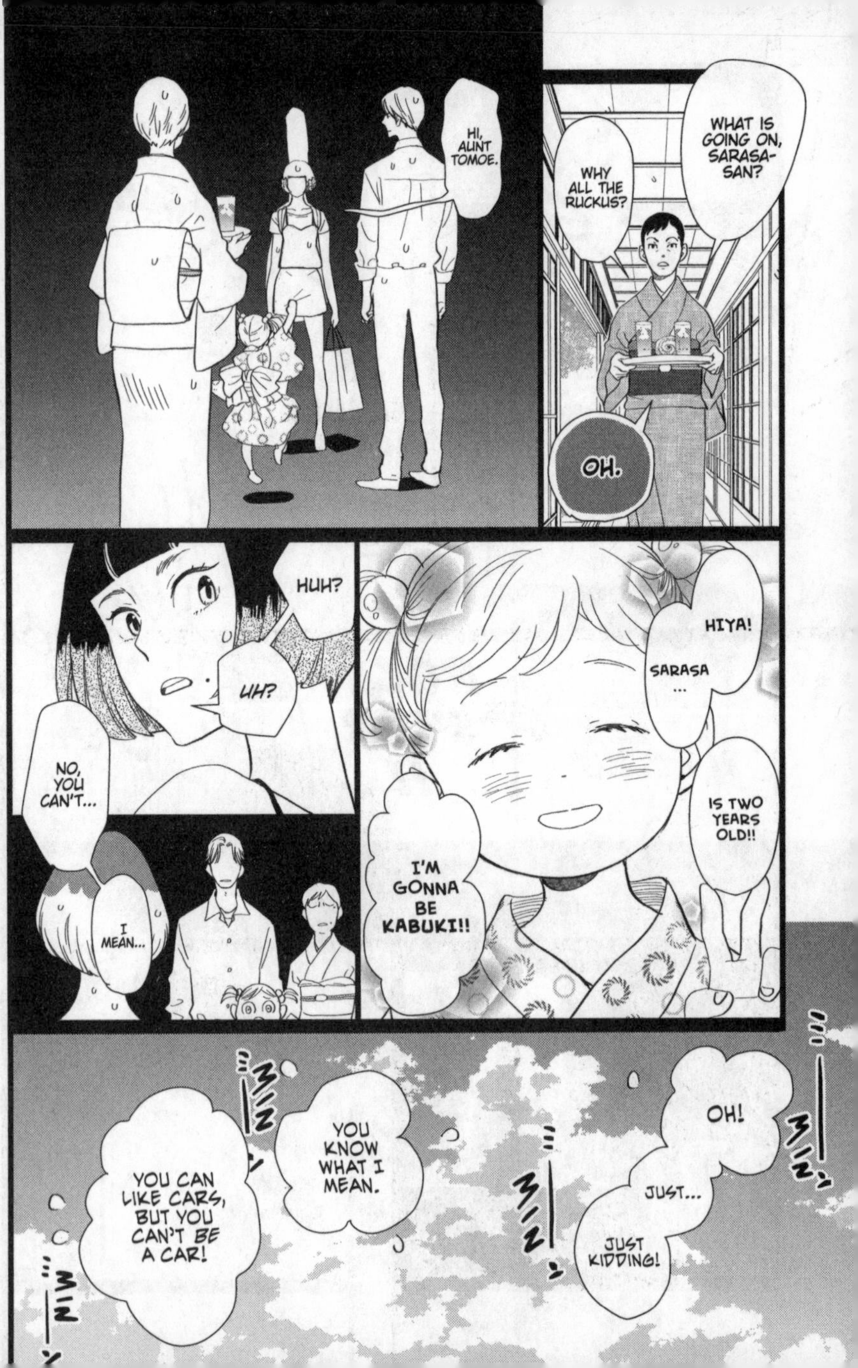
WHAT IS GOING ON, SARASA-SAN?
WHY ALL THE RUCKUS?
OH.
HI, AUNT TOMOE.
HIYA!
SARASA...
IS TWO YEARS OLD!!
I'M GONNA BE KABUKI!!
HUH?
UH?
NO, YOU CAN'T...
I MEAN...
OH!
JUST...
JUST KIDDING!
MIN
MIN
YOU KNOW WHAT I MEAN.
MIN
YOU CAN LIKE CARS, BUT YOU CAN'T BE A CAR!
MIN

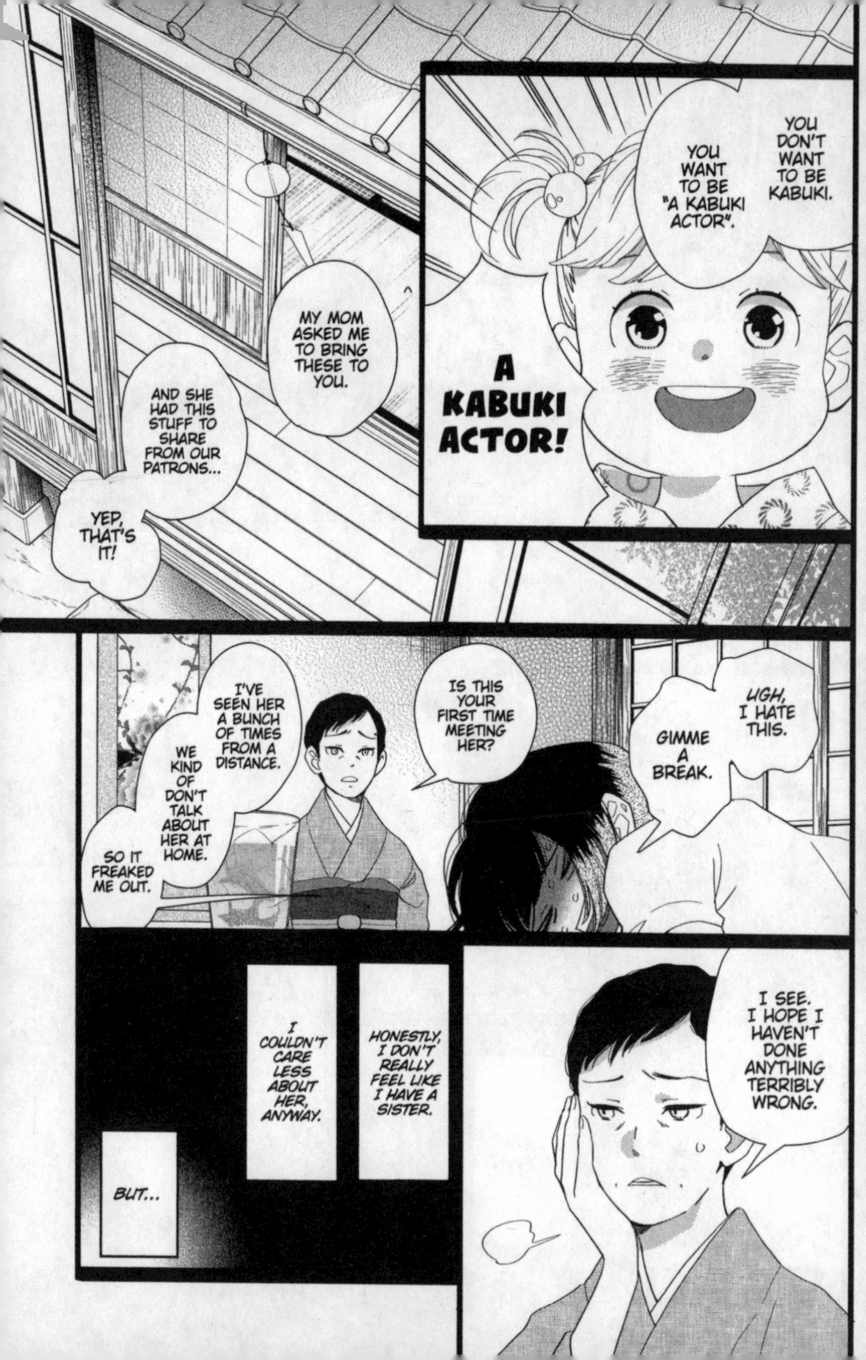

YOU DON'T WANT TO BE KABUKI.
YOU WANT TO BE "A KABUKI ACTOR".
A KABUKI ACTOR!
MY MOM ASKED ME TO BRING THESE TO YOU.
AND SHE HAD THIS STUFF TO SHARE FROM OUR PATRONS...
YEP, THAT'S IT!
UGH, I HATE THIS.
GIMME A BREAK.
IS THIS YOUR FIRST TIME MEETING HER?
I'VE SEEN HER A BUNCH OF TIMES FROM A DISTANCE.
WE KIND OF DON'T TALK ABOUT HER AT HOME.
SO IT FREAKED ME OUT.
I SEE. I HOPE I HAVEN'T DONE ANYTHING TERRIBLY WRONG.
HONESTLY, I DON'T REALLY FEEL LIKE I HAVE A SISTER.
I COULDN'T CARE LESS ABOUT HER, ANYWAY.
BUT...

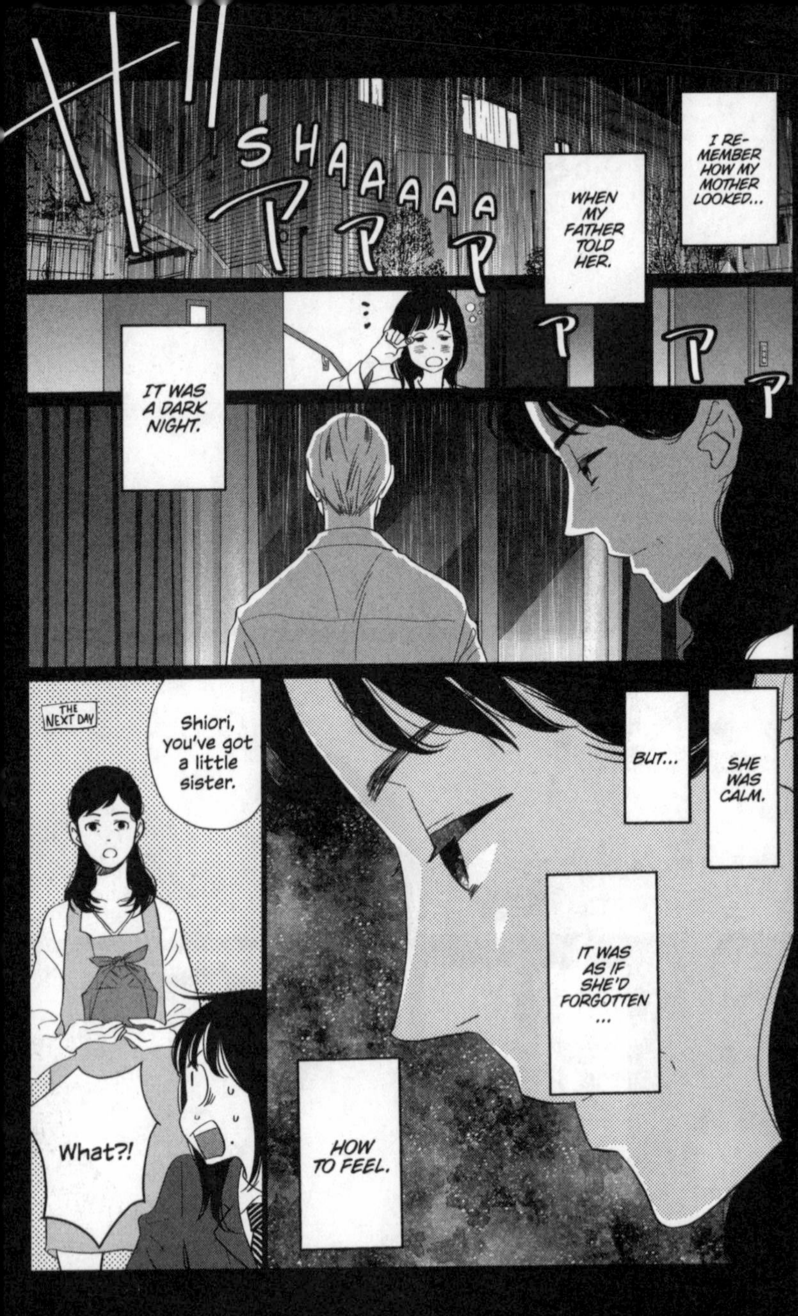
SHAAAAA
I RE-MEMBER HOW MY MOTHER LOOKED...
WHEN MY FATHER TOLD HER.
IT WAS A DARK NIGHT.
SHE WAS CALM.
BUT...
IT WAS AS IF SHE'D FORGOTTEN ...
HOW TO FEEL.
THE NEXT DAY
Shiori, you've got a little sister.
What?!

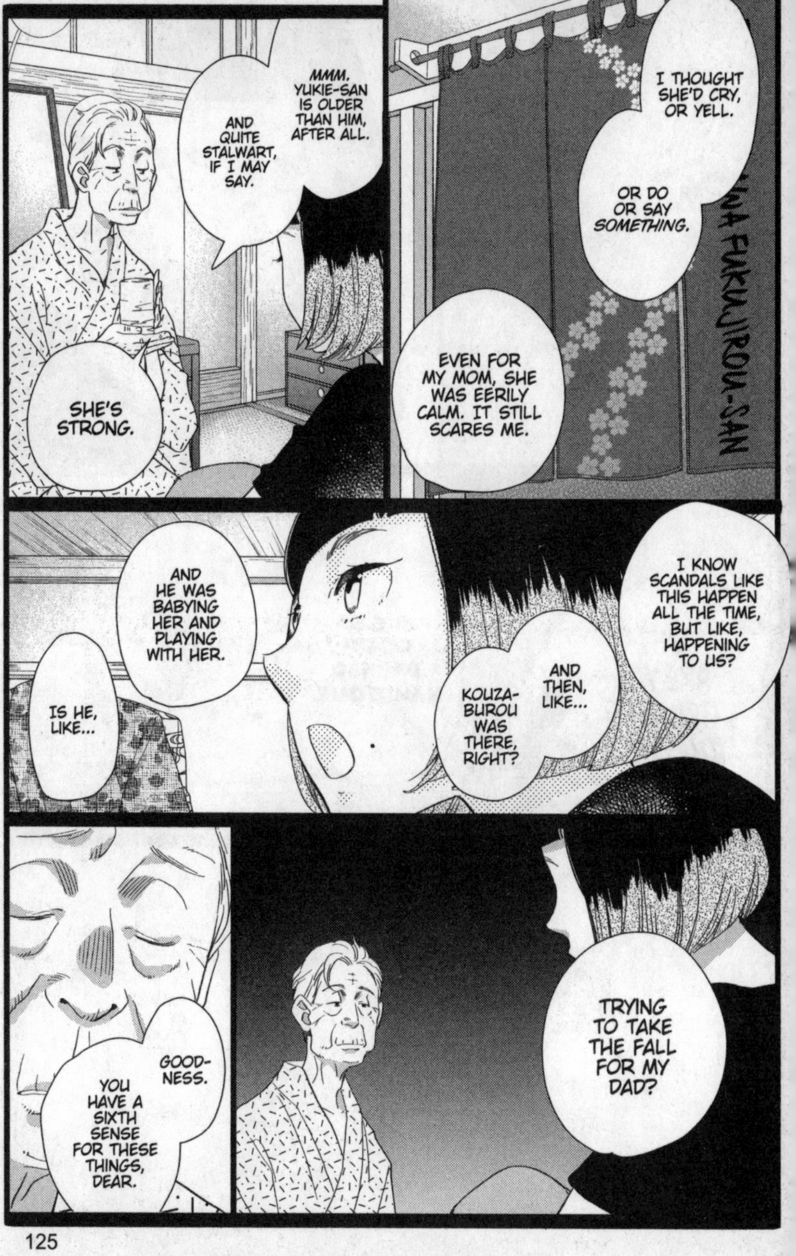
I THOUGHT SHE'D CRY, OR YELL.
OR DO OR SAY SOMETHING.
FUKUJIROU-SAN
EVEN FOR MY MOM, SHE WAS EERILY CALM. IT STILL SCARES ME.
MMM. YUKIE-SAN IS OLDER THAN HIM, AFTER ALL.
AND QUITE STALWART, IF I MAY SAY.
SHE'S STRONG.
I KNOW SCANDALS LIKE THIS HAPPEN ALL THE TIME, BUT LIKE, HAPPENING TO US?
AND THEN, LIKE...
KOUZA-BUROU WAS THERE, RIGHT?
AND HE WAS BABYING HER AND PLAYING WITH HER.
IS HE, LIKE...
TRYING TO TAKE THE FALL FOR MY DAD?
GOOD-NESS.
YOU HAVE A SIXTH SENSE FOR THESE THINGS, DEAR.

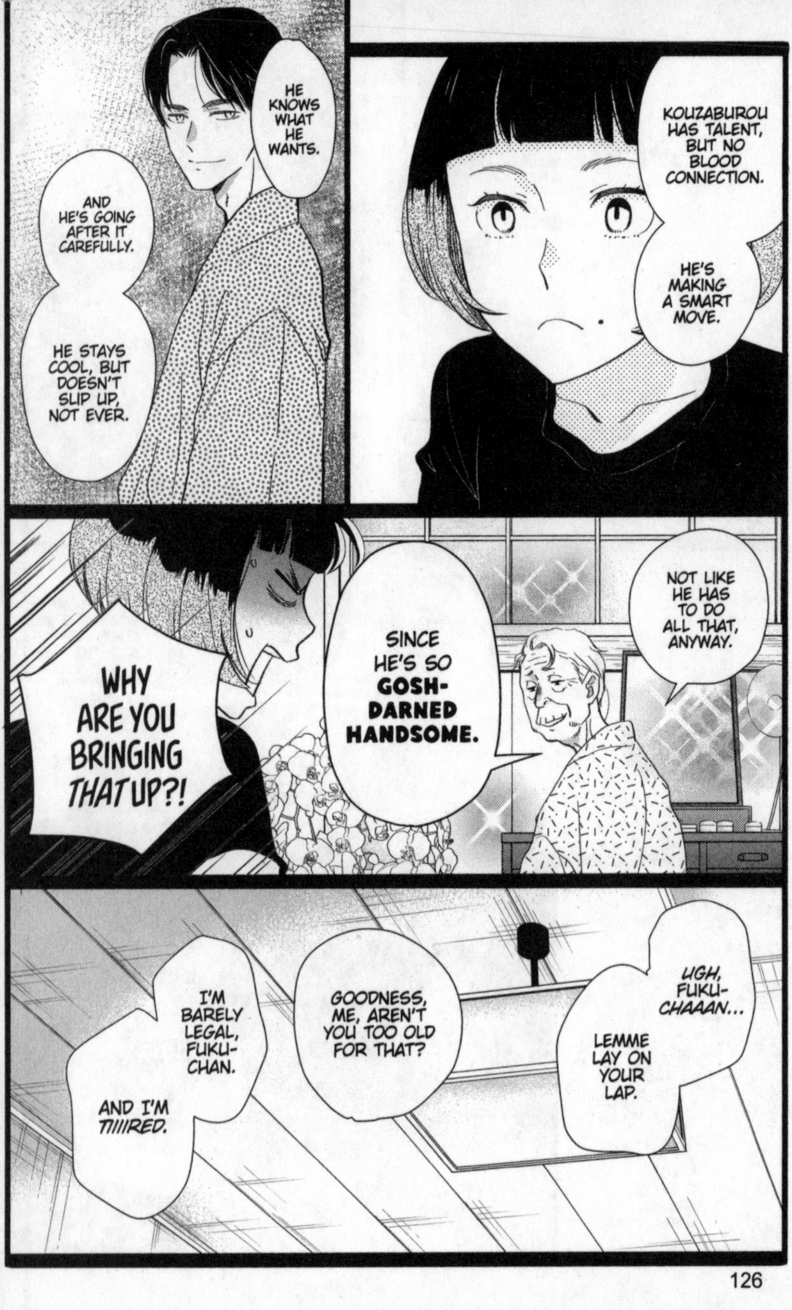
KOUZABUROU HAS TALENT, BUT NO BLOOD CONNECTION.
HE'S MAKING A SMART MOVE.
HE KNOWS WHAT HE WANTS.
AND HE'S GOING AFTER IT CAREFULLY.
HE STAYS COOL, BUT DOESN'T SLIP UP, NOT EVER.
NOT LIKE HE HAS TO DO ALL THAT, ANYWAY.
SINCE HE'S SO **GOSH-DARNED HANDSOME.**
WHY ARE YOU BRINGING *THAT* UP?!
UGH, FUKU-CHAAAN...
LEMME LAY ON YOUR LAP.
GOODNESS, ME, AREN'T YOU TOO OLD FOR THAT?
I'M BARELY LEGAL, FUKU-CHAN.
AND I'M *TIIIIRED.*

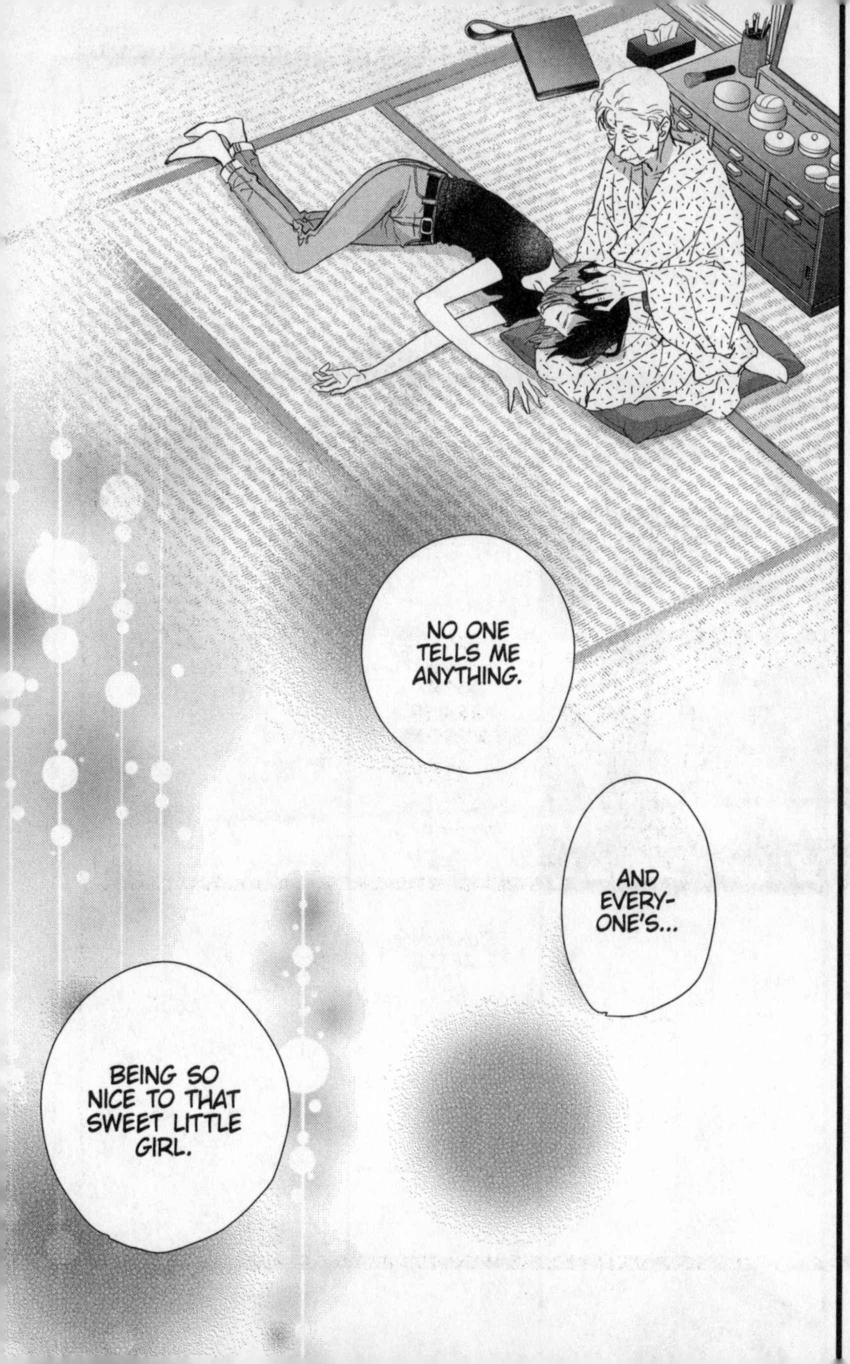
NO ONE TELLS ME ANYTHING.
AND EVERY-ONE'S...
BEING SO NICE TO THAT SWEET LITTLE GIRL.

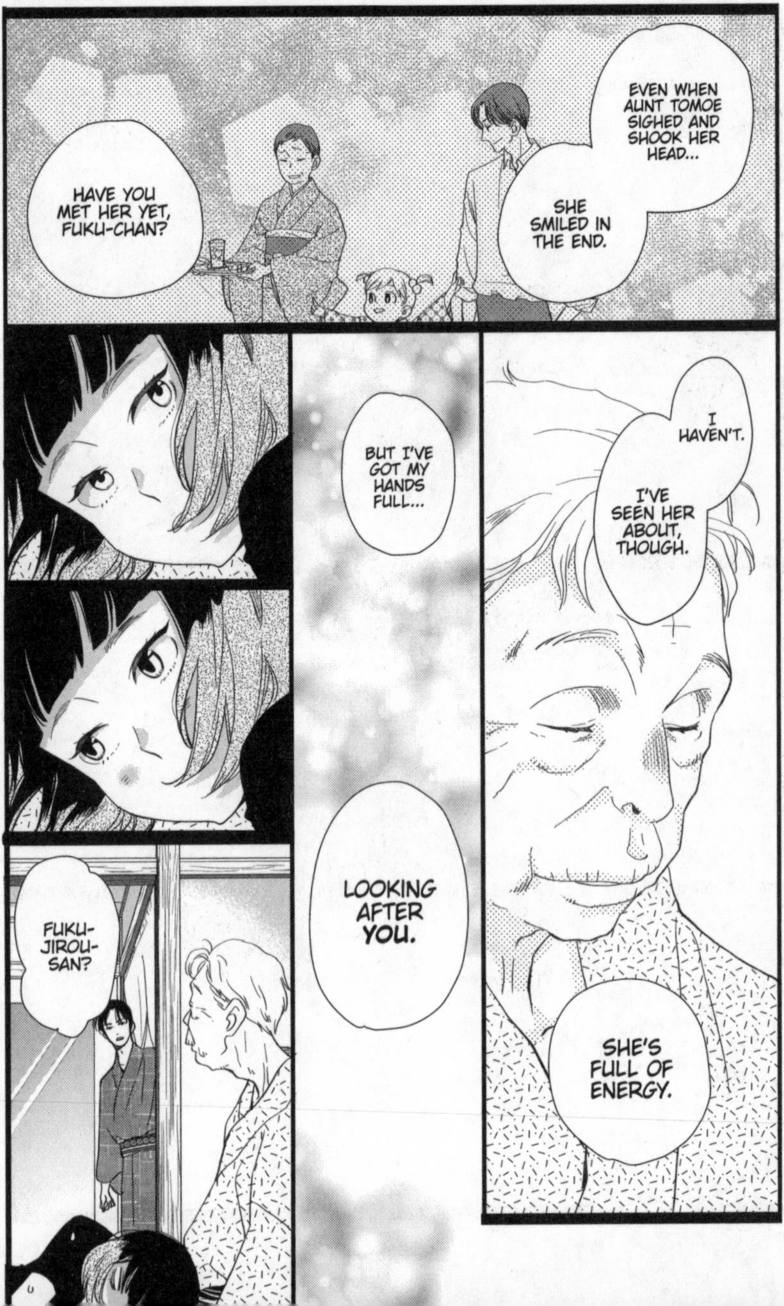
EVEN WHEN AUNT TOMOE SIGHED AND SHOOK HER HEAD...
SHE SMILED IN THE END.
HAVE YOU MET HER YET, FUKU-CHAN?
I HAVEN'T.
I'VE SEEN HER ABOUT, THOUGH.
SHE'S FULL OF ENERGY.
BUT I'VE GOT MY HANDS FULL...
LOOKING AFTER YOU.
FUKU-JIROU-SAN?

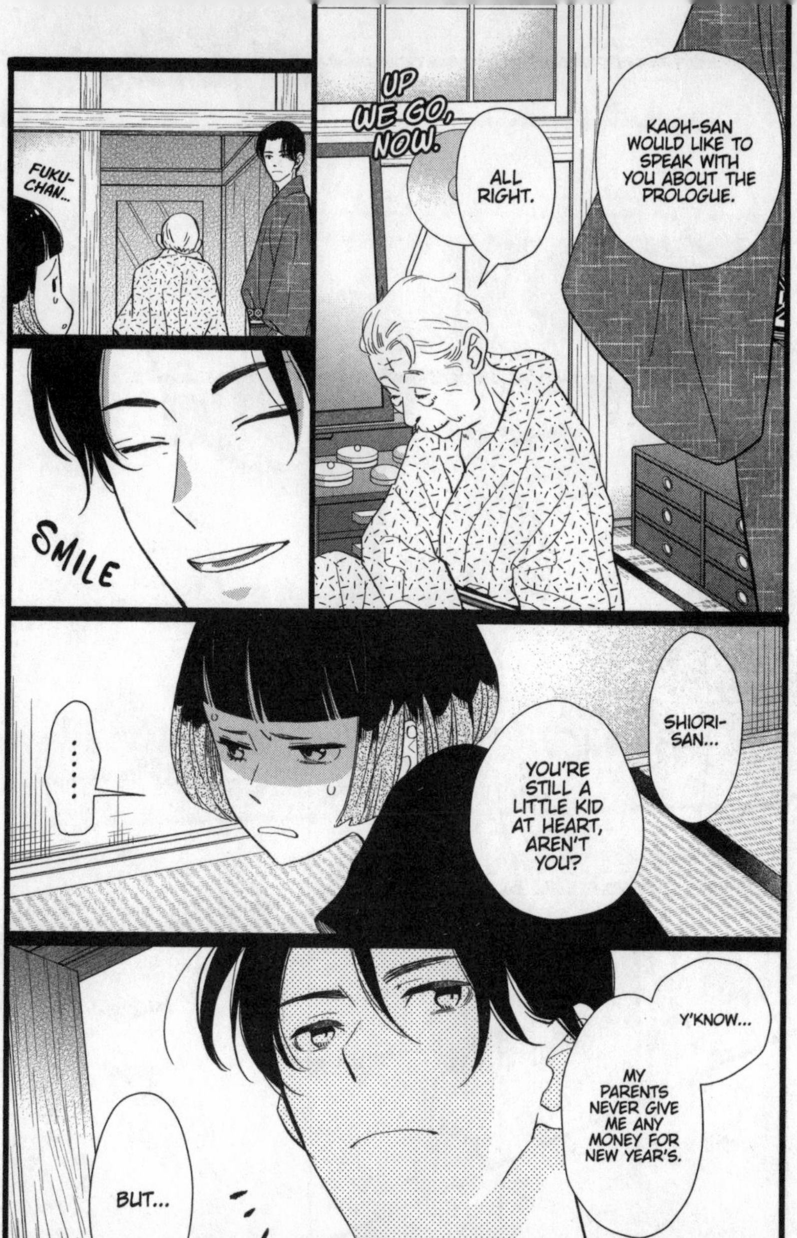
KAOH-SAN WOULD LIKE TO SPEAK WITH YOU ABOUT THE PROLOGUE.
ALL RIGHT.
UP WE GO, NOW.
FUKU-CHAN...
SMILE
SHIORI-SAN...
YOU'RE STILL A LITTLE KID AT HEART, AREN'T YOU?
......
Y'KNOW...
MY PARENTS NEVER GIVE ME ANY MONEY FOR NEW YEAR'S.
BUT...

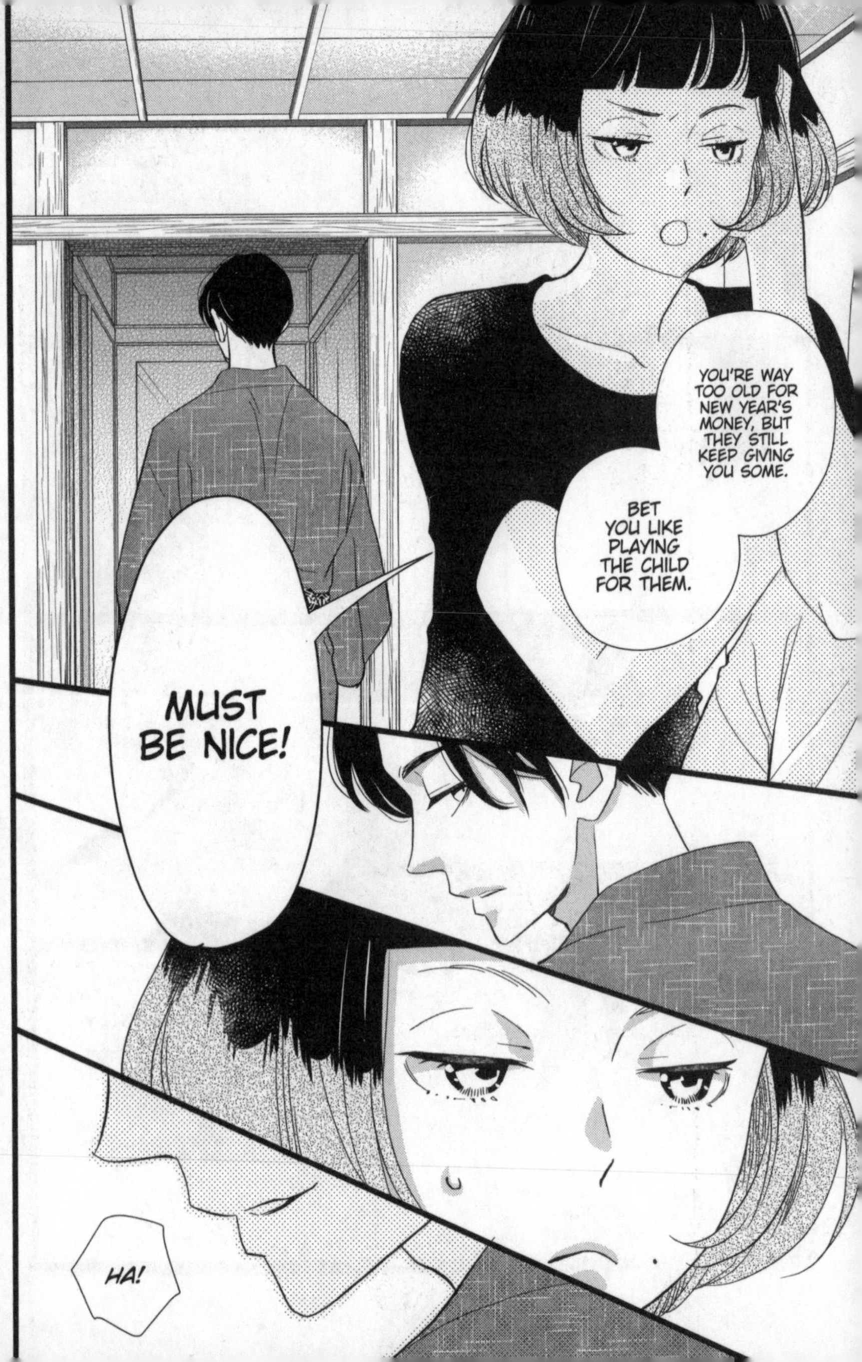
YOU'RE WAY TOO OLD FOR NEW YEAR'S MONEY, BUT THEY STILL KEEP GIVING YOU SOME.
BET YOU LIKE PLAYING THE CHILD FOR THEM.
MUST BE NICE!
HA!

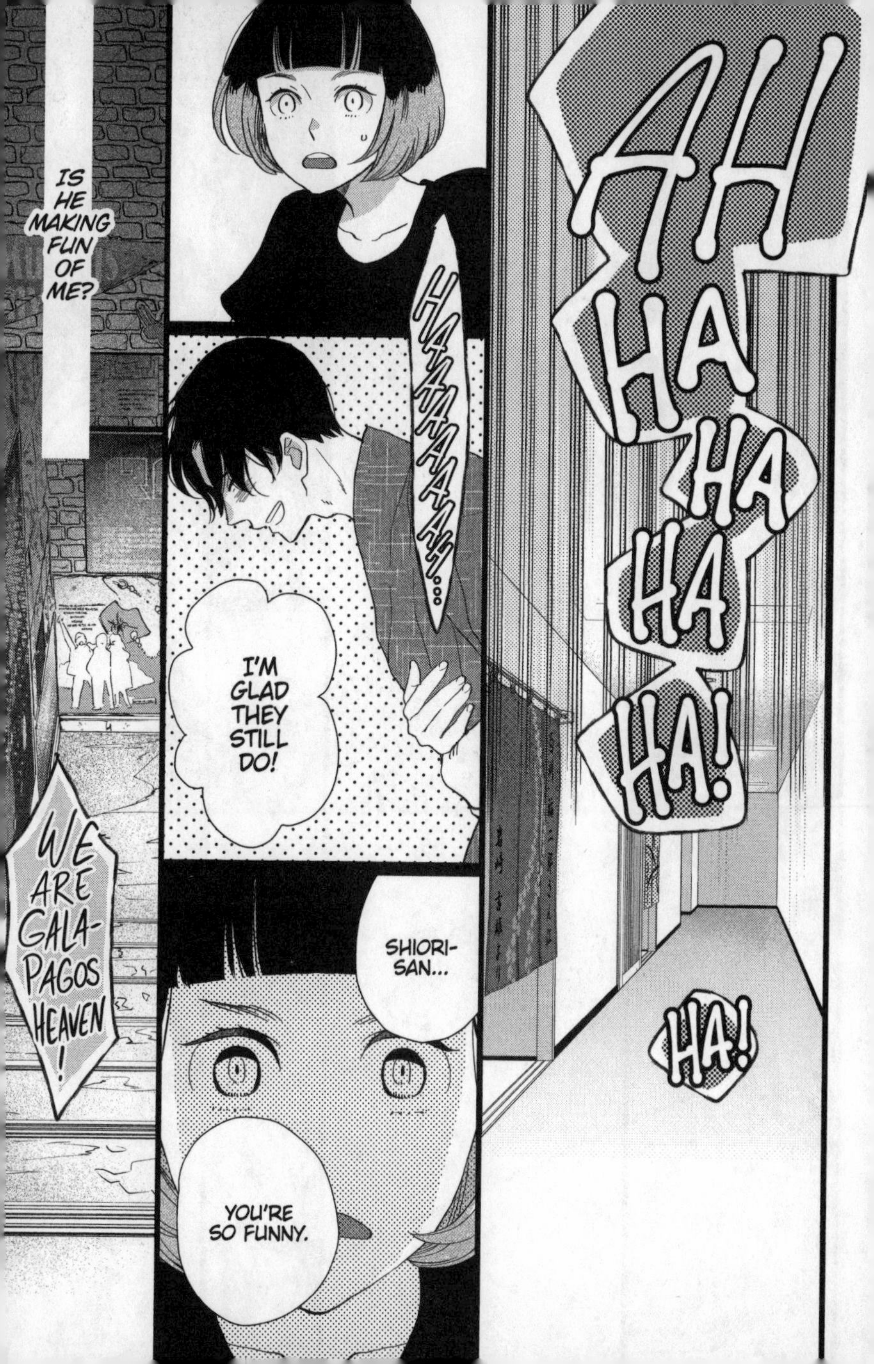
AH HA HA HA HA!
HA!
HAAAAAAAH...
I'M GLAD THEY STILL DO!
SHIORI-SAN...
YOU'RE SO FUNNY.
IS HE MAKING FUN OF ME?
WE ARE GALA-PAGOS HEAVEN!

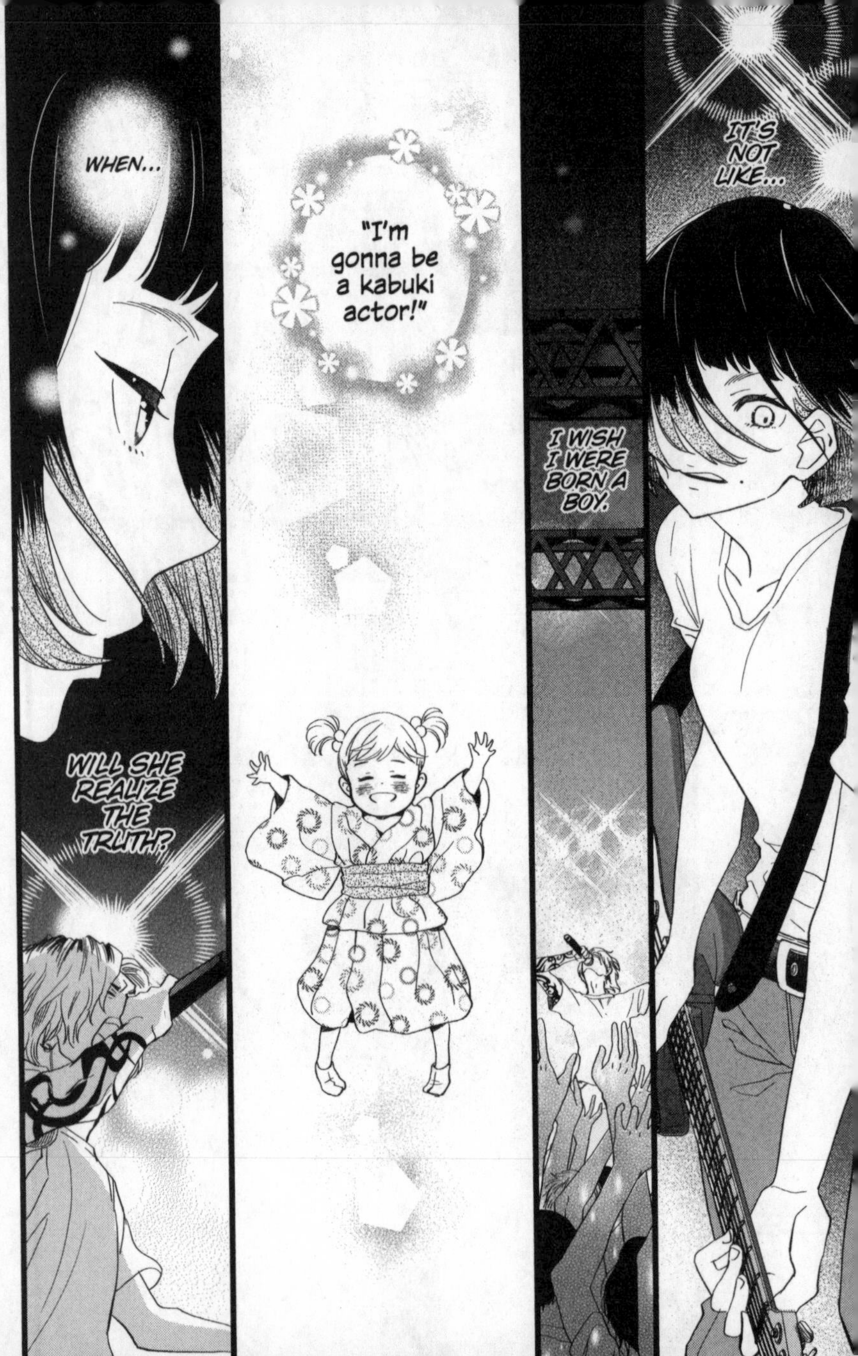
IT'S NOT LIKE...
I WISH I WERE BORN A BOY.
"I'm gonna be a kabuki actor!"
WHEN...
WILL SHE REALIZE THE TRUTH?

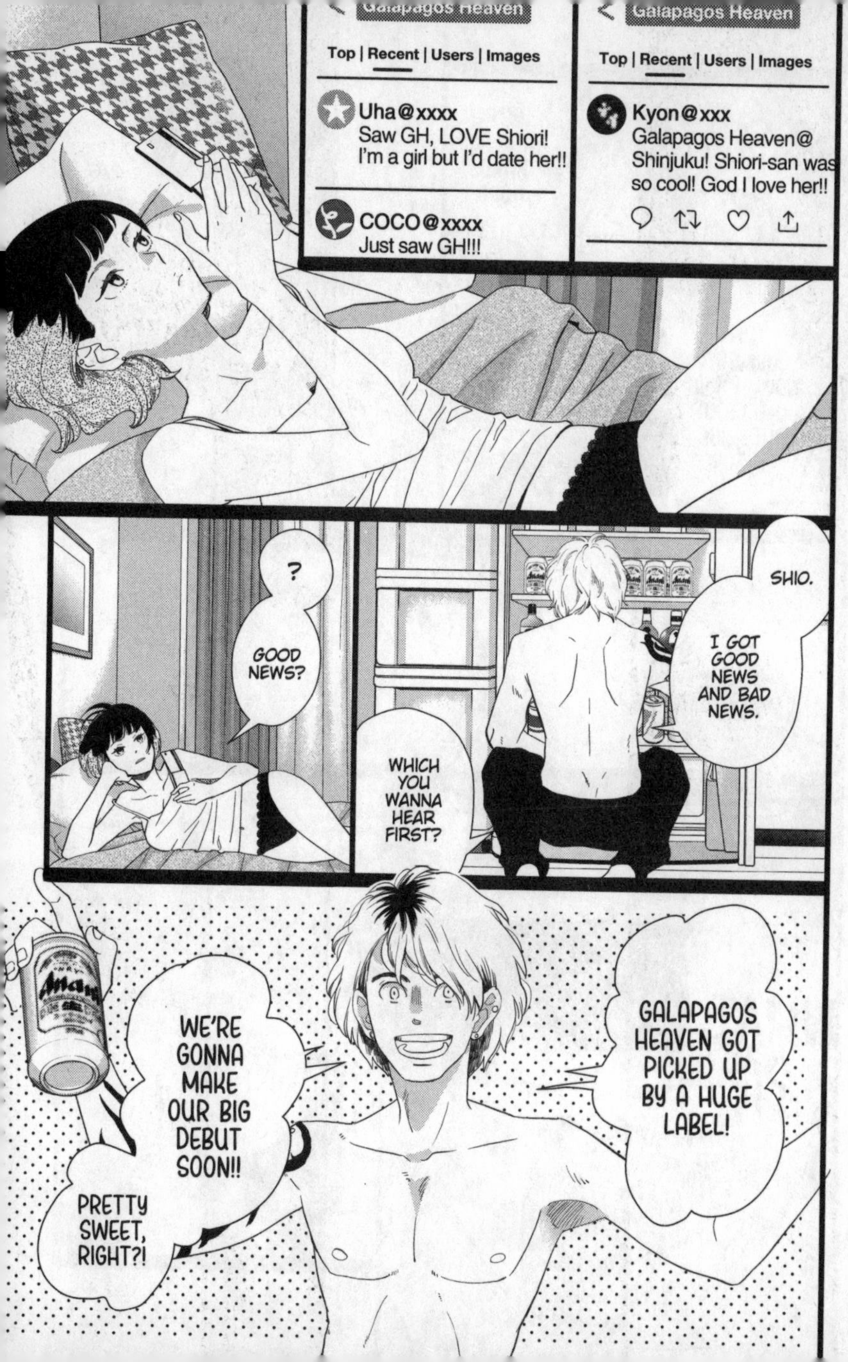
Galapagos Heaven
Top | Recent | Users | Images
Kyon@xxx
Galapagos Heaven@ Shinjuku! Shiori-san was so cool! God I love her!!
Top | Recent | Users | Images
Uha@xxxx
Saw GH, LOVE Shiori! I'm a girl but I'd date her!!
COCO@xxxx
Just saw GH!!!
SHIO.
I GOT GOOD NEWS AND BAD NEWS.
WHICH YOU WANNA HEAR FIRST?
?
GOOD NEWS?
GALAPAGOS HEAVEN GOT PICKED UP BY A HUGE LABEL!
WE'RE GONNA MAKE OUR BIG DEBUT SOON!!
PRETTY SWEET, RIGHT?!

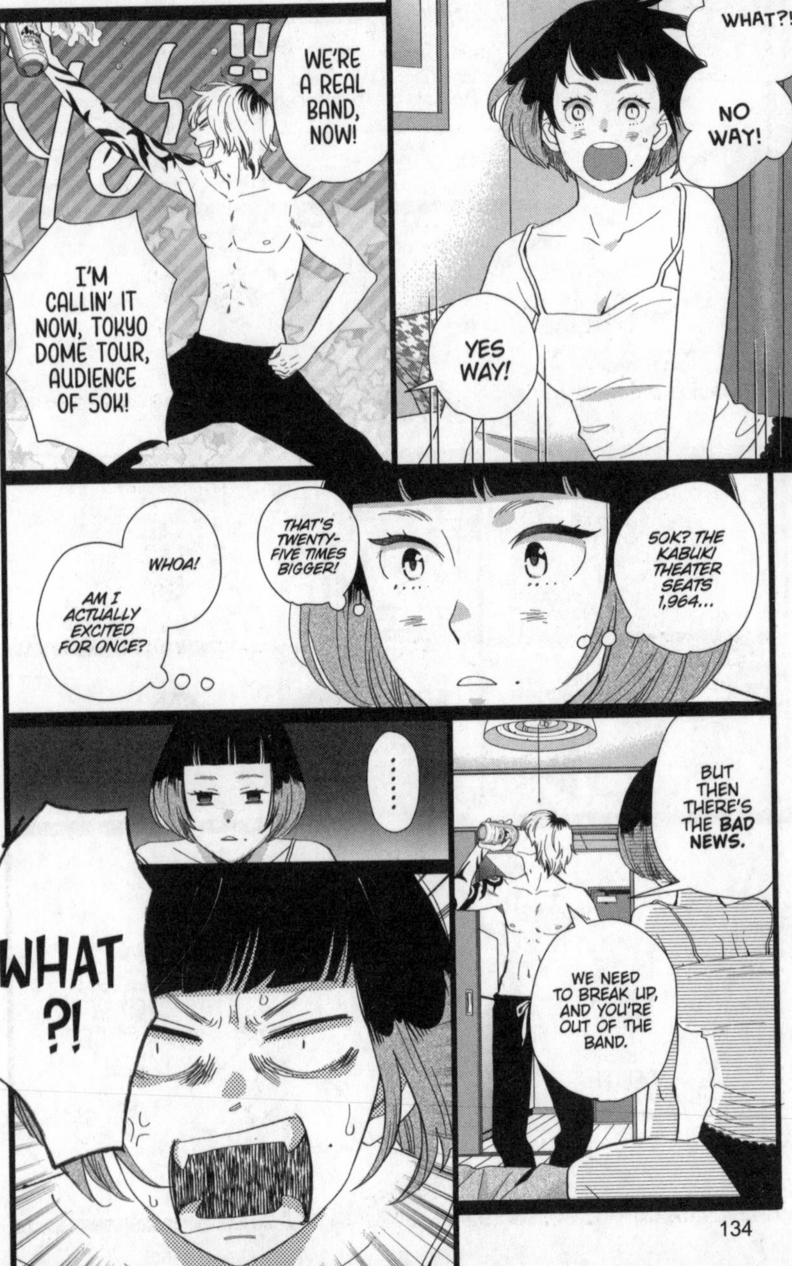
WHAT?!
NO WAY!
YES WAY!
Yes
!!
WE'RE A REAL BAND, NOW!
I'M CALLIN' IT NOW, TOKYO DOME TOUR, AUDIENCE OF 50K!
50K? THE KABUKI THEATER SEATS 1,964...
THAT'S TWENTY-FIVE TIMES BIGGER!
WHOA!
AM I ACTUALLY EXCITED FOR ONCE?
BUT THEN THERE'S THE BAD NEWS.
WE NEED TO BREAK UP, AND YOU'RE OUT OF THE BAND.
......
WHAT ?!

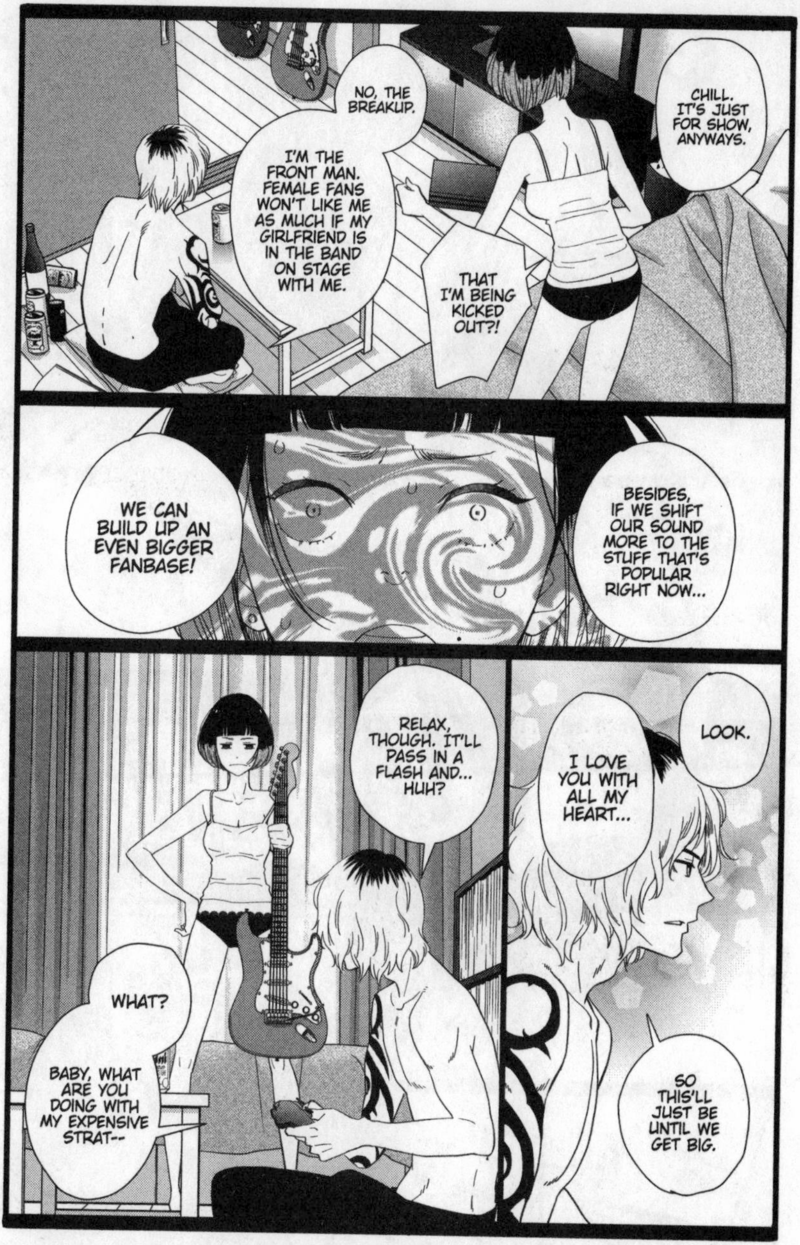
CHILL. IT'S JUST FOR SHOW, ANYWAYS.
THAT I'M BEING KICKED OUT?!
NO, THE BREAKUP.
I'M THE FRONT MAN. FEMALE FANS WON'T LIKE ME AS MUCH IF MY GIRLFRIEND IS IN THE BAND ON STAGE WITH ME.
BESIDES, IF WE SHIFT OUR SOUND MORE TO THE STUFF THAT'S POPULAR RIGHT NOW...
WE CAN BUILD UP AN EVEN BIGGER FANBASE!
LOOK.
I LOVE YOU WITH ALL MY HEART...
SO THIS'LL JUST BE UNTIL WE GET BIG.
RELAX, THOUGH. IT'LL PASS IN A FLASH AND... HUH?
WHAT?
BABY, WHAT ARE YOU DOING WITH MY EXPENSIVE STRAT--

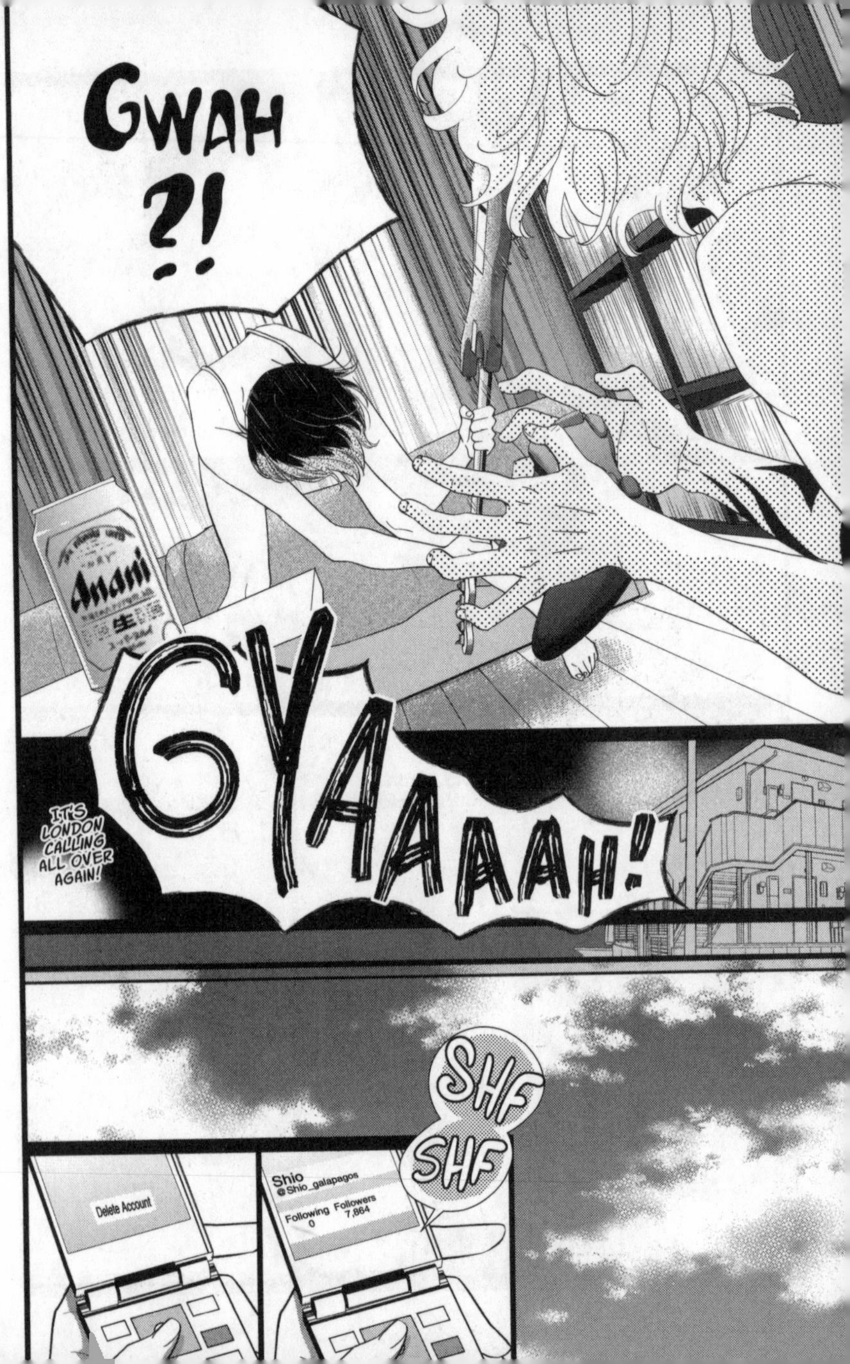
GWAH ?!
Anani
GYAAAAH!
IT'S LONDON CALLING ALL OVER AGAIN!
SHF SHF
Shio
@Shio_galapagos
Following 0 Followers 7,864
Delete Account

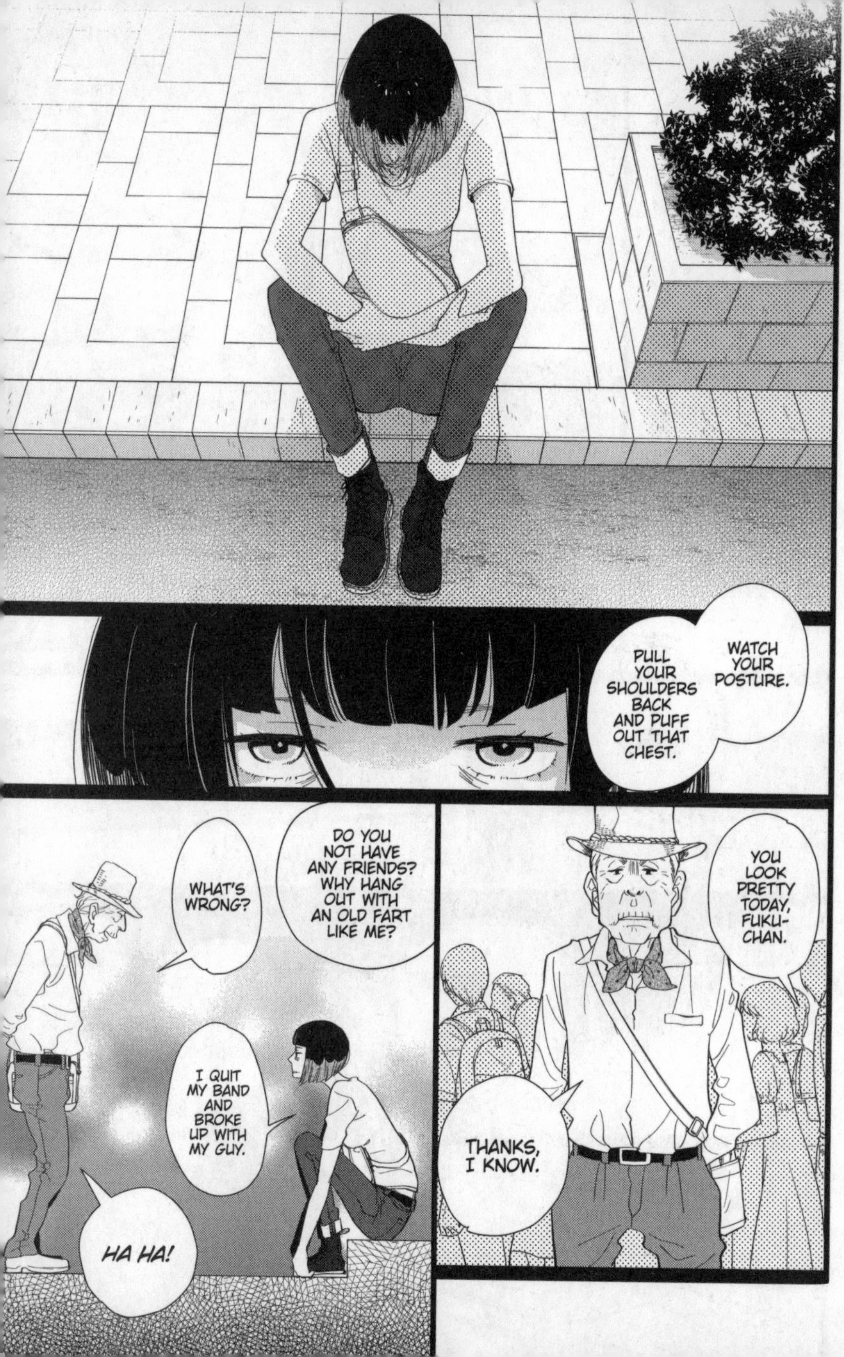
WATCH YOUR POSTURE.
PULL YOUR SHOULDERS BACK AND PUFF OUT THAT CHEST.
YOU LOOK PRETTY TODAY, FUKU-CHAN.
THANKS, I KNOW.
DO YOU NOT HAVE ANY FRIENDS? WHY HANG OUT WITH AN OLD FART LIKE ME?
WHAT'S WRONG?
I QUIT MY BAND AND BROKE UP WITH MY GUY.
HA HA!

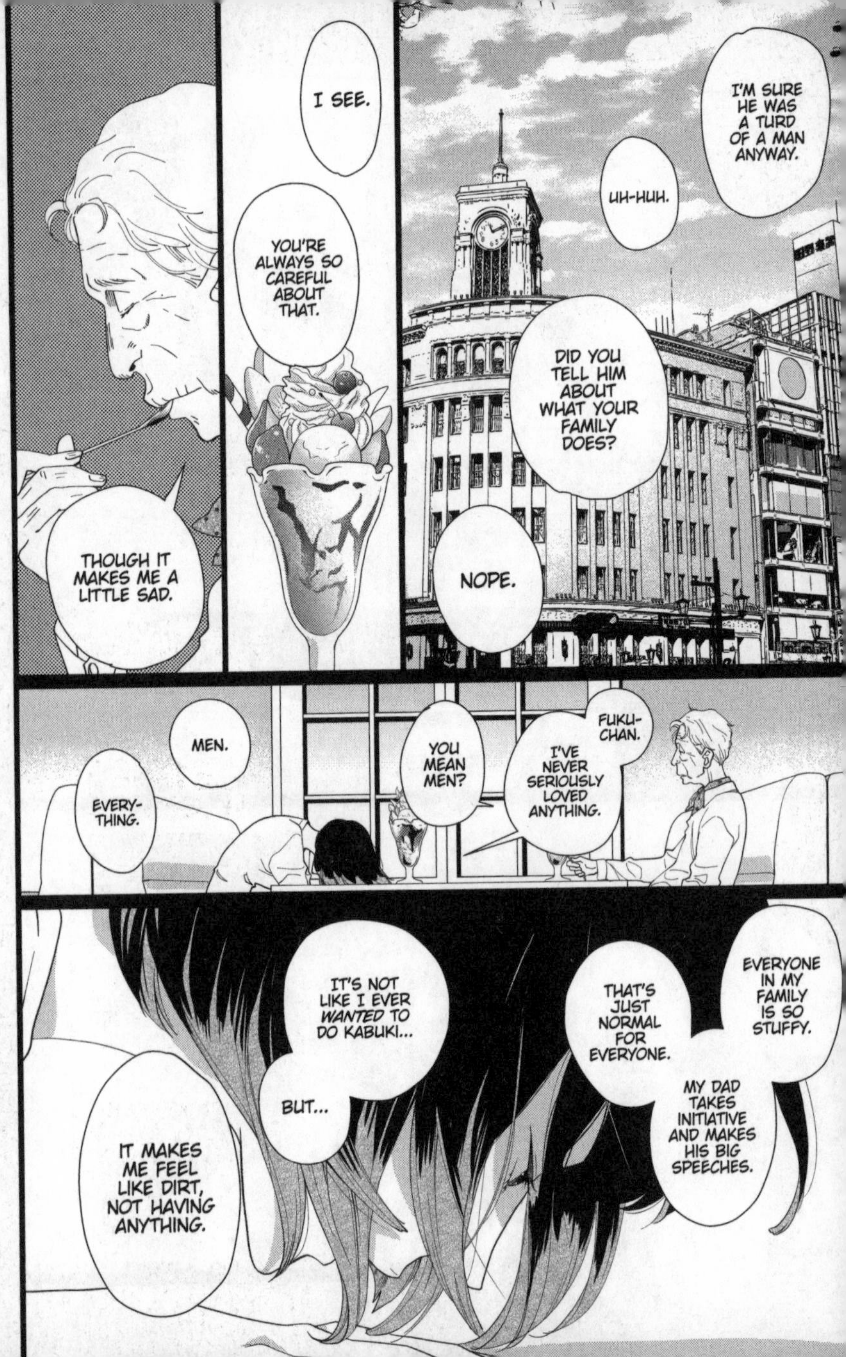
I'M SURE HE WAS A TURD OF A MAN ANYWAY.
UH-HUH.
DID YOU TELL HIM ABOUT WHAT YOUR FAMILY DOES?
NOPE.
I SEE.
YOU'RE ALWAYS SO CAREFUL ABOUT THAT.
THOUGH IT MAKES ME A LITTLE SAD.
FUKU-CHAN.
I'VE NEVER SERIOUSLY LOVED ANYTHING.
YOU MEAN MEN?
MEN.
EVERY-THING.
EVERYONE IN MY FAMILY IS SO STUFFY.
THAT'S JUST NORMAL FOR EVERYONE.
MY DAD TAKES INITIATIVE AND MAKES HIS BIG SPEECHES.
IT'S NOT LIKE I EVER *WANTED* TO DO KABUKI...
BUT...
IT MAKES ME FEEL LIKE DIRT, NOT HAVING ANYTHING.

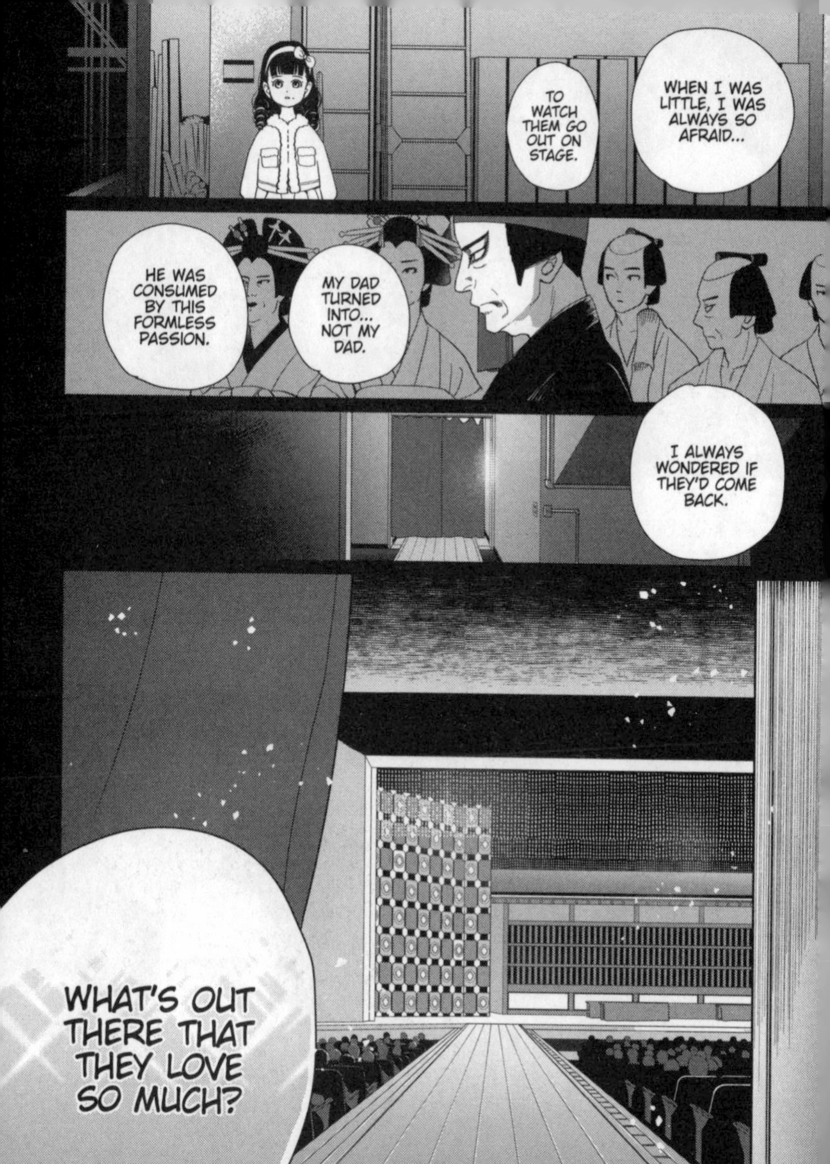
WHEN I WAS LITTLE, I WAS ALWAYS SO AFRAID...
TO WATCH THEM GO OUT ON STAGE.
MY DAD TURNED INTO... NOT MY DAD.
HE WAS CONSUMED BY THIS FORMLESS PASSION.
I ALWAYS WONDERED IF THEY'D COME BACK.
WHAT'S OUT THERE THAT THEY LOVE SO MUCH?

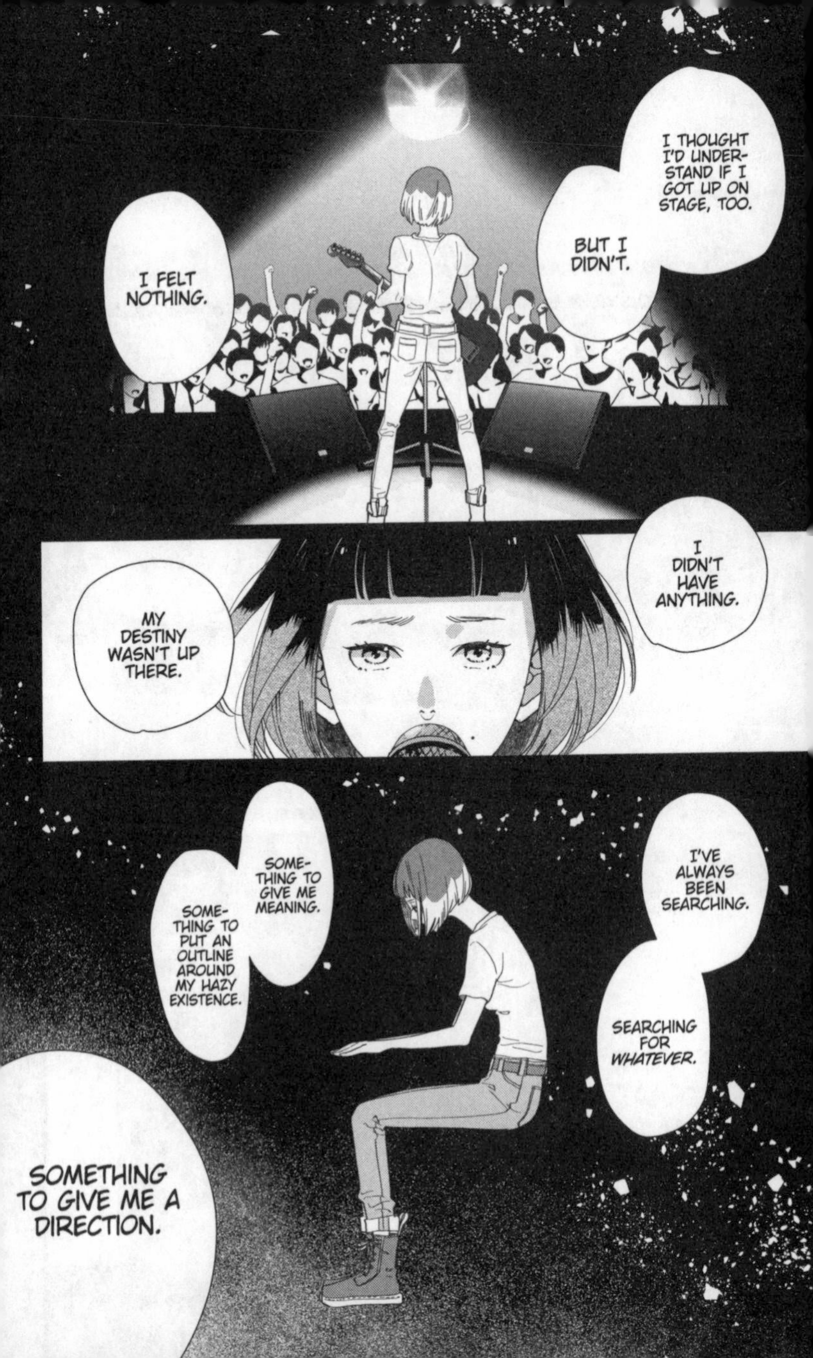
I THOUGHT I'D UNDER-STAND IF I GOT UP ON STAGE, TOO.
BUT I DIDN'T.
I FELT NOTHING.
I DIDN'T HAVE ANYTHING.
MY DESTINY WASN'T UP THERE.
I'VE ALWAYS BEEN SEARCHING.
SEARCHING FOR *WHATEVER.*
SOME-THING TO GIVE ME MEANING.
SOME-THING TO PUT AN OUTLINE AROUND MY HAZY EXISTENCE.
SOMETHING TO GIVE ME A DIRECTION.

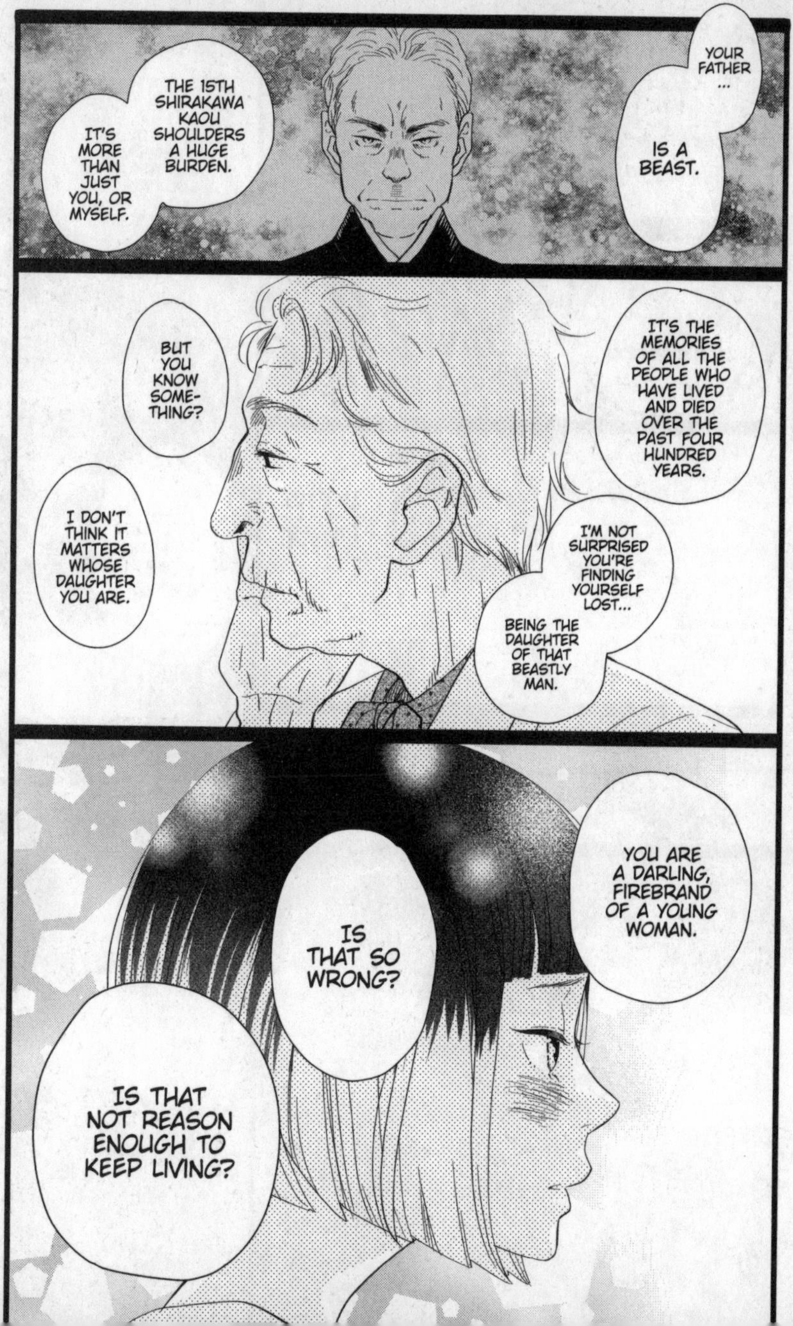
YOUR FATHER ...
IS A BEAST.
THE 15TH SHIRAKAWA KAOU SHOULDERS A HUGE BURDEN.
IT'S MORE THAN JUST YOU, OR MYSELF.
IT'S THE MEMORIES OF ALL THE PEOPLE WHO HAVE LIVED AND DIED OVER THE PAST FOUR HUNDRED YEARS.
BUT YOU KNOW SOME-THING?
I'M NOT SURPRISED YOU'RE FINDING YOURSELF LOST...
BEING THE DAUGHTER OF THAT BEASTLY MAN.
I DON'T THINK IT MATTERS WHOSE DAUGHTER YOU ARE.
YOU ARE A DARLING, FIREBRAND OF A YOUNG WOMAN.
IS THAT SO WRONG?
IS THAT NOT REASON ENOUGH TO KEEP LIVING?

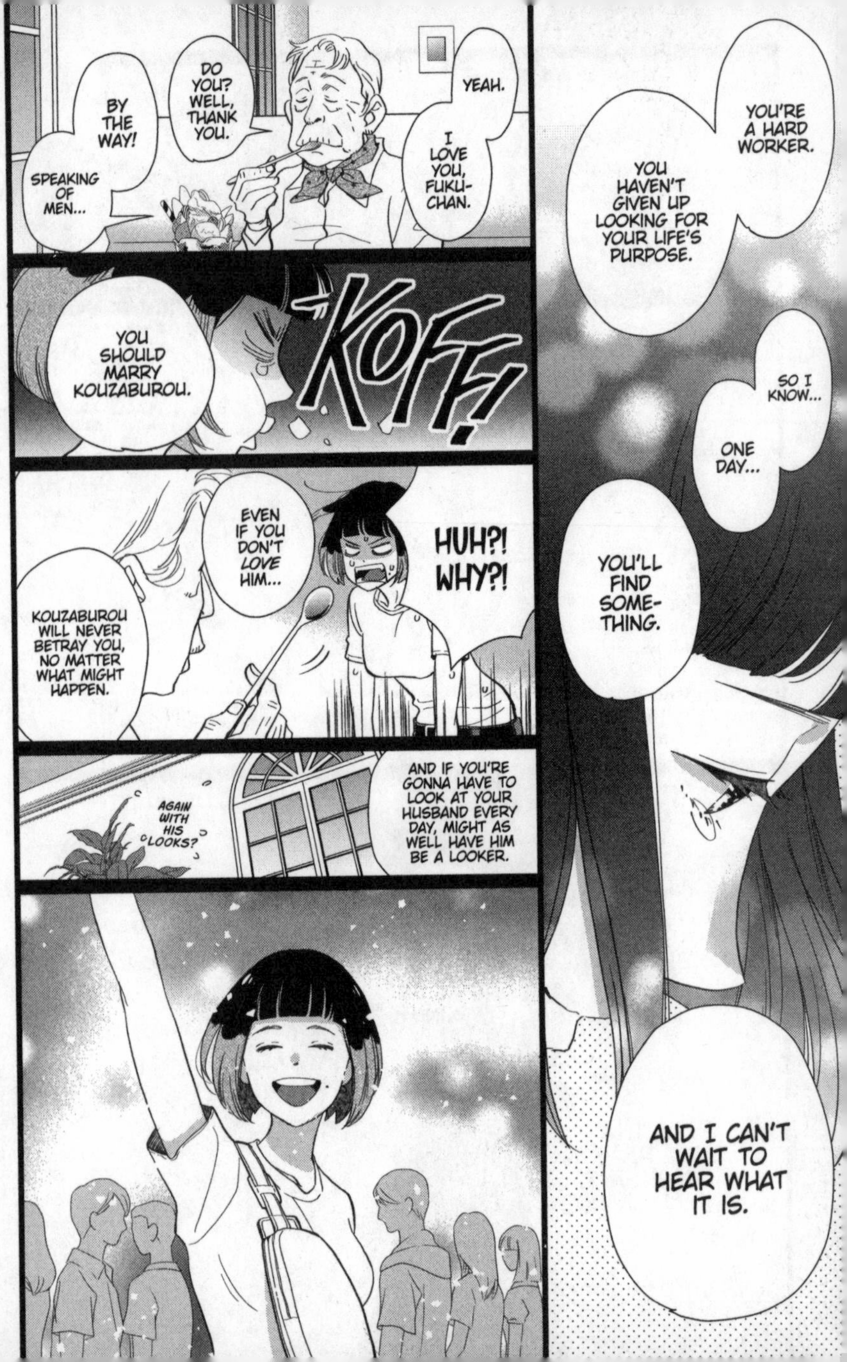
YOU'RE A HARD WORKER.
YOU HAVEN'T GIVEN UP LOOKING FOR YOUR LIFE'S PURPOSE.
SO I KNOW...
ONE DAY...
YOU'LL FIND SOME-THING.
AND I CAN'T WAIT TO HEAR WHAT IT IS.
YEAH.
I LOVE YOU, FUKU-CHAN.
DO YOU? WELL, THANK YOU.
BY THE WAY!
SPEAKING OF MEN...
KOFF!
YOU SHOULD MARRY KOUZABUROU.
HUH?! WHY?!
EVEN IF YOU DON'T LOVE HIM...
KOUZABUROU WILL NEVER BETRAY YOU, NO MATTER WHAT MIGHT HAPPEN.
AND IF YOU'RE GONNA HAVE TO LOOK AT YOUR HUSBAND EVERY DAY, MIGHT AS WELL HAVE HIM BE A LOOKER.
AGAIN WITH HIS LOOKS?

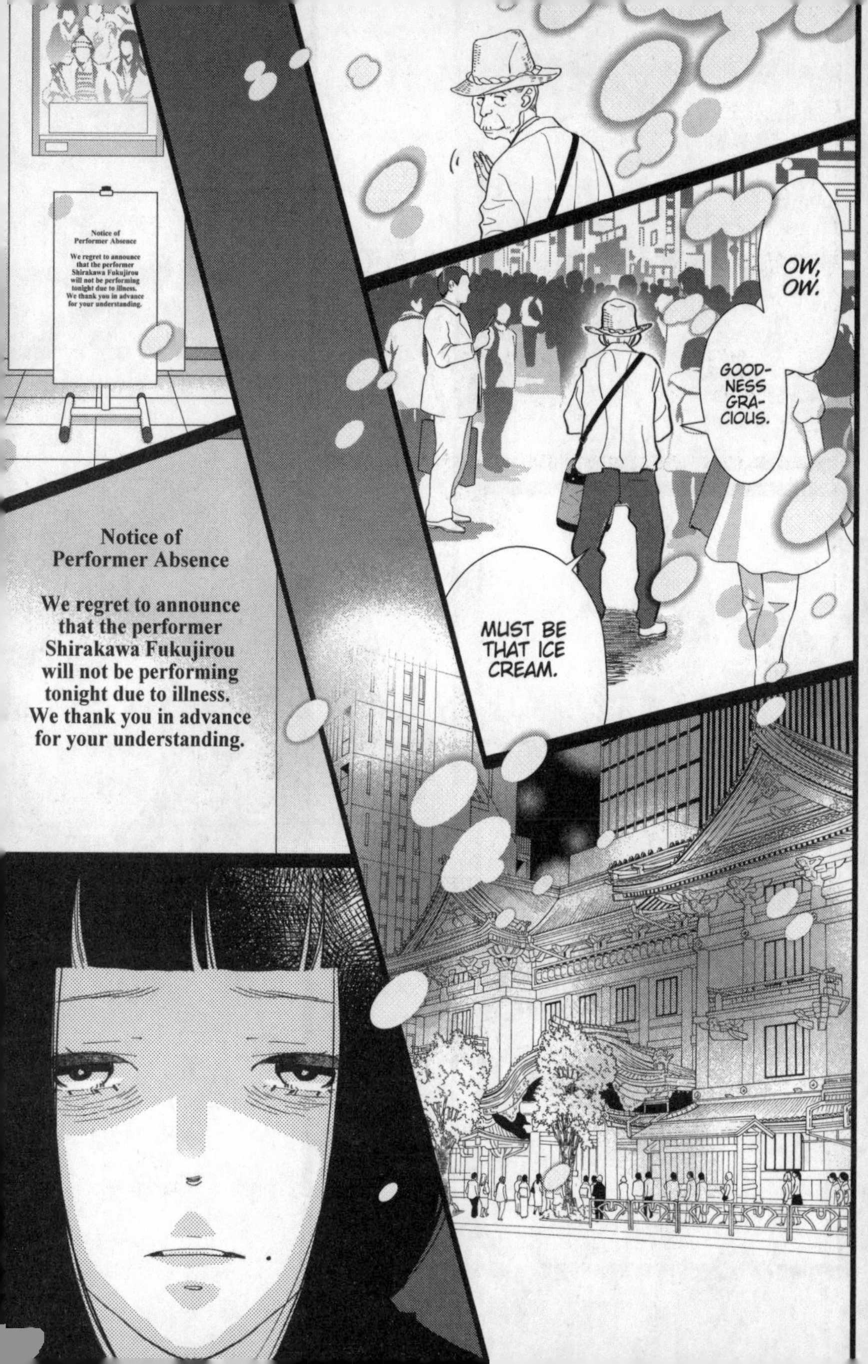
OW, OW.
GOOD-NESS GRA-CIOUS.
MUST BE THAT ICE CREAM.
Notice of Performer Absence
We regret to announce that the performer Shirakawa Fukujirou will not be performing tonight due to illness. We thank you in advance for your understanding.
Notice of Performer Absence
We regret to announce that the performer Shirakawa Fukujirou will not be performing tonight due to illness. We thank you in advance for your understanding.

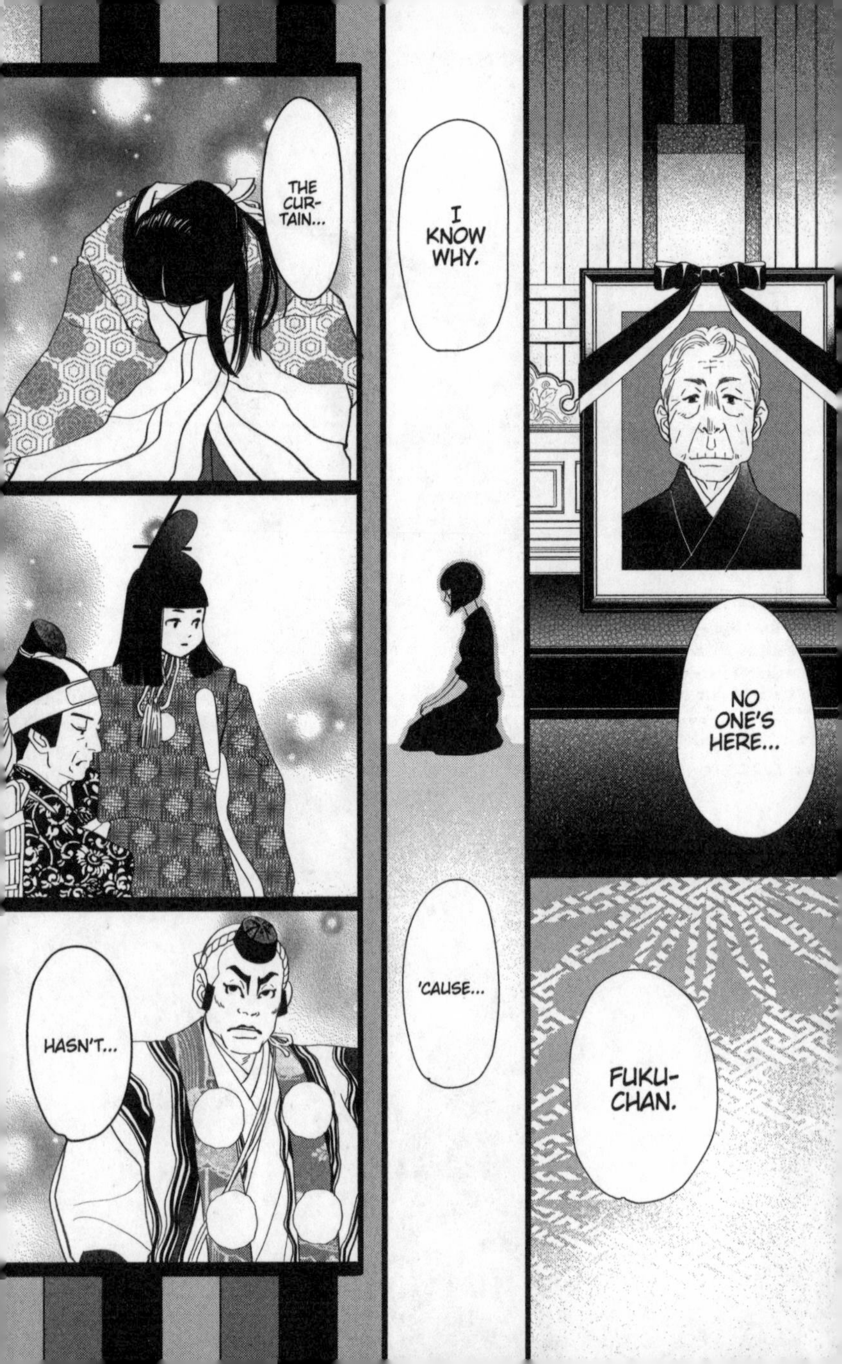
NO ONE'S HERE...
FUKU-CHAN.
I KNOW WHY.
'CAUSE...
THE CUR-TAIN...
HASN'T...

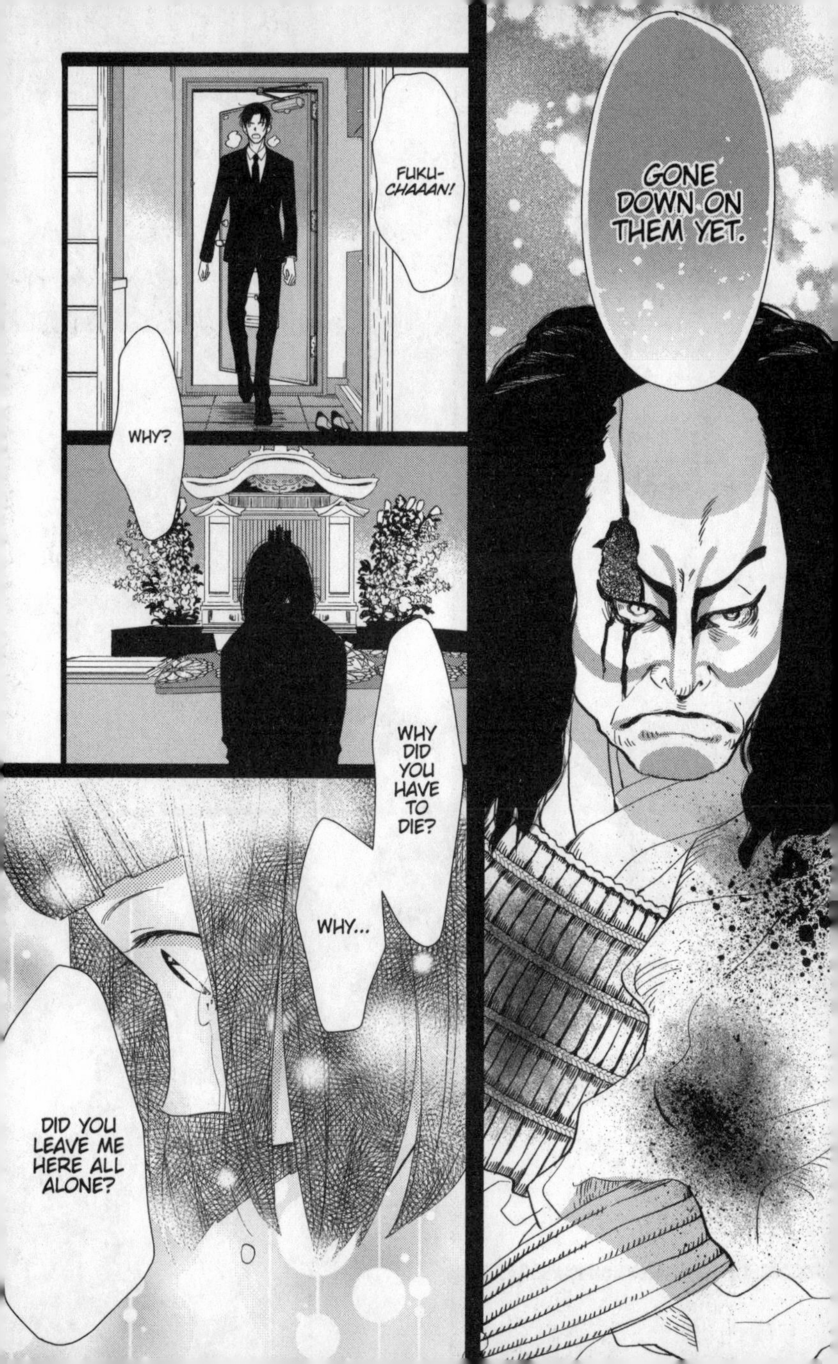
GONE DOWN ON THEM YET.
FUKU-CHAAAN!
WHY?
WHY DID YOU HAVE TO DIE?
WHY...
DID YOU LEAVE ME HERE ALL ALONE?

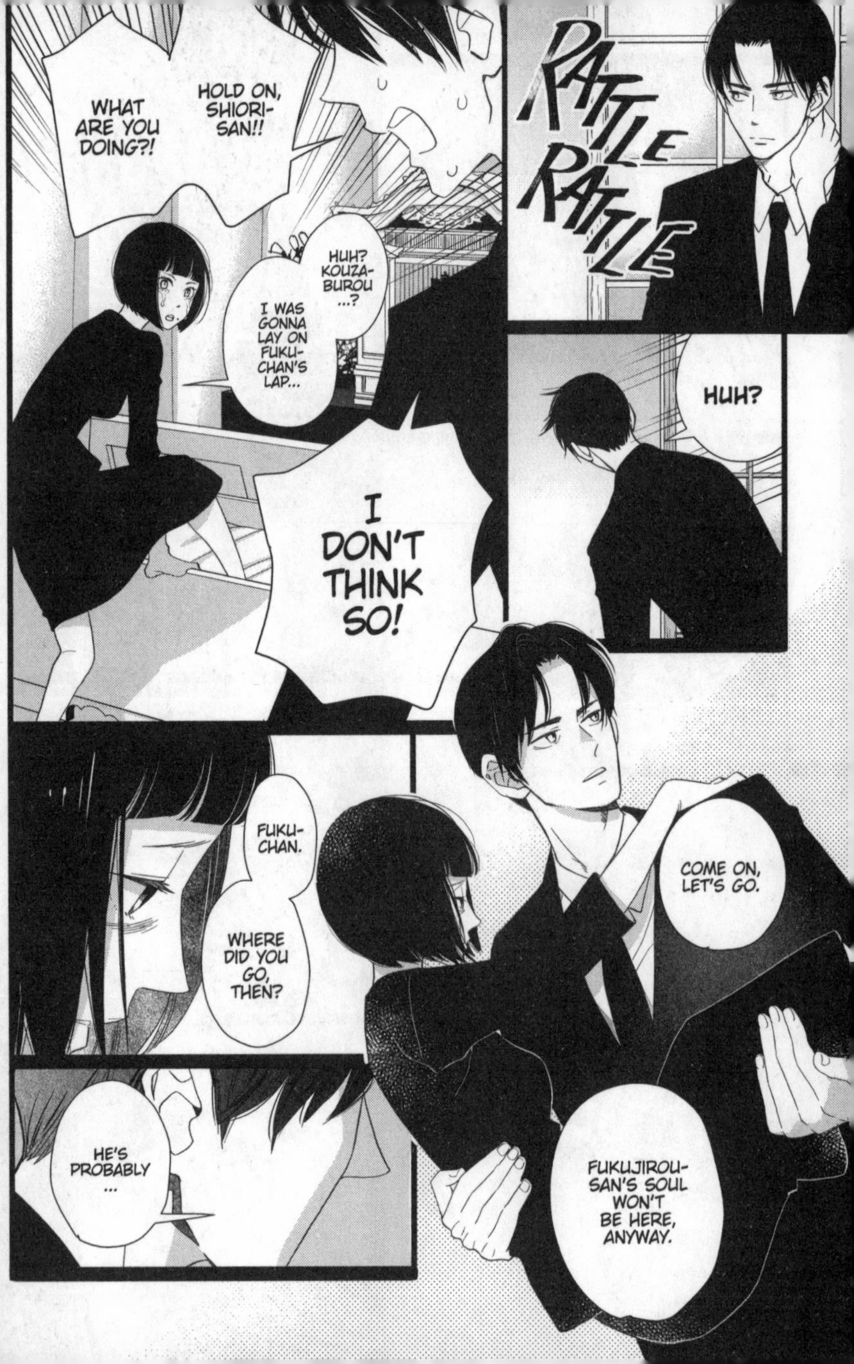
RATTLE RATTLE
HUH?
HOLD ON, SHIORI-SAN!!
WHAT ARE YOU DOING?!
HUH? KOUZABUROU ...?
I WAS GONNA LAY ON FUKU-CHAN'S LAP...
I DON'T THINK SO!
COME ON, LET'S GO.
FUKUJIROU-SAN'S SOUL WON'T BE HERE, ANYWAY.
FUKU-CHAN.
WHERE DID YOU GO, THEN?
HE'S PROBABLY ...

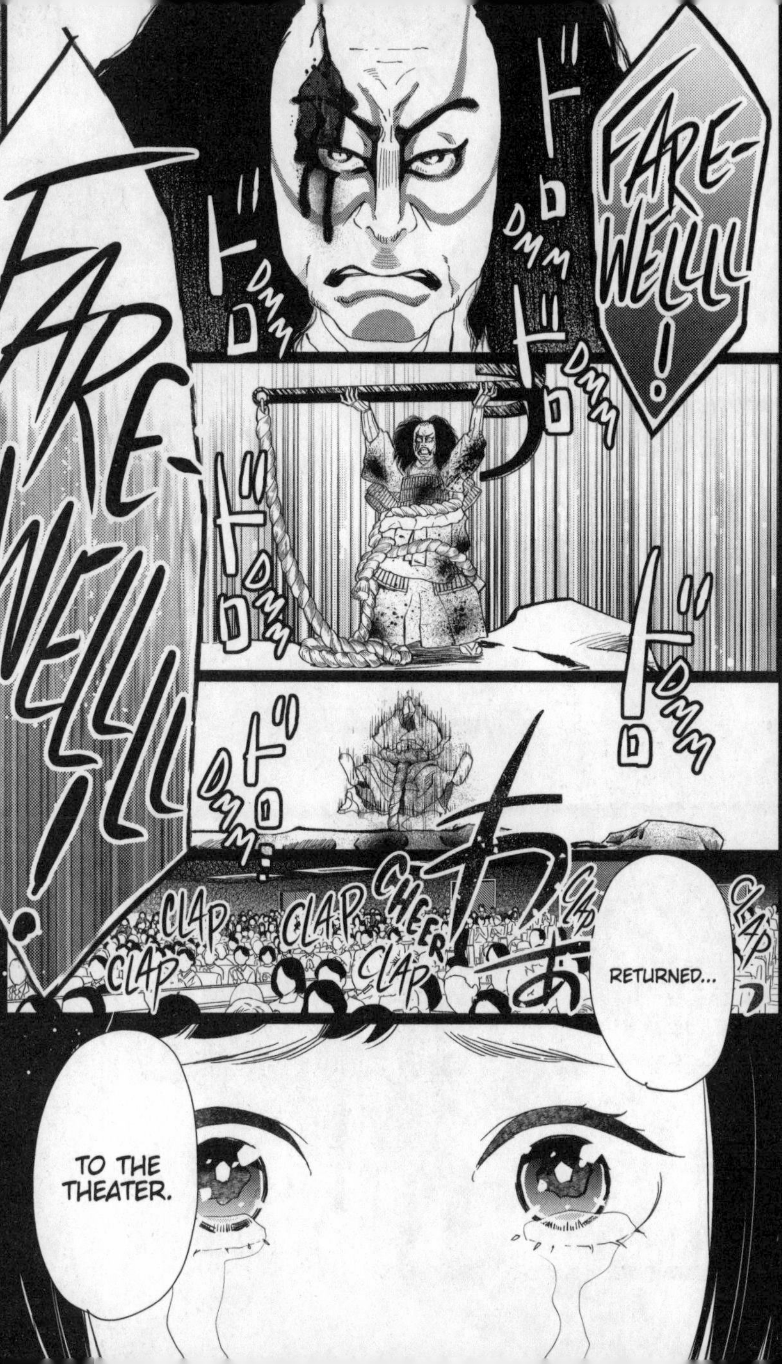
FARE-WELLL!
DMM
DMM
DMM
FARE-WELLLL!
DMM
DMM
DMM
CLAP
CHEER
CLAP
CLAP
CLAP
CLAP
RETURNED...
TO THE THEATER.

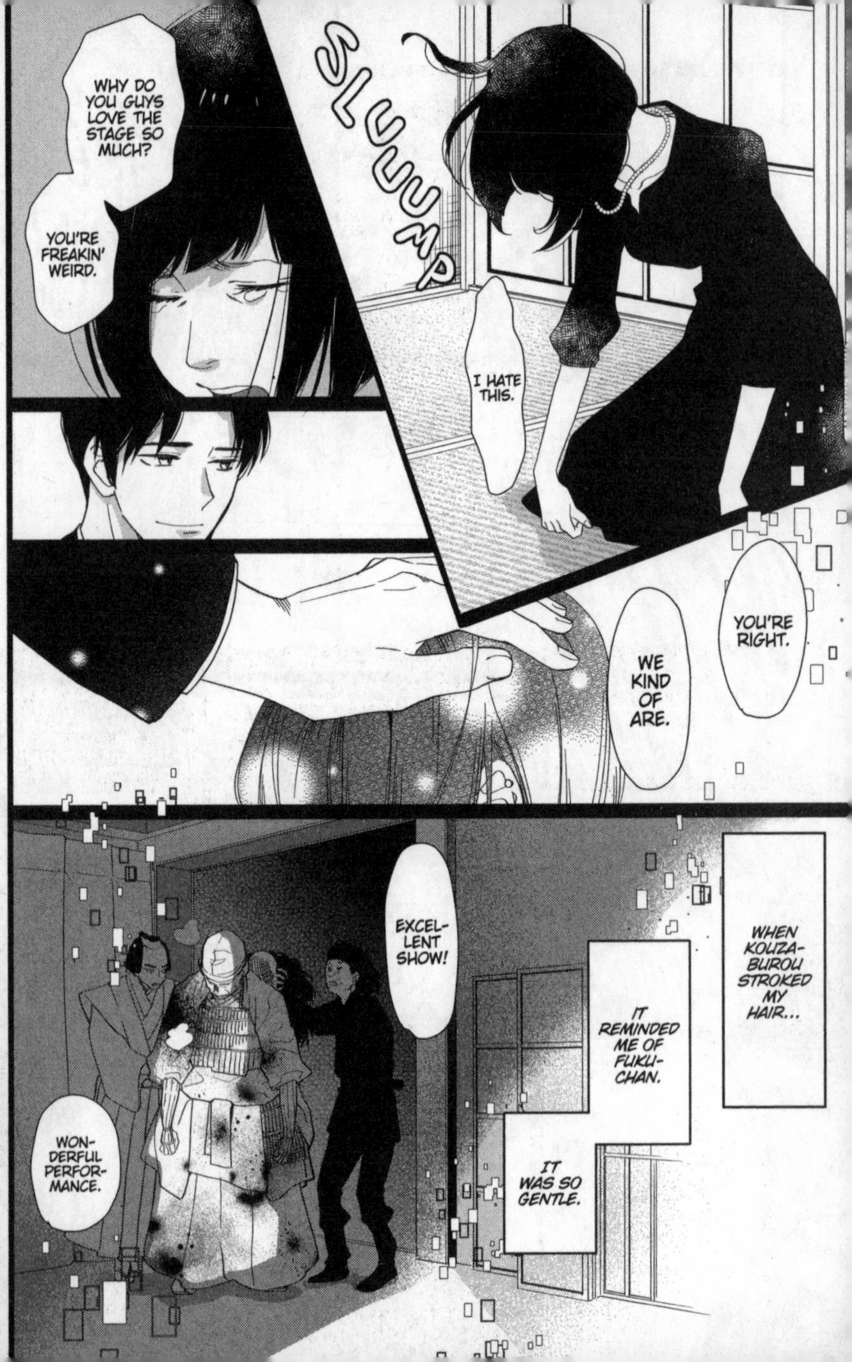
SLUUMP
I HATE THIS.
WHY DO YOU GUYS LOVE THE STAGE SO MUCH?
YOU'RE FREAKIN' WEIRD.
YOU'RE RIGHT.
WE KIND OF ARE.
WHEN KOUZABUROU STROKED MY HAIR...
IT REMINDED ME OF FUKU-CHAN.
IT WAS SO GENTLE.
EXCELLENT SHOW!
WONDERFUL PERFORMANCE.

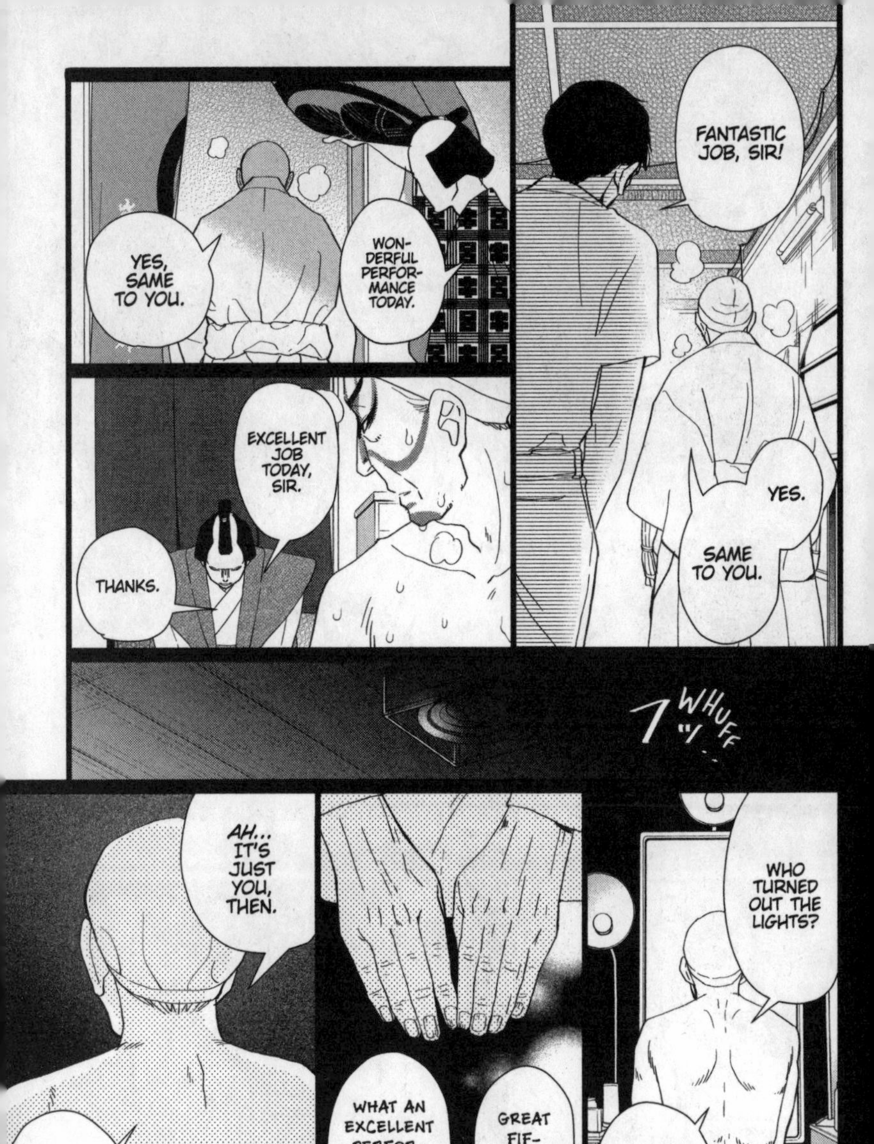
FANTASTIC JOB, SIR!
YES. SAME TO YOU.
WON-DERFUL PERFOR-MANCE TODAY.
YES, SAME TO YOU.
EXCELLENT JOB TODAY, SIR.
THANKS.
フッ...
WHUFF
WHO TURNED OUT THE LIGHTS?
I'VE GOT TO GET MY--
GREAT FIF-TEENTH.
WHAT AN EXCELLENT PERFOR-MANCE TONIGHT.
AH... IT'S JUST YOU, THEN.
WHY ARE YOU HERE?

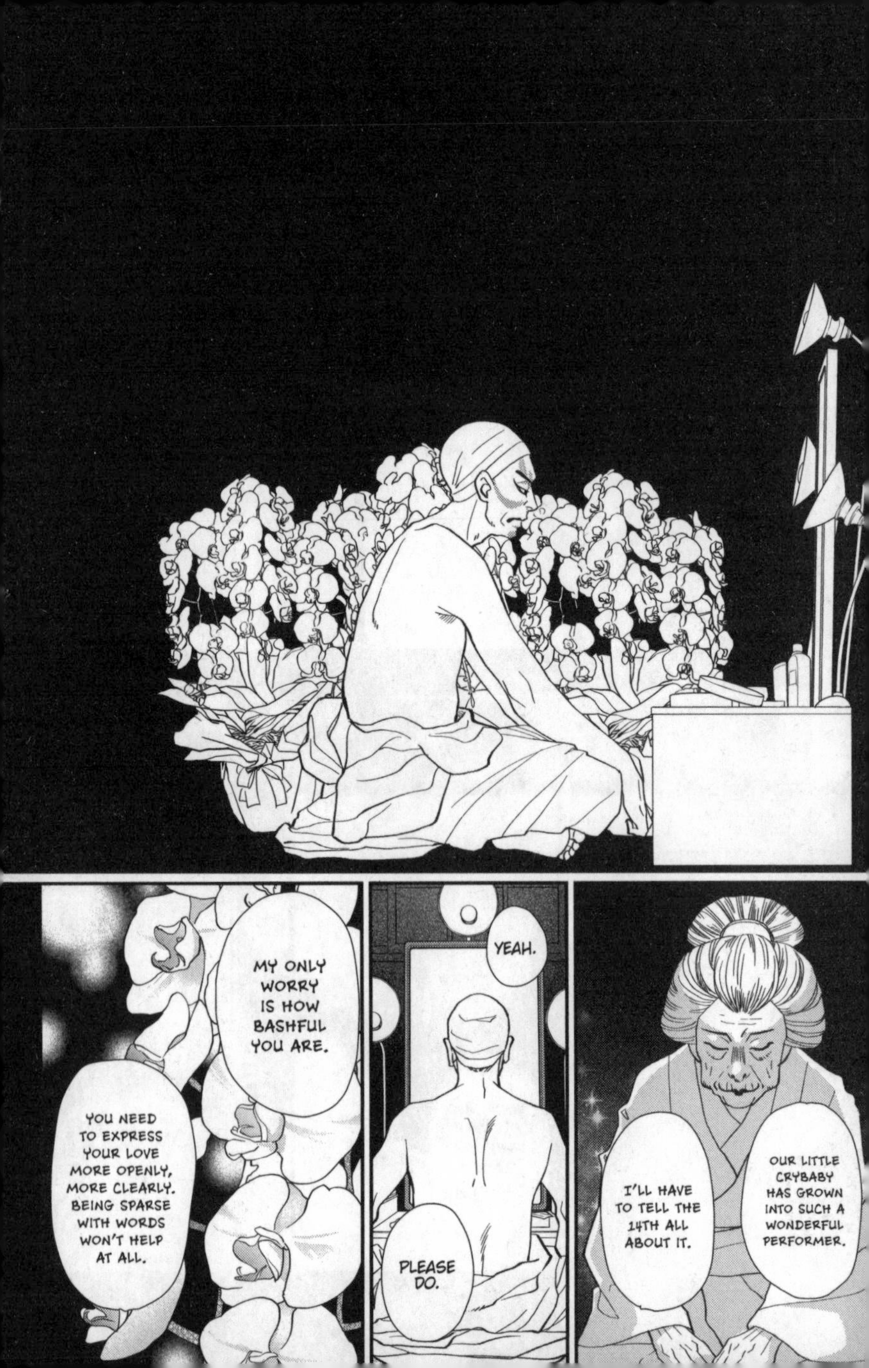
OUR LITTLE CRYBABY HAS GROWN INTO SUCH A WONDERFUL PERFORMER.
I'LL HAVE TO TELL THE 14TH ALL ABOUT IT.
YEAH.
PLEASE DO.
MY ONLY WORRY IS HOW BASHFUL YOU ARE.
YOU NEED TO EXPRESS YOUR LOVE MORE OPENLY, MORE CLEARLY. BEING SPARSE WITH WORDS WON'T HELP AT ALL.

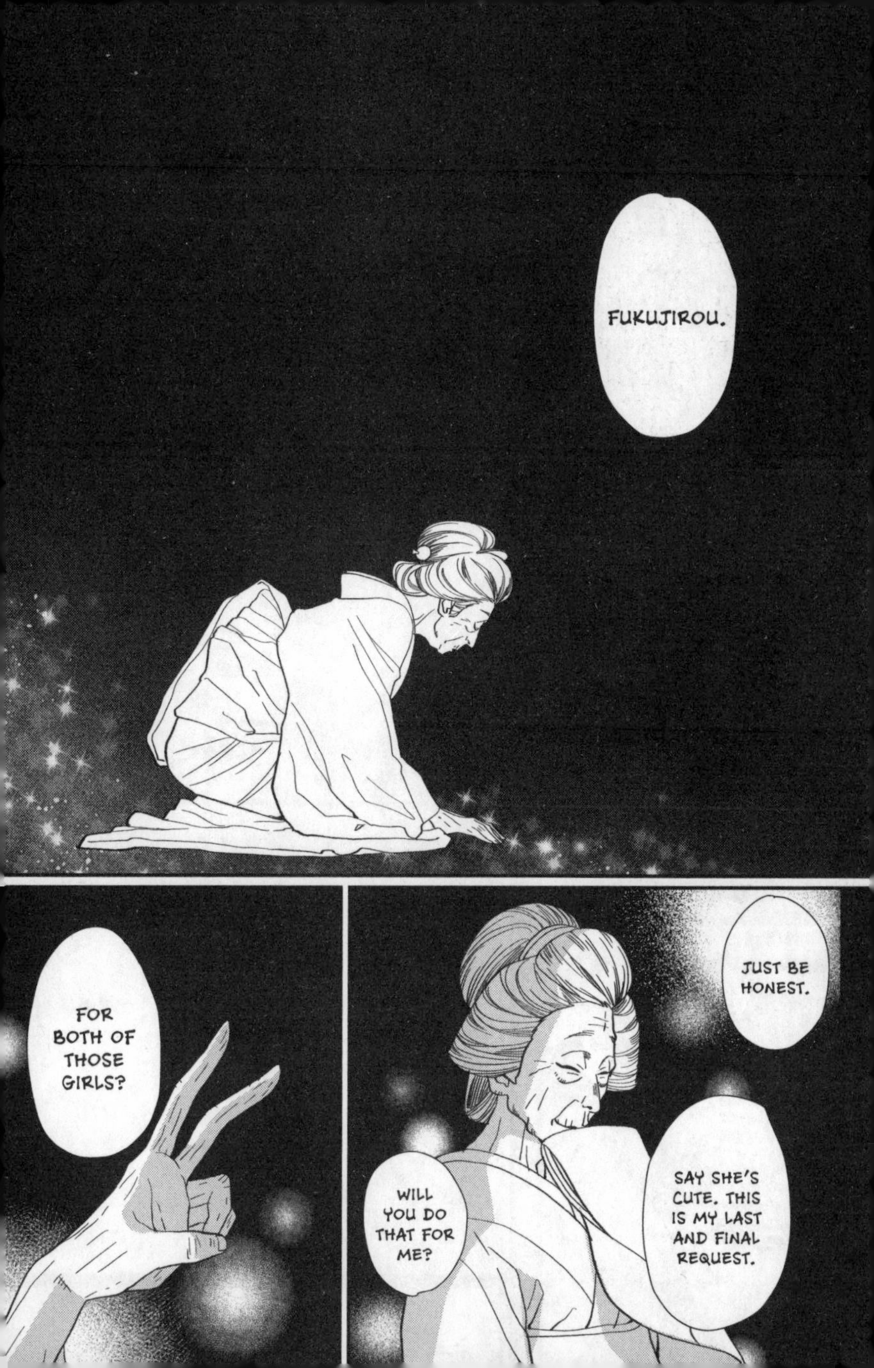
FUKUJIROU.
JUST BE HONEST.
SAY SHE'S CUTE. THIS IS MY LAST AND FINAL REQUEST.
WILL YOU DO THAT FOR ME?
FOR BOTH OF THOSE GIRLS?

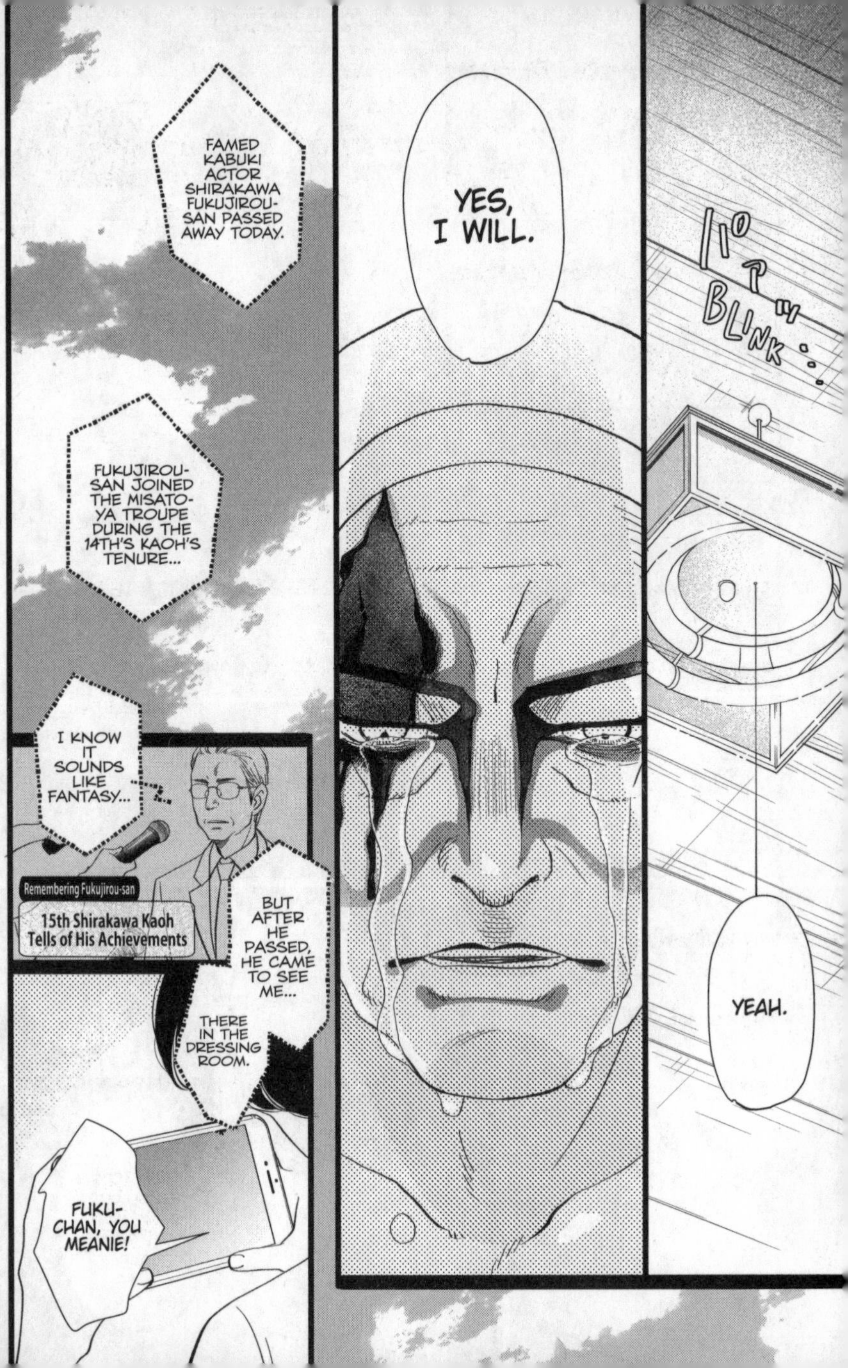
BLINK
YEAH.
YES, I WILL.
FAMED KABUKI ACTOR SHIRAKAWA FUKUJIROU-SAN PASSED AWAY TODAY.
FUKUJIROU-SAN JOINED THE MISATO-YA TROUPE DURING THE 14TH'S KAOH'S TENURE...
I KNOW IT SOUNDS LIKE FANTASY...
Remembering Fukujirou-san
15th Shirakawa Kaoh Tells of His Achievements
BUT AFTER HE PASSED, HE CAME TO SEE ME...
THERE IN THE DRESSING ROOM.
FUKU-CHAN, YOU MEANIE!

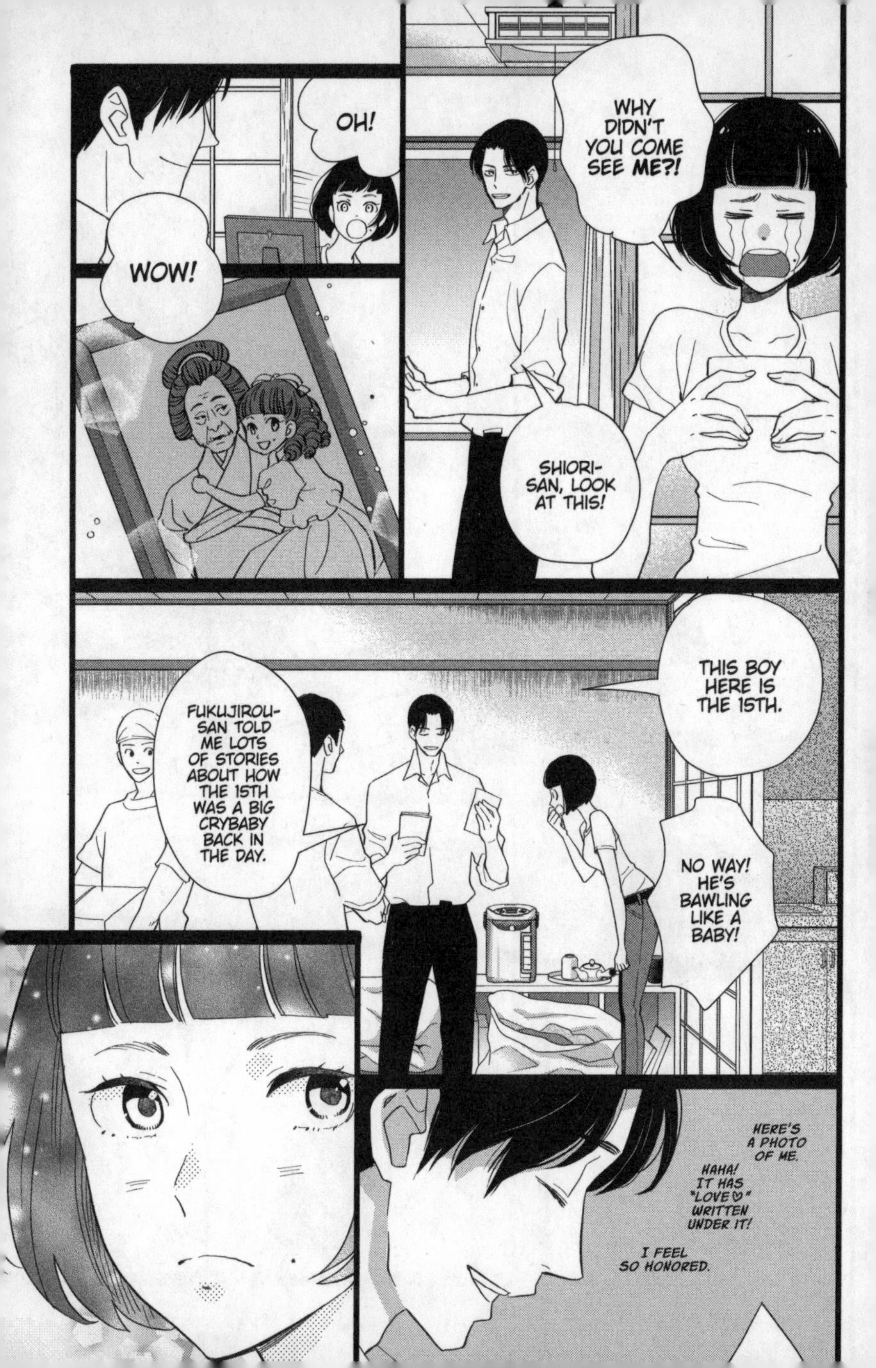
WHY DIDN'T YOU COME SEE ME?!
SHIORI-SAN, LOOK AT THIS!
OH!
WOW!
THIS BOY HERE IS THE 15TH.
NO WAY! HE'S BAWLING LIKE A BABY!
FUKUJIROU-SAN TOLD ME LOTS OF STORIES ABOUT HOW THE 15TH WAS A BIG CRYBABY BACK IN THE DAY.
HERE'S A PHOTO OF ME.
HAHA! IT HAS "LOVE♡" WRITTEN UNDER IT!
I FEEL SO HONORED.

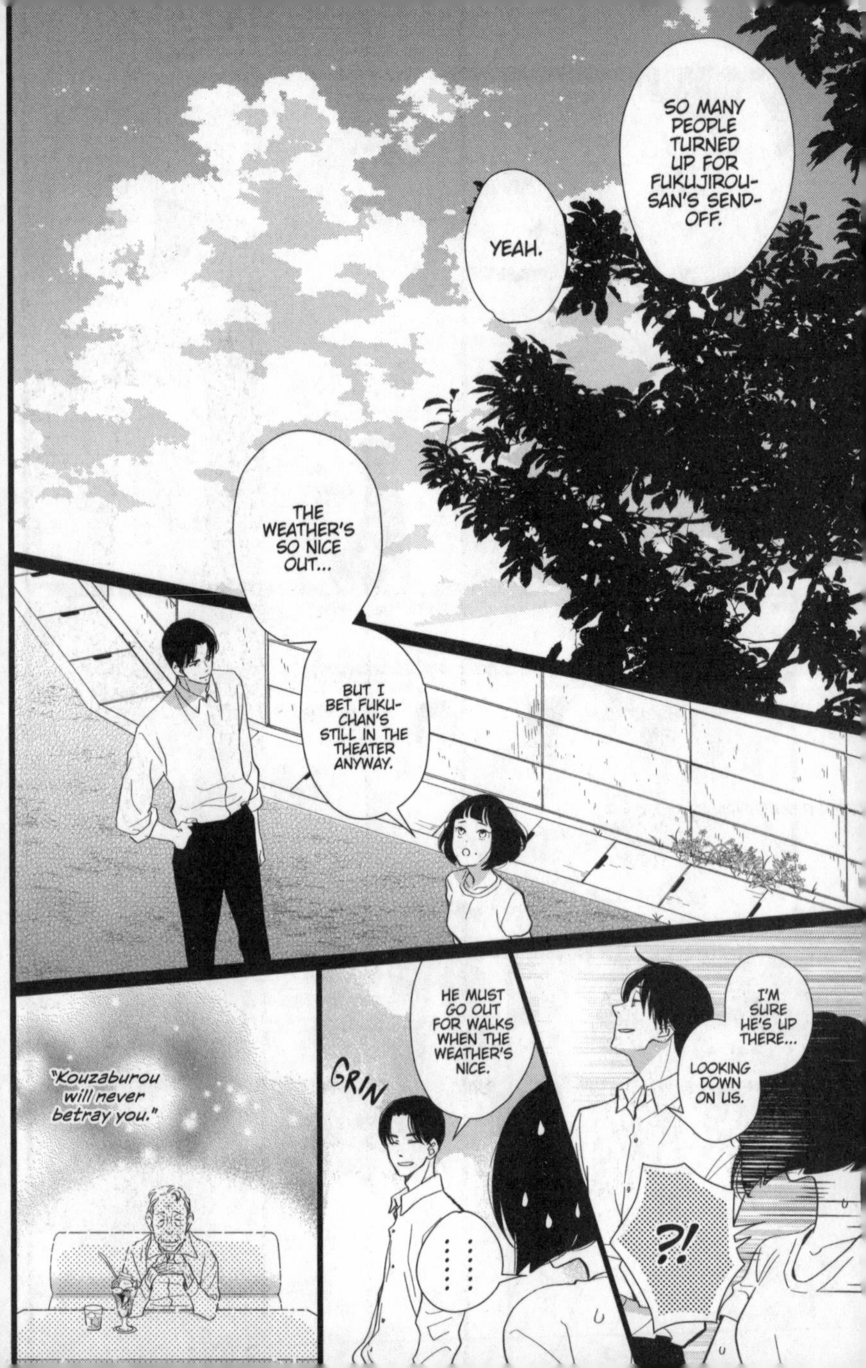
SO MANY PEOPLE TURNED UP FOR FUKUJIROU-SAN'S SEND-OFF.
YEAH.
THE WEATHER'S SO NICE OUT...
BUT I BET FUKU-CHAN'S STILL IN THE THEATER ANYWAY.
I'M SURE HE'S UP THERE...
LOOKING DOWN ON US.
?!
HE MUST GO OUT FOR WALKS WHEN THE WEATHER'S NICE.
GRIN
......
"Kouzaburou will never betray you."

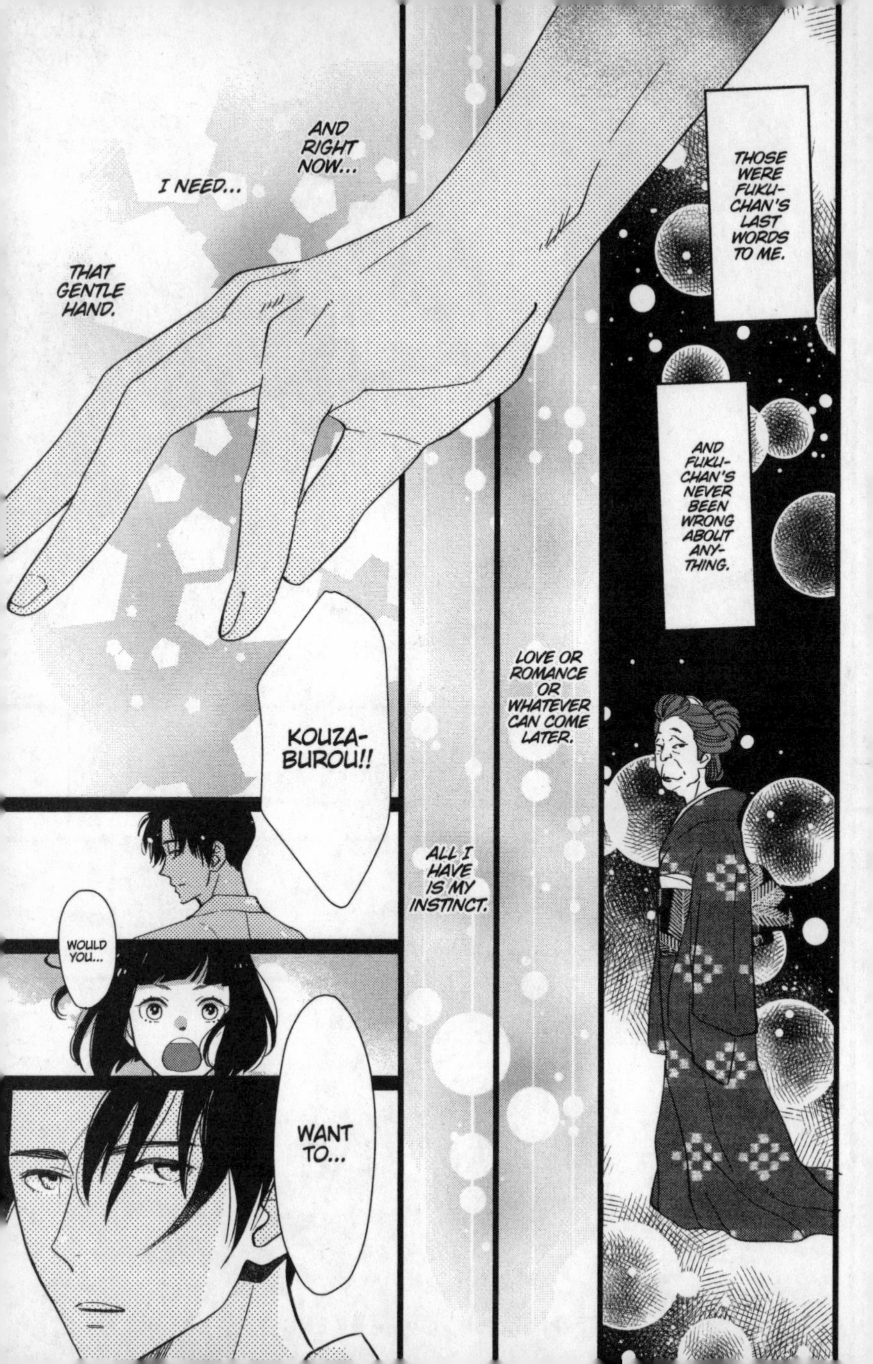
THOSE WERE FUKU-CHAN'S LAST WORDS TO ME.
AND FUKU-CHAN'S NEVER BEEN WRONG ABOUT ANYTHING.
LOVE OR ROMANCE OR WHATEVER CAN COME LATER.
ALL I HAVE IS MY INSTINCT.
AND RIGHT NOW...
I NEED...
THAT GENTLE HAND.
KOUZA-BUROU!!
WOULD YOU...
WANT TO...

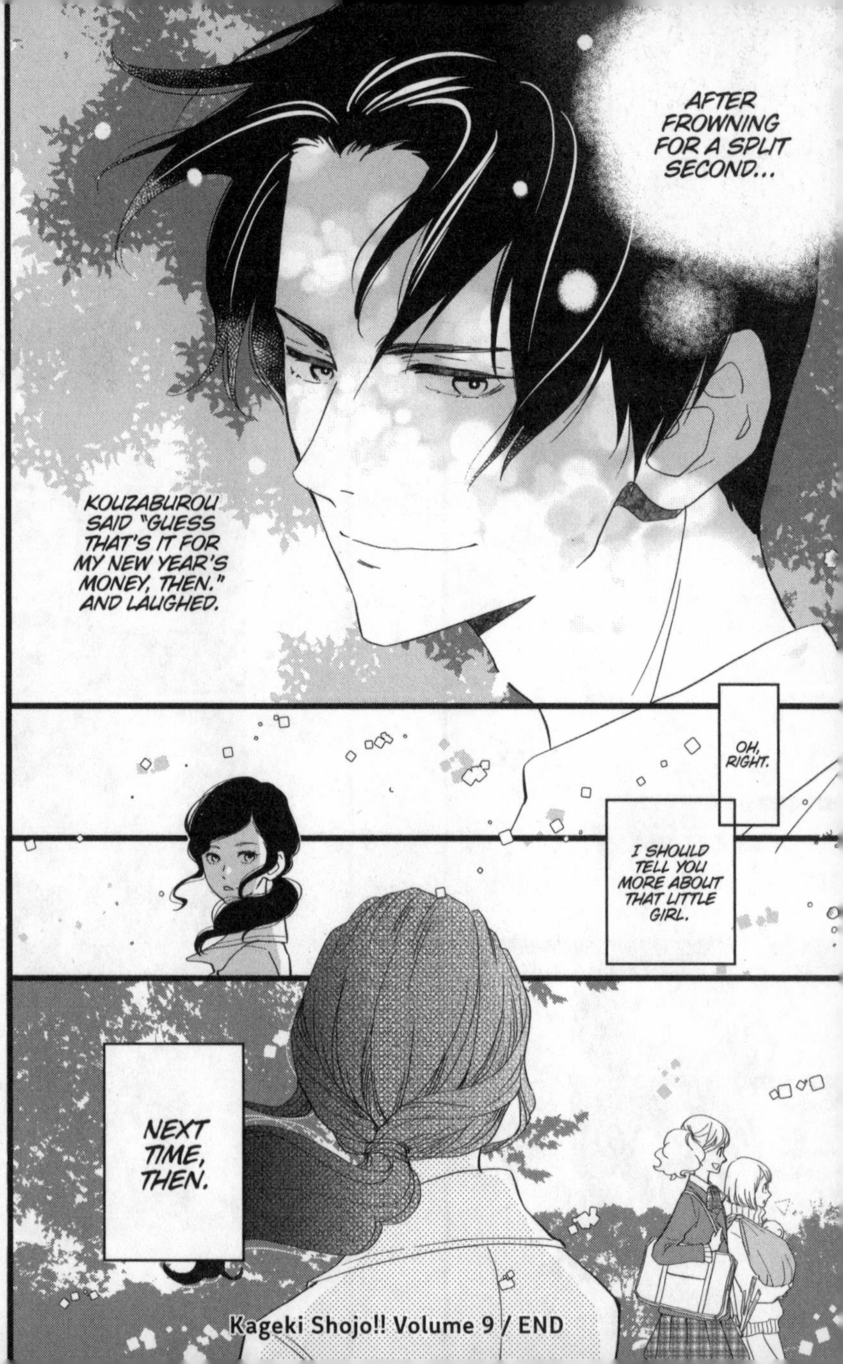
AFTER FROWNING FOR A SPLIT SECOND...
KOUZABUROU SAID "GUESS THAT'S IT FOR MY NEW YEAR'S MONEY, THEN." AND LAUGHED.
OH, RIGHT.
I SHOULD TELL YOU MORE ABOUT THAT LITTLE GIRL.
NEXT TIME, THEN.
Kageki Shojo!! Volume 9 / END

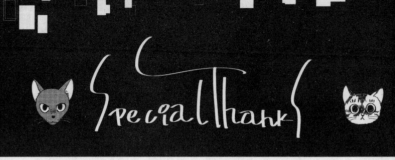

Special Thanks

Asai-san
Momo-san
Okada-san
Yasuhara-san
Ino-san

Kitano-san (3D Modeling)
Takisawa-san
Kuroki-san
Morita-san

Nono & Jill

♡all of my readers♡

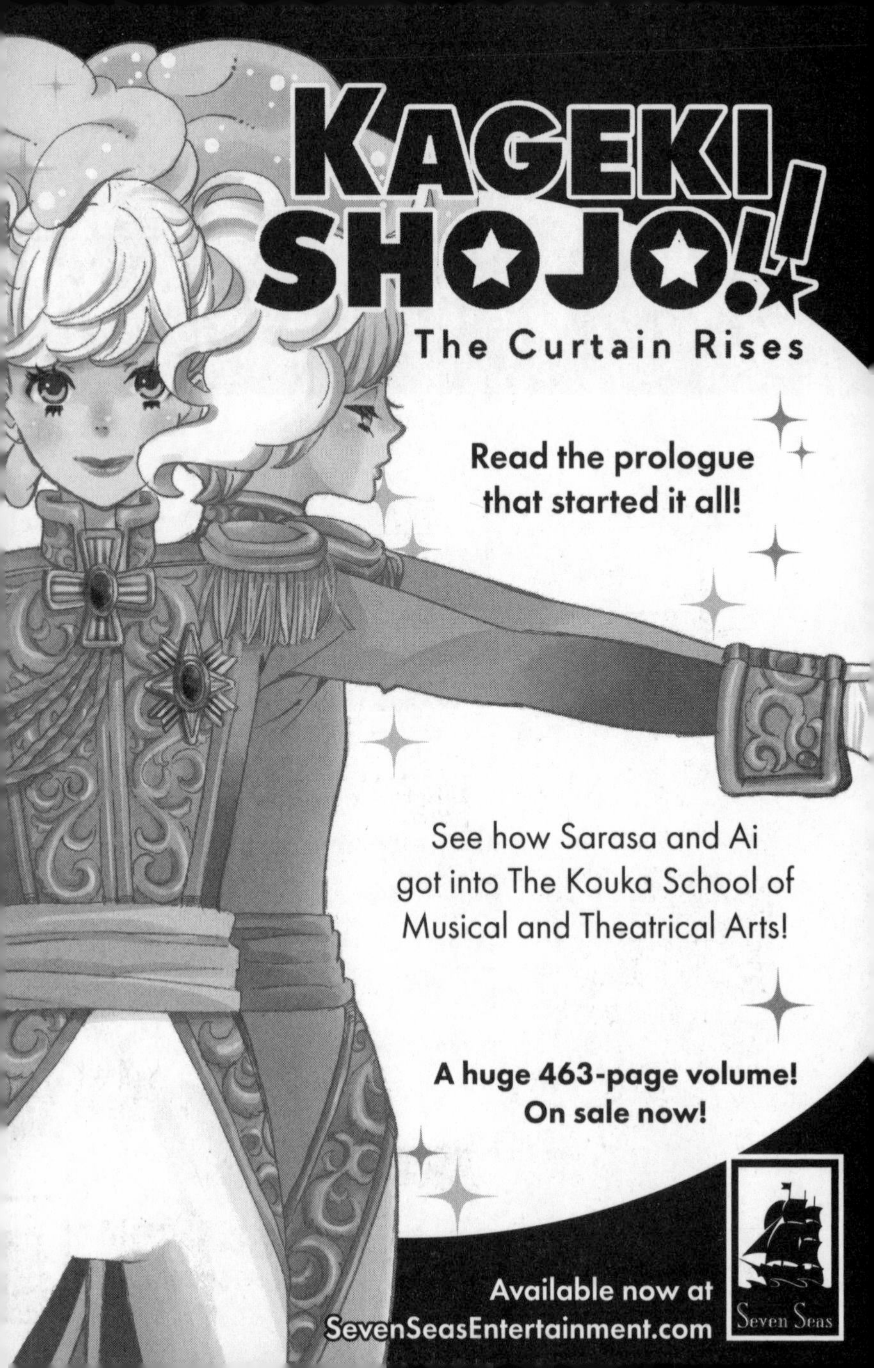

SEVEN SEAS ENTERTAINMENT PRESENTS

KAGEKI SHOJO!!

story and art by **KUMIKO SAIKI** **VOLUME 9**

TRANSLATION
Katrina Leonoudakis

LETTERING
Aila Nagamine

COVER DESIGN
H. Qi

LOGO DESIGN
Courtney Williams

PROOFREADER
Alyssa Honsowetz

SENIOR EDITOR
Shannon Fay

PRODUCTION DESIGNER
Christina McKenzie

PRODUCTION MANAGER
George Panella

PREPRESS TECHNICIAN
Melanie Ujimori
Jules Valera

MANAGING EDITOR
J.P. Sullivan

EDITOR-IN-CHIEF
Julie Davis

ASSOCIATE PUBLISHER
Adam Arnold

PUBLISHER
Jason DeAngelis

First published in Japan in 2020 by HAKUSENSHA, INC., Tokyo.
English language translation rights arranged with HAKUSENSHA, INC.,
Tokyo through TOHAN CORPORATION, Tokyo.

Seven Seas press and purchase enquiries can be sent to Marketing Manager Lianne Sentar at press@gomanga.com. Information regarding the distribution and purchase of digital editions is available from Digital Manager CK Russell at digital@gomanga.com.

ISBN: 978-1-63858-834-4
Printed in Canada
First Printing: June 2023
10 9 8 7 6 5 4 3 2 1

READING DIRECTIONS

This book reads from ***right to left***, Japanese style. If this is your first time reading manga, you start reading from the top right panel on each page and take it from there. If you get lost, just follow the numbered diagram here. It may seem backwards at first, but you'll get the hang of it! Have fun!!

1
2
3
4
5
6
7
8
9

Follow us online: www.SevenSeasEntertainment.com

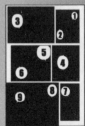